DAILY LIFE IN JAPAN
at the time of the Samurai

LOUIS FRÉDERIC

DAILY LIFE IN JAPAN
AT THE TIME OF
THE SAMURAI
1185 - 1603

Translated from the French by
Eileen M. Lowe

CHARLES E. TUTTLE COMPANY
SUIDO 1-CHOME, 2–6, BUNKYO-KU, TOKYO

Published by the Charles E. Tuttle Company, Inc., of
Rutland, Vermont and Tokyo, Japan, with editorial offices
at Suido 1-chome, 2–6, Bunkyo-ku, Tokyo, Japan, by special
arrangement with George Allen & Unwin, Ltd., London.

First Tuttle edition, 1973
Second printing, 1984

PRINTED IN JAPAN

To my wife, Hiroko

CONTENTS

ILLUSTRATIONS

INTRODUCTION

Towards the end of the twelfth century, while Western Europe was still wavering between a dying Roman influence and a dawning Gothicism, preliminaries to a medieval era which would make possible the development of a world-wide humanism, Asia had already lived through her classical period and, sinking into decay, was preparing to face a long period of political and spiritual unrest. While India was beginning to suffer under the yoke of the victorious Mussulman, who had come down on her from the mountains of Afghanistan and the plains of Iran, and while the domination of the Khmers was reaching its climax at Angkor, China, under pressure from the barbarians of the north, was withdrawing to the south where the Song empire, thinking itself safe from invasions, continued to live a life of luxury. Finally Japan, isolated in her islands, was experiencing political and social upheavals which were destined to change her structure from top to bottom and in consequence to lead to the formation of the Japanese nation.

In four turbulent centuries, from the twelfth to the sixteenth, the whole world evolved in a diversity of ways, each country in its own particular fashion. Early seventeenth-century man was nearly everywhere different from the man of the twelfth century. The West was suffering from growing pains; absolute monarchies followed feudal forms of government throughout the confusion bred of a practically endemic state of warfare. Frontiers changed, empires were established and as quickly overthrown. Europe was in search of stability. No sooner was America discovered than it became the pawn of a close struggle between nations, a prelude to the birth of colonialism. India became progressively Islamic, China was invaded by the Mongols, the Khmers were reduced to impotence by the rise of the Thai and pressure from Vietnam: the world at that time was in a ferment.

Until then Japan might have thought herself safe; but the infection spread to her and she, in her turn, suffered from growing pains.

For four centuries there were head-on clashes between men and ideas under the aegis of the shôgun dynasties or the military dictatorships, but gradually a new Japanese civilization, still alive and active now beneath its Western veneer, asserted itself. These changes remained localized, however, only affecting the Japanese Islands. They were internal, not influenced by any invasion or powerful external pressure. There was no real usurpation of power to be seen here, no class struggles, still less racial conflicts: in Japan, whatever might befall, the emperor, regarded as a descendant in direct line from the sun-goddess, Amaterasu Ômikami, was and remains the protector of the nation, if not its ruler. The shôgun only acted as the emperor's representatives. The development of the Japanese people in the Middle Ages was closely linked with the economic conditions of the country, with its geographic and climatic characteristics. The will of the masses was of small account. The supreme spiritual entity was personified in the emperor, and the secular power in the shôgun, regents, ministers and other officials; as for the people, they possessed no power of any kind. Beyond classification and supporting one or the other according to circumstances, were the religious orders.

This was so in theory: in actual fact, the emperor and his court excepted, there were the aristocrats (the nobles and the majority of the religious orders), and there were masses, the first knowing nothing whatever about the second. Until the twelfth century, it was the aristocracy that ruled and set the fashion. Scholarly and artistic, it legislated, concerning itself with religious and moral questions. Peaceable, it owned the land and enjoyed its revenues. Through intermediaries, it traded with foreign countries, meaning China and Korea. The illiterate multitude neither possessed the earth nor enjoyed its fruits; overburdened with taxes, it had nothing but its traditions to live for. But it had a deep love for that same earth made fertile by its labour, loved its trees and its forests; it worshipped the mountains, and gloried in the blossoming of springtime, in the fiery glow of autumn. To the nobleman, the populace was a matter of wonder: if he met a peasant on the roadside, he was filled with amazement and would ask him quite ingenuously what kind of animal he was. And yet it was from this poverty-stricken people, from its passion for work, its highmindedness, its faithfulness to its code, from its courage, from its contempt of death, too, that new social concepts arose. Finally, it was thanks to it that the social structure of Japan was completely refashioned. The reversal of the situation, to be seen at the end of the twelfth century in Japan was, in the long run, nothing but the natural outcome of a combination of events independent of the will of a single class.

In politics, as in everyday life, the Japanese way of thinking appears different from ours. Indeed, perhaps it is, from some angles. But, though not Cartesian, it is none the less remarkably efficient. And it must not be forgotten that Japanese criteria of the Middle Ages were not altogether the same as those of modern Japan, no more, it must be added, than they were the same in Europe at that time.

There are countless ways of getting to know a race, countless ways of understanding it. Moreover, the Japanese themselves are the first to have extremely diverse and contradictory ideas and points of view about their country. It is enough to glance through Japanese history books to realize the diversity of their opinions, to say nothing of their antagonisms. If this is so as far as political or factual history is concerned, what can we say when it is a question of the lives of men, whose existences make up the indestructible web into which, by way of embellishment, mighty deeds and historical incidents are woven? How is one to describe the life this nation led for four centuries, a nation doomed to endless changes, to repeated reverses of fortune, to a state of wretchedness, that very few races have experienced to this degree?

The choice we have made in selecting this epoch for our book is undoubtedly open to criticism. But, allowing for the uncertainty of the information about it that is available to us, we chose it because, in our opinion, and in view of the compass of such a study, it offered the best means of portraying the everyday life of medieval Japan by following the method of logical progression. It is quite obvious that classification constrains one to define categories, to put things into compartments. But a practical method of exposition does not necessarily square with reality completely; the categories that we have artificially created: the city, the country, war, religion, etc., did not exist so rigidly in the life of medieval Japan. The objection might be raised that the world of the aristocrat was entirely different from that of the common man. But if this is true about the Heian period, the situation is very much more confused at the time our story begins, because of the coming to power of a new class of men. The aristocrats, on the downward track, continued to lead an aimless life in the capital, Kyôto, while the rest of the country was living through heroic, vigorous, and stirring times.

Compared with the sources at our disposal about the luxury-loving Heian epoch (794–1185) and which deal in the main with the life of the nobles of Kyôto, those concerning medieval Japan may seem dull. Setting aside some rare architectural remains, on the whole of little value in the study of the everyday life of men, and artistic evidences whose documentary interest is somewhat limited, literature offers practically our only source of information. Now, very few Japanese works of that period have been translated into any European language. Fortunately for our purposes, these Middle Ages have bequeathed to us a quantity of *emakimono* or 'illuminated scrolls', more likely to be concerned with the life of the common people than with that of the court aristocrats. The monks used them to expound their teachings, and writers and story-tellers to illustrate their works or those of their predecessors, and to put them within reach of a greater number of people: these 'picture-scrolls' (some measure more than ten metres in length) still remain our most reliable source of information. We have made ample use of them in our endeavour to reconstitute the daily life of the Japanese people at the time of the samurai. We are likewise indebted for a great deal of our information to various authors, both Japanese and European who, for their part, have studied them in the minutest detail! But the fact remains that these *emakimono* leave us in the dark over many questions.

In order to shed some light on these scrolls, we have had recourse to unfinished works, historic, religious or artistic, which were already recognized at that time. The men of letters in medieval Japan took little trouble to describe the lives of their contemporaries with any accuracy, unless the latter were high-born. It is only possible to recount the life of the common man by making certain extrapolations, by putting forward certain assumptions, sometimes dangerous ones. However, we have tried to avoid the latter as often as possible. In spite of all these accumulated difficulties, it seemed to us an exciting challenge to recount, however briefly (the compass of this work not lending itself to exhaustive treatment of the subject, and at the risk of almost unavoidable mistakes), the everyday life of the men and women of Japan at the time of the samurai. We hope the reader will be as interested in it as the author,

and will be kind enough to show indulgence in forgiving the latter
the mistakes and flights of fancy which imagination, in its effort
to re-create, has undoubtedly made him commit.

We thought it advisable to keep throughout the work the Japanese spelling of names, which have been transcribed according to
the Hepburn method, and not to add French plurals to Japanese
words, because it might have led to some confusion. We also hope
it will be remembered, in the course of reading, that there is no
diphthong in the Japanese tongue, and that every vowel is pronounced separately. Furthermore, the letter 'u' is pronounced like
'ou' in French, 'c' becomes 'tch', 'g' is always hard. Thus the word
samurai will be pronounced 'samourai', the name *Nobunaga* as
'Nobounaga', etc. Long vowels have been indicated by a circum-
flex accent. We have kept to the Japanese way of naming individuals: surname first, then personal name. Reference notes, a brief
bibliography and a few tables, which may be of use in understanding
this 'Daily Life' are to be found at the end of the book.

We would like, at this point, to express our sincere thanks to
M. Jacques du Bouëtiez de Kerorguen for his kindness in reading
the proofs of this work and for suggesting several corrections.

Finally, the author considers that he would not have been able
to carry out his task successfully without the assistance of his wife,
Hiroko, who, by translating many original texts, has given him the
opportunity of drawing from sources which would otherwise have
remained closed either by reason of language difficulties, or by reason of a context difficult for a European to appreciate with all its
nuances. This work owes much to her, and the author owes even
more.

Tôkyô–Paris, 1967   L. F.

CHAPTER ONE

BIRTH OF THE MIDDLE AGES

JAPAN AT THE DAWN OF THE TWELFTH CENTURY

The whole history of Japan, from the end of the prehistoric era and the official introduction of Buddhism and Chinese civilization in the middle of the sixth century, until feudal times in the Middle Ages, is one of rivalries among the clans round the person of the emperor, of the conquest of the northern part of the country from the Ainu aborigines and, primarily, of the struggles of the nobles themselves for the possession of the land. At that time there was no such thing as national consciousness, but only the feeling of belonging to a group, a city, or a district. So as to understand more easily how the Japanese people, far from freeing themselves from servitude – for, uneducated as they were, they would not have known how to make use of a freedom they had not sought – created new masters instead, it is necessary to take a quick look at the centuries during which the aristocracy came into power and kept it, and also to examine the reasons which allowed a military type of government to supplant the peaceable authority of the Fujiwara regents.

In Japan, every social or political movement was closely bound up with the land. The bulk of the Japanese had always been farmers, and this despite the very small area of land that is level enough for cultivation. The part played by agriculture was all the more important in that, owing to the scarcity of money, barter was mainly carried on according to the productivity of the soil. To own land (with, of course, its peasantry, the manpower required for farming it) was as good as possessing wealth, and consequently, power. Now, ever since the seventh century the land had been nationalized under a system adopted from the Chinese. Every registered peasant farmer had been granted a plot of land (*handen*) whose size depended upon the sex of the recipient and the number of people in the family. This distribution of land was accompanied by a set of rules chiefly relating to taxes and called *ritsuryô*. State lands were thus loaned for life but it was forbidden to sell or lease them. This system (which, it must be added, did not work in China) could possibly have shown satisfactory results if taxation had not been so heavy and, above all, if the state from 743 had not brought in an amendment with catastrophic results: it was a question of allowing certain farmers, monasteries and aristocratic families to hold direct (with all the rights ascribed to them) the newly cleared lands, or lands conquered from the Ainu tribes and situated mostly in the northern part of the country.

This had two results: firstly, so as to make the most of these new lands, the nobles or religious landowners leased them at a low price to the peasant farmers who chose to cultivate these domains for which the overlords were exacting only a comparatively moderate tax, to the detriment of the 'state controlled' lands where the excessively heavy taxes and duties would leave them scarcely enough to subsist on. This led to an increasingly marked desertion of the 'nationalized' farmers. Secondly, nobles and monasteries, having been granted tax exemption by the state, soon controlled, entirely for their own benefit, the peasant farmers who had come and settled down on their domains, thus creating virtually self-governing territories or manors called *shôen*. The 'lord of the domain', a kind of feudal baron before his time, administered his domain as he pleased, levying taxes, assigning tasks to his farmers and dispensing justice. He was in actual fact supreme ruler of his own territory. In order to defend this land against the incursions of the Ainu in the north, or against the greed of his neighbours, he set up a kind of armed militia. The most powerful of these nobles, who preferred to reside in Kyôto rather than in their own domains, more often than not delegated their powers to representatives in whom they could place complete confidence. Thus, countless *shôen* were formed throughout the Heian period (794–1185).

Owing to the almost complete conquest of the north of the island of Honshu from the Ainu, the lands newly opened to cultivation were exceedingly wide-spread. The lords lived in magnificent style, whereas the nationalized lands, gradually abandoned, yielded less and less to the state. In order to increase their revenues still more, certain lords, whose holdings chanced to lie along the coast, devoted themselves to commercial and maritime enterprises, even to piracy. It happened also, owing to the difficulty of communications be-

1 Minamoto no Chikafusa, Japanese historian (1293–1354)
Drawing by Kikuchi Yôsai (1788–1878)

tween distant provinces and the capital, that a good many of the representatives of lords residing in Kyôto in their turn declared themselves independent. The peasant farmers living on these privileged holdings, since they enjoyed comparative freedom, banded together under the leadership of the ex-representative, now a local lord, so as to resist, if need be, the claims of the nobles of Kyôto or of the government officials. It was, therefore, quite natural for bonds of dependence to be forged between the heads of families or of clans of farmer warriors and the actual, if not lawful, lords.

The government, not having an adequate army at its disposal, was compelled, in order to put down local uprisings, to call upon the forces of these clan leaders. The latter were not slow to enter the contest for the acquisition of power. Two of the greatest of these clans, the Minamoto (or Genji) and the Taira (or the Heishi, or Heike), savagely attacked each other. After many disorders, arising directly from political causes, but inevitable considering that a new class of men had arisen in opposition – as much by its character as by its way of life – to that of the aristocracy, the province revenged itself on the capital. After the Taira clan had been overthrown in

23

1185 following a bitter struggle, a military dictatorship or *bakufu* was soon set up at Kamakura by the head of the victorious clan, Minamoto-no-Yoritomo, allied to the main leaders of the clans of the north and the east.

MEDIEVAL JAPAN

When Yoritomo received the coveted title of *Seii-Taishôgun* (Commander-in-Chief), from the emperor in 1192, he already controlled virtually half of Japan. With the emperor rendered powerless for want of money and troops, the bakufu endeavoured to impose its rule on the whole of Japan: this was the beginning of the time of the samurai. It took four centuries for these warriors to assert themselves, four centuries of vicissitudes, battles, political and social disorders of all kinds. The entire country was entering an active phase, like a volcano wakening after lying dormant for a long period of time. At the end of the twelfth century it seemed as if a complete change was about to take place, a total eruption in all the domains. In point of fact, the outcome of a great many developments meant that there was no real eruption: Japan had roused herself from her torpor, and was about to come to life. But what she sought most of all, throughout rebellions, wars, unremitting rivalries and vicissitudes of every description, was stability. This period of confusion, which witnessed the triumph of the samurai class, can be called 'the Middle Ages of Japan', although this title does not correspond exactly to a coherent social structure any more than to a clearly defined policy.

This medieval period was in fact made up of changes and alliances between the opposing parties, which were no sooner entered into than broken. Political systems were unstable, one reform followed another, decided on from one day to the next. Whereas, during the Heian period it was the imperial city of Kyôto (then called Heiankyô) which alone, or almost alone, 'shaped' the life of the country, it was now the turn of the provinces, rent by cruel factions, to set an example to the nation. The Buddhist monks seemed to have foreseen this medieval disruption. They were forever prophesying, on the strength of an old tradition, the end of the Buddhist law and the beginning, from the year 1052, of a time of public disturbances and atrocities called *mappô*. Religion and literature reflected the new

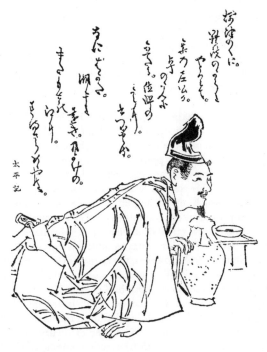

2 Hojo Tokiyori (1227–1263), fifth regent of the Kamakura
bakufu *Drawing by Kikuchi Yôsai (1788–1878)*

state of mind: while the aristocrats of the court at Kyôto continued
to devote themselves to the art of polite behaviour, the style of the
writers of that feverish era was apt to be the one usually associated
with the recording of heroic exploits. Art, linking up with a tradition dating from the Nara period, reverted to realism before being
once more completely transformed and revalued by the advent of
the teaching of Zen.

At first there was an attempt to stem the Heian tide. Then, with
the return of the military government to Kyôto under the Ashikaga
shôgun, the savage energy of the warrior class blended with the
decadent affectation of an imperial court weakened to the last degree.
The development of ideas, like the behaviour of men, suffered an

astonishing irregularity, at one time violent and cataclysmic, at another vacillating, sometimes still hesitant as if in despair of ever reaching a satisfactory conclusion. This was an epoch characterized by the deepest pessimism, glimpsed in the teachings of a popularized form of Buddhism, in the prophecies of the famous Nichiren, as in the final acceptance of a death synonymous with freedom, salvation and peace.

Historians have a habit of splitting up this long 'Middle Ages' into three phases. The first, called the 'Kamakura' period, dating from 1185 to 1333, saw the setting up, at Kamakura (not far from present-day Tokyo) of a prefeudal shôgunate, administered on behalf of the shôgun, by a line of regents who were all members of the Hôjô family. This era was disturbed by two Mongol attacks in 1274 and 1281 which, mobilizing all the forces of the country over a protracted period, utterly exhausted it. The imperial court, with the aid of some samurai malcontents, took advantage of this to rebel and overthrow the Kamakura bakufu: this meant the 'Restoration of the Kemmu Era'. However, the Emperor Go-Daigo remained on the throne for a very short time: a samurai, Ashikaga Takauji, drove him out in order to establish in Kyôto itself, another military dictatorship. Then came the second period, called the 'Ashikaga' period or again the 'Muromachi' period from the name of a district in Kyôto, and beginning in 1336. A war of rivalry between two imperial courts, one in the south (the rightful one) and the other in the north, upheld by the Ashikaga, put the country to fire and sword until 1392. In the following century, endless civil wars witnessed the senior samurai or *daimyô* opposing one another: then followed the epoch of real feudalism. Finally, some of the more powerful samurai succeeded in bringing the other lords to their senses and imposing their will on the country. This was the era of the dictator-administrators, Oda Nobunaga and Toyotomi Hideyoshi which, from 1568 (or 1573 by some accounts), led in 1603 to the setting up of a stable shôgunate under the protection of the Tokugawa shôgun, a form of government which endured for three centuries, in fact until 1868.

These different phases, briefly considered here, present very varied characteristics, now and then affording rather strange contrasts. Nevertheless, they correspond to stages on the road to the awakening of a national consciousness in a people which saw its leaders constantly changing, its aspirations disappointed, its hopes blighted.

THE COURT AT KYÔTO

It is more than likely that the sovereigns of Kyôto, having remained devoutly 'Heian', as much in their way of life as in their demeanour, lived, in the twelfth and thirteenth centuries, in the same style as the emperors of whom the great ladies of the court[1] speak in their writings of the tenth and eleventh centuries. The extra-feudal position of the emperor, which made him a theoretical head of state without any real power, compelled him to lead a secluded life and, while he might appoint the shôgun, he was forced to hand over virtually all his powers, only retaining a religious and traditional authority in principle. Although a few emperors, such as Go-Toba and Go-Daigo, had attempted, on more than one occasion, to take over the reins of government, their sacred character spared them neither humiliation nor even deportation.

The emperor and his court usually lived at Kyôto in the imperial palace, that is when the latter was neither destroyed by fire nor undergoing reconstruction (the Chronicles state that, during Ichijô's reign alone, from 980 to 1011, the palace was burnt down on an average once every four years![2]). Quite often, however, their majesties would live in one of their minor palaces, either one belonging to their father-in-law or brother-in-law, who was nearly always a Fujiwara regent. They travelled little, except for official visits to state sanctuaries. Life in the palace, as much for the sovereign as for the nobles of his household, would have been intolerably dull and devoid of interest were it not for the many festivals, mostly religious, which took place at regular intervals and so broke the monotony of the passing days and seasons.

However refined and elegant the tastes and aesthetic sensitivity of the great aristocrats might be, they lacked the most elementary comforts of life. One might be inclined to picture the existence of the Japanese nobles as luxurious. It was nothing of the kind, at least in the sense that we, in accordance with our Western criteria, understand luxury. Winter is extremely cold in the basin formed by the plain of Kyôto. For all that, the emperor had nothing to warm himself by but a simple brazier, giving just enough heat to enable him to thaw the tips of his fingers. He remained nearly all day seated on a thick straw cushion covered with woven grass, sheltered alike from observation and insidious draughts by screens of wooden lattice covered with paper. Everything he used pointed to an exquisite

27

elegance but was hardly practical. The only light he had came from oil lamps. There was little or no furniture – just a few chests. Summer time, being hot and humid was, however, more bearable: Japanese houses are designed for hotter climates on the whole. There is a free movement of air in them and the wooden screens are then replaced by light hangings. It was quite cool in the palace but it was very dark inside, a place of perpetual twilight.

Whereas the lesser nobles could travel, ride horseback and enjoy exercise, the emperor and empress could not take part in these invigorating distractions without contravening the accepted code of behaviour: they spent their time sitting down, everlasting lookers-on. Great nobles and emperors did little walking as a rule, for it was customary for them to be carried in palanquins when they had to travel. The Emperor Go-Daigo, attempting to flee from the island to which he had been exiled, experienced such difficulty in walking that Tadaoki, one of his faithful adherents who had come to rescue him, was obliged 'to pull him along by his hands and push him by his hips'. To enable him to reach the harbour more speedily, a peasant hoisted the sovereign on to his back.[3] It is easy to understand, therefore, why sovereigns, readily agreed to abdicate in favour of one of their sons and to submit to the tonsure: as monks, they became freer to travel, freer to talk, freer also to govern in their own way, the titular sovereign being powerless to go against their will, powerless likewise to take any decisive step, being but a puppet in the hands of the Fujiwara regents.

Distractions were comparatively rare and, although great nobles and sovereigns might take pleasure in playing the flute and in writing poems, their life wore on with intolerable tedium. A sense of propriety and polite behaviour would not allow them to make the slightest alteration in this state of affairs. And the writings of that period sometimes give us an impression of frightful boredom hanging over the life of the court. So it is that 'flirting' played an important part in the lives of both the men and women of the aristocracy. Polygamy was customary, and licence permitted on the understanding that the woman was discreet. The 'good-folk' of Heian-kyô, disdaining to concern themselves with what went on around them, deliberately ignored the rest of Japan and gave their minds to aesthetic practice and religious devotions.[4]

Religious feeling wavered between divinatory practices, together with the observance of countless interdicts governing the most trifling of human activities, and the Buddhist sense of the imperma-nence of all worldly things, not to mention the solemnities of Shintô worship. Retreats, pilgrimages and endless rituals punctuated the life of the 'gentry' of Heian-kyô, utterly absorbed as it was with details of dress or a fleeting aesthetic emotion. Idleness seemed to constitute the essence of refinement.

Needles to say, the townsfolk of Kyôtô itself pulsated with vulgar, clamorous life, as ready for brawls as for dissipation, loving, hating, working from dawn to dusk without haste or respite, making it possible, through their sufferings, for the handful of idlers, who were oblivious to these sufferings, and believed themselves to be different from the rest of the world, to live a life of elegant boredom. Never-theless, at Kamakura in the east of the country, in the 'Tent dis-trict' (*bakufu*) of Minamoto-no-Yoritomo, history, rekindled by the warmth of combat, incited to rebellion a people which, unlike its aristocratic masters, refused to remain static in an outmoded pre-sent. While the nobles of Kyôtô were writing poetry, the masses in the provinces were raising their voices.

CHAPTER TWO

MEDIEVAL MAN

BIRTH

To reach manhood in this feudal Japan, one had first of all to survive, for the law of natural selection dealt very harshly with the newly born. The severity of the climate and a complete lack of hygiene were responsible for an incalculable number of deaths. Births took place in private, as they still do today in the more remote provinces of Japan. No one appeared to know that a child was being born in the next house for women never cried out with the pains of childbirth,[1] perhaps for fear of losing face or of afterwards being considered immodest. Yet a birth was very much an everyday occurrence, married women finding themselves pregnant practically every year; but it was not seemly to let the family or villagers know about it in case the child did not survive the ordeal of childbirth and this was most probably the reason for keeping any imminent births a secret.

The day before the confinement which, among well-to-do families, had to take place in a room away from the main part of the house, sisters and close relatives of the mother-to-be, having come to assist in the delivery, covered up any openings in the room with white curtains, and spread out in the middle of the floor a plain white linen cloth or a *tatami* edged with a white fabric specially prepared for the occasion. When ' · time came, the expectant mother, also dressed in white, was taken into the room which had been prepared for her. Outside, during the whole time she was in labour a man, either a hunter or a warrior-monk, as the case might be, or even a Shintô priest, would pluck a bow-string so as to ward off evil spirits and to attract the attention of the *kami* or 'divine spirits'[2]; sometimes a monk, seated in front of a small folding table, on which had been placed vertically seven strips of paper or of white cotton kami tokens, recited prayers of purification (*harai*). Inside the room, the woman in labour would be in a squatting position on the white fabric or the tatami now covered with a thick padding, supporting herself on the shoulders of women sitting at either side of her. In some cases a *miko* (a kind of Shintô priestess), squatting not far away and equipped with a rosary, would also offer up prayers to the kami, while servants came and went, bustling about, bringing buckets of hot water and setting out close at hand, ready for use, a stack of sheets of thin paper which in those days served as linen. The baby was received on to a piece of white material held by one of the midwives helping the new mother, and the umbilical cord was cut at once with a bamboo knife. Then the baby was wiped clean while the mother lay down and servants and helpers cleaned and put the room to rights;[3] next, a sign was hung up outside the room betokening a taboo (usually a sprig of willow which was credited with powerful prophylactic properties[4]) and indicating that no visitor could be admitted, the new mother, according to ritual, being considered defiled, likewise all those who had gone near her. It was for this reason that the confinement had, preferably, to take place in a room separated from the main building.[5]

Probably the event took place in very much the same way in poorer families, except for the white clothing, *tatami*, servants and priests. Then it was the father himself who had to act as devil-chaser by plucking his bow-string. Of course, the neighbours were fully aware of what was happening, but they pretended not to know anything about it as long as they had not been officially told. The baby was hardly ever bathed right after its birth, but merely wiped clean. The first bath (*ubuyu*) was only given several days later. In aristocratic circles, it took on the significance of a rite. Jewels were dropped into the bath water, pledge of the child's future prosperity, and over the surface of the water, so as to be reflected in it, was held a small statue or picture of a dog or a tiger, as these animals were thought to possess healing virtues and to have the power to safeguard the health of children. The bath over, the child was clothed in his first garments.[6] Until then, he had been left naked, in direct contact with his mother's breast. In the poorest families, the first bath was simply accompanied by the plucking of a bow-string.

The Japanese of former days believed that from birth, and for thirty days after, the soul of the child was not firmly attached to his body, so the greatest precautions were taken, neither the child nor the mother being allowed to go out during this lapse of time. For the first two days, the baby was not fed. On the third day, when the mother gave it the breast for the first time, the midwife and close relations gathered together in an intimate little ceremony in order to choose the name the child would bear.[7] Then the taboo sign was removed, except from the room where the mother and child were. After he had been purified (through the ministrations of a Shintô priest in the case of wealthy families, by a simple bath in others), the father of the new-born child welcomed his guests and set before them a light meal served with *sake* (rice wine). Then a child's name was chosen. If it was a question of an heir, the name usually had to end in -*maru* or -*maro*. If it was the couple's first-born, the marriage was considered definitely sealed. The next procedure (but this was sometimes done later) was the baby's first hair-cut, with scissors. The tiny locks were then enclosed in a box and buried in the village shrine, to intimate to the kami (*ujigami*) that the child was being entrusted to his care.[8]

The birth of twins was not as a rule welcome, the mother feeling rather ashamed of having given birth 'like the animals' and popular belief maintaining that misfortune would dog the lives of children so born. Therefore, in order to ward off evil influences, they were given particularly felicitous names.[9]

Although childbirth was surrounded by a certain amount of mystery, the emotions that it never failed to arouse in parents were often described in the novels of the time. And, in the *Gikeiki*, a story relating the vicissitudes of the unfortunate Yoshitsune in the north of the country, the narrator even makes us witness the birth of the outlaw's son in the forest:

'As for Hitachibô, he too joined his hands in prayer while Kane-fusa gave a great sigh. Yoshitsune was resting, as if exhausted, near his wife. "Ah! how it hurts!" exclaimed the lady, holding tight to Yoshitsune's arm when she recovered consciousness (for she had fainted a few minutes before while Benkei, Yoshitsune's faithful servant, had gone to the foot of the hill looking for water). Benkei set about massaging her back and the child was born without further difficulty. Benkei wrapped the wailing baby in his monk's cowl, awkwardly cut the umbilical cord and washed the infant with water from the jug.

' "We must name him right away. We are in the mountains of Kamewari. Since *kame* means tortoise and since the latter is said

1 *Ginkaku-ji*—tea-house of the Shôgun at Kyôto. On the top is a *hô-ô* (phoenix of gold-plated metal)

2 'Threshing of rice' from *Shiki Kōsaku Zu* ('Painting of the Four Seasons') by Kanō Yukinobu (1513–75). Ink on

to live for a long time, let us add *tsuru*, crane, which some say lives for a thousand years, so we must call him Kametsuru!" he suggested.

' "Poor helpless child! Will he ever grow up?" moaned Yoshitsune. "If my future were brighter, everything would be perfect. It would be better to abandon him in these mountains while he is still to young to be aware of it!"

'His wife forgot her recent sufferings: "Shame on you for saying such a thing!" she began to shout. "Now that he has been fortunate enough to enter the land of the living, how dare you speak of killing him before he has even had time to set eyes on the moon and the sun! Kanefusa, take the baby if his Lordship is dissatisfied! He must not die, even if you and I have to go back to the capital with him!" '[10]

In every family, although they often tried not to show it, a birth was always considered a happy event, and the first to rejoice in it were, obviously, the parents. At the court, however, girls were more passionately longed for than boys, for they could always hope to make a marriage above their station. When a young woman had just been raised to a very high rank, the *Taiheiki*, which tells us this story, comments on this fact, adding: 'Her glory was reflected upon her family, somewhat strangely, however, and in such a way that the people in the locality of the court had nothing but scorn for boys, only longing in future for girls. . . .'[11] Nevertheless, a son brought great joy also, for here was an event one could be proud of, especially if it was a question of a first-born. After the birth of Genji's son the Emperor showed as much impatience to see Fujitsubo's child as the father himself.

'To this end, Genji visited his wife's palace at a time when there were still very few people about, and had a note taken to her telling her that, in view of the state of impatience the Emperor was in, and since etiquette prevented him from coming himself before several weeks had gone by, he begged her to be kind enough to let him see the child so that he could describe him to the Emperor.'[12]

On the thirty-first day for boys and the thirty-third for girls, the mother, accompanied by a few relatives, went out for the first time and visited the Shintô shrine with her child. After being presented to the priest, the mother would clap her hands to attract the attention of the kami of the place and light a lamp.[13] Next, a meal was prepared at the house, to which all those who were present on the day of the child's birth, as well as intimate friends, were invited. The child was then considered to be officially part of the community. Every taboo then being finally lifted, the father could once more approach his wife. From that day, the baby (at least among common folk) would leave its mother's arms to be carried around on her back. Weaning generally took place very belatedly, parents instinctively putting off this stage of development which was thought, at that time, to be a danger to the life of the baby. At this juncture, it was given a little water in which rice had been cooked, to begin with, then some rice or other cereals in the form of gruel.

Towards the hundred and twentieth day after the birth, it was customary for the parents to invite the family and a few friends, and the baby then received its first solid food. This ceremony was called *tabezome*. A small table was made ready for the baby, a table set with such things as bowls and chopsticks, black for a boy, black and red for a girl. After thanking the guests for the interest they were showing in the child's health, the mother would take the baby on to her knees, sit down at the table and, with the help of chopsticks, lift a grain of rice into its mouth.[14] Thereupon, everyone offered wishes for the baby's health. At last came the so-much dreaded day when weaning was complete, from which time the child was no longer fed only on pap made from cereals. Not much distinction was made between the children while they were very young, although the feeling about the law of primogeniture was instilled into the first-born very early on – he was always the first served, and slightly favoured in comparison with his younger brothers.

THE WORLD OF CHILDHOOD

The first birthday (*tanjōbi*) was an occasion of great rejoicing both in the child's life and the parents', even among the poorest people. At this time friends of the family offered the baby its first toys, usually dolls made of wood or rag, or little, painted terra-cotta dogs. Age was reckoned in the following manner: at its birth, the baby was already considered as a year old (the period of gestation counting as a year); then at the beginning of the year following the one it was born in, another year was ascribed to it. So a baby born on the last day of the year was, from the next day, two years old.

When the child began to talk properly, generally at about five for boys and four for girls, the hair-cutting ceremony, called *kamisogi*,[15] took place. The child was made to stand on a *go* board and the operation was carried out with scissors. As a rule the hair was merely bobbed, the cut locks being placed on a tray. However, this custom was not observed everywhere and, in most cases, especially among country-folk, children's hair was summarily clipped or even at times not cut at all. Their heads were shaved when they had too many lice. Where the girls were concerned, they usually kept a complete head of hair; they were only obliged to cut it if they renounced the world or became widows and did not want to marry again.

Japanese children's games were the same as those of all children the world over. When very young, they amused themselves with dolls made out of wood, rag or straw, with figurines of painted clay, sometimes mounted on wheels and which they pulled along behind them.[16] Little boys, of course, played at war with bows, and with wooden swords of their own making, or else they teased the dogs to be found, in any number, in the courtyard of every house. In summer little boys, especially of the lower orders, would run about stark naked. From a certain age, they were dressed in a kind of very short kimono tied round the waist by a band of material stitched to the garment, and barely long enough to hide the drawers made of coarse hempen cloth which they occasionally wore. It must be added that this kimono was so short only because the child had grown too quickly. Only the children of nobles or very rich people wore clothes made to measure. The hair-style of young boys and girls of 'good family' was different from that of youngsters who had reached their 'majority'. Boys' hair was generally cut to shoulder length, then gathered into a bunch on the crown of the head and tied up with a bit of cord, while girls' hair was gathered into heavy curls held back off the face by ribbons.[17] But very often boys and girls had their hair done and were dressed in the same way and it was difficult, at first sight, above all with children of the common people, to make out to which sex they belonged.

When they were about five, the belt, which until then had been sewn on to the children's kimonos, was now worn separately;[18] then at about seven for boys, and six for girls, a little family ceremony took place designed to bless their real 'coming out' of babyhood. The boys then put on (for the first time) a *hakama*, a kind of very

35

full pair of breeches slit at the sides and slipped on over the kimono, and the girls were given a real kimono. This festival was generally held on the day corresponding to November 15th, before going to the shrine to give notice of the occasion to the kami. Children of the samurai were then presented to the chief of the clan, those of great nobles to the emperor, the others to the headman of the village or to some person of consequence in the city, a governor or some such dignitary. From that time onwards, the child had the right to wear a head-dress made from a triangle of paper or of black stiffened cloth tied high on his forehead by a ribbon: such was his first head-dress, or *hitai-eboshi*.[19] Children were thereafter free to come and go with relatively little supervision: they were allowed to do as they pleased. They were very rarely beaten; when they had done something naughty, they were merely scolded severely. Children were almost looked upon as holy: it was believed that it pleased certain divinities to be reincarnated in their likeness.

From the first fine days of spring, children virtually lived out of doors, giving themselves up with all the fervour of youth to a multiplicity of games: a kind of pall-mall consisting of driving a ball with a curved stick[20] (a ritual called *gicchô*[21] which the adults enjoyed on New Year's Day), races on stilts,[22] wrestling contests, and every kind of team game, as well as dances and songs. Of course, there were fights and blows were exchanged. In most cases, the children of both sexes took part in the same games. The girls were no less enthusiastic than the boys in hunting crickets, fire-flies and various singing insects for which they constructed minute cages of bamboo or grass. The boys, especially, liked to capture dragon-flies (*tombo*), those gracefully flying 'nymphs' (so numerous that Japan was sometimes poetically styled 'The country of the dragon-flies') and to make them fight each other. The warriors used to call these warlike insects *kachi-mushi*, or 'victory insects', and the clothes of men going into battle would be tied up with special knots in the shape of a dragon-fly. The girls preferred to collect great quantities of fire-flies and to keep them in little cages. They did not kill them, in the fond belief that these fire-flies were the lost souls of the dead.[23]

Yet, the lives of children more than six or seven years old in ancient Japan were not always just fun and games. Boys and girls had to go to school at a very early age in noble families. The education of girls was from this point of view somewhat neglected: they were merely taught to read and write the *kana* (syllabic symbols numbering only fifty-one). The education of the boys, on the other hand, was more strict: in addition to Japanese writing, Chinese literature and writing, they had to learn by heart many Chinese classics, Buddhist *sûtra* and ancient poems contained in the anthologies put together by scholarly Emperors. For the young nobleman of those days, outdoor games alternated with extremely serious lessons in writing and literature. In his leisure moments he would delight his mind by composing verses.[24]

The children of the masses and of the small farmers were fortunate: in most cases, as their parents could neither read nor write, and since there were no schools for the common people, they were saved the worry of studying. On the other hand, these boys and girls had much to learn on the practical side. They accompanied their parents wherever their work took them, in the field or at home, helping them as best they could, gradually being initiated into country life, learning to recognize plants and animals, seasons and crops; they cut grass for the oxen and horses, gathered mulberry leaves for the silkworms, collected dead wood for the fire, led the horses or oxen, or helped in the kitchen.

In the cities the craftsman initiated his son, as soon as the latter was old enough to understand, into the secrets of his craft and would entrust him with tasks that were within his capabilities. The warrior's son proudly carried a wooden sword and, at a very early age, learned all about arms and horses. As for the girls, before anything else, they had to be thoroughly instructed in their duties as future wives and mothers of families: their main task was to bring up their smaller brothers and sisters, in particular to carry them around on their backs. Boys and girls were constantly together. Sleeping in the same room as their parents (among the common people), very early initiated into sexual matters, they grew up without false shame, and nature held no secrets for them: sexuality was part of everyday life and no one attached any more importance to it than was necessary.

The nobles often entrusted their children, from their earliest years, to the care of the monasteries: there the monks undertook to educate and instruct them until they reached their majority. These children were cherished by the monks and priests, to whom they served as pages. Their clothes were sumptuous, they had their eyebrows shaved and were made up like women. They were the pride of the monasteries which often boasted of possessing the pret-

37

tiest and most talented pages in the district. These *chigo* studied with the utmost diligence. When Yoshitsune, Yoritomo's brother, then called Ushiwaka, was sent as page to the monastery of Kurama, the *Gikeiki* tells us that 'he spent every day with his master reciting *sûtra* and bending over the Chinese classics. When the sun sank in the west, he went on reading with his master until the lamp went out. He studied day and night, working at his books until dawn. . . .'[25] And later, Yoshitsune, in order to escape more easily disguised as a monk, transformed his wife into a page:

' ". . . since you have to travel with a party of ascetics, it is better for you to look like a page. It will seem natural for you to use make-up and your age will present no difficulty."

'Benkei drew his sword "Cleaver of Rocks" and remorselessly chopped off her beautiful hair until it was just level with her breast. Then he combed it (to look like a boy's), arranged it on top of her head, applied a little make-up to her face and painted a delicate pair of eyebrows high on her forehead. She dressed herself in five under-kimonos. . . . Next she put on a pair of breeches fastened high up on her legs, a loose overgarment and a silk hakama . . . straw sandals and a hat of newly-plaited bamboo. At her side she hung a brilliantly coloured fan and a sword with a red wooden hilt. She carried a Chinese flute made of bamboo (which obviously she could not play as she was a woman) and Benkei had hung around her neck a bag of midnight blue brocade containing five chapters of the *Lotus Sutra*.'[26]

These *chigo* throughout the feudal period – when homosexuality was not uncommon (and was accepted) in monastic communities as in the warrior class – looked exactly like young girls. Some, on their majority, became monks; others returned to their families.

In the families of the lesser nobility and the warriors, children were not sent away to monasteries so often, their education being generally attended to at home, or in the household of some nobleman of the district or the capital. The child was then entrusted to a rich family and, while perfecting his education, was obliged to serve as a page (or waiting-maid). One of the tasks of the lower ranking pages was to attend to the needs of their masters throughout the countless and extremely long religious ceremonies. To this end, they were frequently provided with a long tube of bamboo which they carried hanging from their girdles and which was designed

38

to allow the lord to relieve his bladder without moving from his place during the ceremony.[27]

Sometimes, but chiefly in the families of the lesser nobility, a young man was placed with a skilled craftsman, a sculptor or painter, so that he could be instructed in one of the Fine Arts. As soon as farmers' children were strong enough to work, they took an active part in everyday tasks, working as hard in the family fields as on works of communal interest (irrigation channels, roadways, bridges, a diversity of building operations), and included in these there were the jobs prescribed by the local lord or the government: the child had hardly any leisure except during the winter months when, working in the fields being difficult, the parents stayed at home. The children might then receive a little instruction, either at the local temple where a specially delegated monk sometimes fulfilled the office of teacher, or from the village elders.

At Kôyto, from the fourteenth century, an epoch in which the Zen monks, all-powerful at the court of the Ashikaga shôgun, directed the college patronized by the Uesugi family, the five great Zen monasteries of the capital (*gozan*) welcomed the children of the well-to-do classes and provided them with an education at once theoretical (chiefly the classics and Chinese poetry) and practical (simple arithmetic and good manners). During the Muromachi period, in the majority of their provincial temples (*ankoku-ji*), the Zen monks established schools intended especially for the children of the lower classes. In these schools, the young learned to read and write the *kana* and Sino-Japanese characters, and also the rudiments of polite behaviour from handbooks (whose ethics we would certainly consider dubious) such as the *Teikin Ôrai* or 'Manual of Domestic Instruction.'[28]

As for the warriors' sons, they received, from their most tender years, the education essential to the samurai and consequently became familiar with the two arts indispensable in the eyes of their class: culture (that is chiefly writing and a knowledge of the Chinese classics), and the use of arms. In the *Genpei Seisuiki*, a chronicle dating from the beginning of the fourteenth century, Okazaki Bunzô, teacher of his lord's son, relates: '. . . when he was five or six years old, I taught him to handle a small bow and some arrows of thin bamboo and to shoot at a target, at deer and rabbits and to ride horseback so as to chase rabbits and deer. . . .'[29] Generally the samurai, who made it a point of honour to educate their sons themselves, bent all their efforts to instilling into them the principles of loyalty and courage which would enable them, in their turn, to become samurai worthy of the name. Although 'culture', to very many of them, seems to have been somewhat neglected in favour of the military arts, some warriors took great pride in their learning, going so far as to lend their patronage to temples or shrines which developed into so many schools and important cultural centres.

Their children, while carrying on the profession of arms, entered these monasteries towards the age of ten, to stay there for four or five years, during which time they had to work extremely hard: in the morning there was the reading of *sûtra*, then exercises in calligraphy until midday. After lunch came lectures on general matters, followed by physical exercises. Finally the evening was reserved for poetry and music, for the practice of the horizontal flute or the fipple flute, instruments considered eminently masculine. Reading comprised particularly ancient history, war chronicles, compendiums of law like the *Jôei-Shikimoku* (promulgated in 1232) and collections of exemplary maxims such as the *Dôjikyô* or 'Precepts for the use of children', or again the *Sanjikyô*, 'Epigrams of three characters', all works intended to form the minds of the young samurai.[30]

The children of nobles as a rule received a less practical education. It was above all essential for them to learn, in addition to calligraphy, poetry and the Chinese classics, music and painting, the more social graces such as correct posture and the rules of etiquette – at that time extremely elaborate – and the art of distinguishing between the different kinds of incense perfumes, iris bulbs, shellfish, tea, etc. Young girls learned how to dress with taste and spent their time playing music, composing poems, or dancing. For boys, things were quite different: they took part in hawking expeditions, competed in feats of horsemanship, held archery competitions and played *kemari*, a kind of football.

COMING OF AGE

Lastly the 'coming of age' was reached. In the samurai class it took place at fifteen for boys; in the other classes, generally around thirteen, It was an important occasion, for the child became officially adult. From that moment it was obligatory for the young man to wear breeches, and girls had to forego their participation in boys' games. This time-honoured admission into adult life was recognized by a ceremony. The young man was given a new hakama (breeches), and his hair was arranged in a coil on the top of his head. A lucky day had to be chosen for the ceremony of the donning of a man's head-dress (*eboshi*), a ceremony during which a godparent was required to give the adolescent his man's name, a name which at that time had to be made up of two characters, one hereditary, the other personal.[31] From that day onwards, the young man had the right to use a special mark (*kaô*) for signing his name. He had attained his majority and was free to do as he pleased.

' ". . . I will not go to Ôshû as a page!" said Shanaô to Kichiji. "I must appear wearing a man's headdress, a borrowed one if necessary! See to it!" The high-priest (of the temple where young Shanaô – Yoshitsune's childhood name – found himself at that time) obtained an *eboshi*, put Shanaô's hair up and placed the head-dress on his head. Thereupon, Shanaô said: "If I go to Oshu as I am, I shall have to answer 'Shanaô' when Hidehira asks my name. There will be nothing to show that I have reached manhood. Unless my name has already been changed, Hidehira will be sure to suggest holding a ceremony for the putting on of the hat, but it would set many tongues wagging if the latter were performed by someone whose family is an hereditary vassal of the Minamotos! I want the ceremony to take place here, in the presence of the gods and of Yoritomo's mother!"

'He performed the purification ceremony himself and led the way to the august divinities, followed by the priest and Kichiji.

' "Since I am Yoshitomo's eighth child, I should be called Hachirô, but I have no desire to bear the same name as my uncle, Chinzei Hachirô, who gained such a bad reputation during the disorders of the Hôgen era. As I have no objection to being the last, name me Samakurô (the ninth of the Stables of the Left). And since my grandfather was called Tameyoshi, my father Yoshitomo and my elder brother Yoshihira, let my true name be Yoshitsune."

'Thus, he who the previous day had been called Shanaô left the temple of Atsuta (a famous Shintô shrine at Nagoya) as Yoshitsune from now on.'[32]

Among the samurai, this ceremony, called *gempuku*, took place at the age of fifteen; the young man was then entitled to carry a real sword and to use it. With the nobles of Kyôto, the requisite age was thirteen, and the ceremony was traditionally held in the temple of Hôrin-ji. The parents, on this occasion, addressed their prayers mainly to Kokûzô Bosatsu (Boddhisattva Âkâcagarbha[33]), a divinity of esoteric Buddhism who presided over the Mount of Wisdom.

When girls reached the age of puberty they had to undergo an admission rite marking their renunciation of the state of childhood and their entrance into an adult world. The ceremony, a family one, entailed less pomp than the one for the boys. It mainly consisted of shaving or plucking the eye-brows (*mayuharai*), since it was the fashion for women to paint them, either very fine or thickly curved high on their foreheads. In actual fact, this custom was only observed in noble families or those of high-ranking warriors; the women of the lower classes were satisfied with painting their teeth black. Among the common people, the rite chiefly consisted of a simple hair arrangement where the hair was tied up at the back of the head.

For young girls of 'good society' the only problem was to find a husband, if possible one in a prominent position at court, or at least to become the concubine of a great noble, or even of the Emperor. In Kyôto, the position of imperial concubine was very much sought after among the aristocracy.

In the country, young girls were not in such a hurry to marry, on the one hand because the sexual liberty they enjoyed before marriage was relatively great, and on the other principally because they represented for their family so many hands to be used in the cultivation of the soil; they helped with the planting out of rice seedlings, with the rearing of silkworms, the weaving of cloth and with every kind of house work. The same thing did not hold with the boys who, anxious to increase their family by bringing a wife into the home (always welcome if she showed herself willing to stand up to the work), were more likely to look for a woman able to bear children, and fitted to fulfil her role as mistress of the house. Nevertheless, it was customary to marry young so that children might reach adulthood before their parents' old age, and so allow the latter to retire at the earliest opportunity.

In the cities, where a great number of merchants and craftsmen lived, the young men served an apprenticeship. In this case, the rite of admission to adulthood, *gempuku*, took place earlier, at the age of ten or twelve. The young man entered the service of a merchant or a craftsman as a servant and, while engaged in his menial duties, was gradually initiated into the niceties of his trade. This apprenticeship was generally very long and the 'patron' then virtually took the place of the apprentice's family. When he judged that the young man had gained enough experience and mastery to fend for himself, he sometimes adopted him as a son and successor if he had no heir, or even helped him to set up on his own. Very often, he even gave him the right to use his own name and took it upon himself to find him a wife. Whatever his good qualities and shortcomings, the master was always deeply respected and obeyed, a privilege he shared with his apprentice's parents.

During the Middle Ages, few people, apart from the nobles, possessed a family name. Hideyoshi, the Dictator-Administrator at the end of the sixteenth century, after being honoured by the Emperor with a family name, was nicknamed Kinoshita, which means roughly '(found) under a tree', by reason of his obscure birth. Farmers and the lower classes, called *hyakushônin* or 'men with a hundred names', were only known at that time by their individual nicknames. Craftsmen, artists or other members of a guild often added the name of the latter to their surname. Only the aristocrats in possession of an official post, or belonging to a large family or clan, and the high-ranking samurai, were entitled to an hereditary family name, as were also certain persons of distinction specially honoured by the emperor with a patronymic. In the country districts it often happened that all the inhabitants of a village or a locality were called by the same name: in this way, this toponym eventually became a true family name, valid for all the inhabitants born in that particular place, even if they were not related at all. But in Japan, the formation of family names followed the same rules as in Europe. As far as the educated aristocrats were concerned, they often copied the Chinese fashion which decreed that a person of quality must not be referred to by his name, but only by his *azana*, or substitute name. The artists, the monks (who changed their name when they entered religion), and certain craftsmen, are only known to us by their *azana*.

It was also customary to confer a posthumous name on anyone who died. It is for this reason that the emperors are nearly always referred to in history by the posthumous title decreed by their successor. A common practice was to name the children according to the order of their birth: Ichirô (first son), Jirô, Saburô, Shirô,

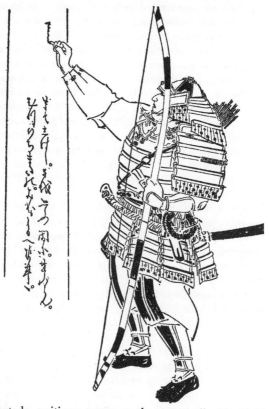

3   Suketada, writing a poem on the stone *torii* with the blood of
his little finger   *Drawing by Kikuchi Yôsai (1788–1878)*

Gorô, etc., if they were of the male sex, or to give them the names of
flowers, qualities or objects if they were of the female sex: Take
(bamboo), Haru (springtime), Yuki (snow), Kiku (chrysanthemum),
Sei (purity), Toshi (goodness), etc.

In the samurai class, each family, as well as a personal name,
possessed a *mon*. This 'symbol' has often been confused with a coat
of arms. In point of fact, the *mon* only represents the distinguishing
sign of a clan, a family or a social group. At first borne by the samurai on their banners, these *mon* were very quickly adopted by their

vassals to show their affiliation, then by the ordinary *bushi* (warriors) themselves who took to displaying their chief's *mon* stitched to their clothing. The fashion spread rapidly and even the nobles of Kyôto adopted this custom. These *mon* generally consisted of a simple geometric design (a circle or a square) representing a plant, an animal, an object, a flower or again some stylized characters. The commoners were not entitled to use these.

High-ranking warriors made a practice of signing their farewell poems or any precious documents, particularly those establishing their allegiance, with their blood. For to sign or to write with one's own blood, in itself exceptional, conferred an immense value on the writing thus authenticated, pledging, as it did, the life of the signatory:

'When Suketada was passing by the stone *torii* (a sacred gateway of Shintô shrines) he caught sight of the poem written by the lay monk Hitomi Shirô who had fallen (in the previous battle) with his father. He bit the little finger of his right hand and wrote a few verses with this finger, thinking: "Here is something which will surely be preserved in the legends of future generations." Thereupon he made his way to Akasaka castle.[34]

As for the uneducated country people, they generally signed by placing their right thumb print on the document. In some cases, the religious classes placed the print of one or of both hands at the bottom of a document; so it is that Hônen wrote, at the bottom of his profession of faith called 'Oath in one page' (*Ichi-mai Kishômon*) dated from the first moon of the second year of the Kenryaku era (1212): 'I here set my two hands as a seal and witness.'

MARRIAGE

Next came the time for marriage, the most important event in the life of a man or woman of that epoch. Marriage, as a general rule, was arranged by the parents with, it is true, the more or less tacit consent of the young people, or else arranged by the young couple themselves, who tried to manage it in such a way that the marriage could not be prevented. In the majority of cases, moreover, the preliminaries prescribed by custom were entrusted to a man or woman go-between. In the country or in the towns, with the common people, the young girl, as soon as her parents had chosen a suitable husband, had to learn to fit in with the ways of her new family by going every day to help with house or farm work. This period of training lasted from one to several months. During this time, the young man she was to marry had the right to go and spend the night with her in the home of his future parents-in-law. This trial marriage was, therefore, doubly probationary, for the family and for the intended husband. Of course, the young girl, if she was not happy in her new family, was entitled to refuse to marry the man.

During the Heian and at the beginning of the Kamakura epochs, polygamy was the rule throughout the aristocracy. It laid upon the man the duty of going to live with each of his wives in turn, usually in the mother-in-law's house. This system, valid for the leisured classes, became difficult to apply when it was a question of those who had to work for a living. So, farmers and craftsmen had found a compromise which provided a solution between having a patri-archal system which was modified by the necessity of living in a matriarchal residence, and a patriarchal system which demanded residence under the patriarchal roof; this became the rule with non-aristocrats from the Kamakura epoch on. For if the great lords could have several wives and concubines, the fighting-men were almost forced to remain monogamous, a fact which, however, did not prevent them in any way from having concubines 'on the side'. With the *buke*, or warrior families, monogamy became the rule but, in the case of a wife's sterility, the men were entitled to take, as had the *kuge* or nobles, 'secondary wives' of the same social class or 'in-ferior-rank mothers' of a lower one. From the fifteenth century on-wards, however, this custom tended to disappear: in this case the absence of a male heir was remedied by the adoption of a relative or a son-in-law.[35]

In the ordinary course of events, marrying took place strictly within the limits of each class. But, as there was no absolutely clear division between classes, frequent interrelationships occurred, generally through concubinage, between the various social strata, which greatly contributed to the mixing of the population. Yet, the farmers seldom married outside their own village or group of vil-lages. Marriages between comparatively close relations were not prohibited except, however, when it was a question of an ascendant or descendant in direct line, of a brother or a sister, or of a half-brother and half-sister. There was no age limit apart from that determined by custom in each district or village. This varied according to the class or the epoch.[36] If, in the samurai class, parental consent was obligatory – the father's opinion generally prevailing – it was not as necessary in the other classes, everything depending essentially upon the conditions under which the marriage was to take place. Generally speaking, parents did their utmost to make their children happy and to encourage a good match.

Marriage was strictly a family matter, at least where the nobles and commoners were concerned. Yet, political interests sometimes turned marriages into affairs of state. As the Fujiwara regents made it a practice to marry their daughters to emperors so as to uphold their privileges and high political standing, a number of clan leaders, too, pursued a policy of matrimonial alliances, giving their daughters in marriage to neighbouring lords or influential persons. With the warriors of the Middle Ages, it was customary to have recourse to this procedure to make sure of allies in case of dissension.

This practice enabled men to strengthen their authority while weakening that of the women whose authority (we should say influence rather than authority), until then had been encouraged by the custom of residence in the matriarchal home, although women continued to hold a chosen place in Japanese society. A certain Masaka, Yoritomo's wife, did not hesitate to take the reins of government into her hands on her husband's death and to engage in open conflict with her father, Hôjô Tokimasa, over her son Yoriie. Women remained in a very strong position in samurai society during the Kamakura epoch; but this position gradually decreased in strength during the struggles which took place in the Muromachi and Momoyama periods, to dwindle into insignificance during the epoch of the Edo bakufu, under the growing influence of the neo-Confucian philosophy of Chu-Hsi.

Before marriage, young girls went secretly to pray to the local kami and attached to the branches of the sacred tree sheets of paper with their name on and the name of the man they wanted to marry, so that the kami, being acquainted with their wish, might look with favour on their union (*en-musubi* or 'marriage-bond').

It sometimes happened that, in some farming families, the parents objected to their daughter's choice. Under these circumstances, the 'theft of the fiancée' was organized by the young man with the help of a few friends. The young girl, forewarned and assenting, left her parents' house crying: 'I'm going away' so that her family might be warned, and took refuge in the home of the man she loved, where the marriage formalities were kept to a minimum. Next day, the young man's friends gave a banquet to which all the young couple's acquaintances were invited, with the exception of the parents who had shown their opposition to the union and who, from that time forward, no longer had the right to refuse their consent to their daughter's marriage. In some districts, trial-marriage was reversed: it was up to the young man to live and work (sometimes for wages) with his parents-in-law during a period of three to five years. After this probationary spell, during which the husband had to behave like a good son towards his future parents-in-law, he returned to his home taking his wife with him. This was known as *nenki-muko* or trial marriage over a determined time.

In the samurai and aristocratic classes, the strict seclusion of women was often offset by a fairly mild paternal authority. And, actually, the times when a young girl was forced to marry against her will must have been few and far between.

The marriage ceremony was conducted in a relatively simple fashion, its degree of ostentation depending above all on the financial circumstances of the parents. Although this ceremony was strictly a family one, sometimes a Shintô priest was asked, on this occasion, to invoke the kami and to beg for protection for the young couple. The essential rite of the marriage ceremony consisted in the exchange between the newly weds of three cups of *sake*, each one to be drunk in three sips.

The ritual exchange of the three cups of *sake*, or *sansankudô* (which is still observed in a marriage ceremony today) has been codified by the *Sangi Ittô Ô-Sôshi* or 'Samurai Rules of Etiquette' (1358–1408) in its final form. But it is more than likely that this rule of conduct endorsed an ancient custom particularly in use among the warriors and aristocrats. The lower classes in their turn took to following this custom. In former times there had been a simple exchange of food.[37] Tables already prepared were first presented to the newly-weds, and then the guests were given theirs and the banquet began. We have very detailed descriptions of these feasts in the *Hôchô-Kikigaki* (Book of Household Rites) and the *Ôgusake Ryôrisho* (Ôgûsa Family Cookery Book) of the Muromachi era, which also give instructions for the preparation of the feast

48

and the development of the ceremony among wealthy people.[38] The ceremony generally took place in the husband's home.[39]

It goes without saying that in families of modest means, the ceremonial was less elaborate. The *sake* flowed and gaiety effervesced, finding an outlet in dancing and licentious songs, and in bawdy pleasantries in which the married women present joined lustily. A meal is always a light-hearted occasion in Japan. It is the time when people forget their cares and feel themselves a little less bound by social conventions; everyone is expected to join in the merry-making and, when the *sake* is flowing freely, it is considered good manners to become slightly drunk. Every little breach of etiquette is overlooked then and no one dreams of reproaching the somewhat tipsy offender. The ceremony was generally held late in the evening. When the banquet was long drawn out, the young couple disappeared, then each in his turn went off into the night. However, the marriage was only considered really valid on the day a child was born.

If the marriage broke down, a comparatively rare event among humble folk, it was always possible to have recourse to a divorce, although this was usually frowned upon. The marriage could be broken either by mutual consent between the two parties, or by repudiation of the woman for some serious reason.[40] The wife then simply went back to her parents: her children always stayed with the husband. On the other hand, the wife of a samurai or a noble who wanted to divorce her husband without his consent, could only do so in one way: by running away. Then, so as to avoid pursuit (at least at Kamakura), she could take refuge in the Tôkei-ji temple founded by Mino-no-Tsubone, one of Yoritomo's waiting-women. The custom had been established in 1285 by the wife of the regent Tokimune, with imperial approval. The fugitive had to stay for three years in the temple, and no one had the right to annoy her or to take her back. After this lapse of time, the divorce became effective. Because these three years were eventually considered too long a time, the Abbess Yôdô, daughter of the Emperor Go-Daigo (1318–39) reduced it to two years.[41] This temple, also called Enki-ridera, the temple of divorce, gave sanctuary every year to anything from seventy to eighty women of 'good society'.

The husband had the legal right to beat his wife, albeit lightly. He must not hurt her under any circumstances, otherwise he would incur a severe penalty.[42]

THE AGES OF MAN

The most important event in the life of a Japanese of the Middle Ages, after his birth, his coming to man's estate and his marriage, was – his death. But in the course of his life there were phases that were considered difficult or dangerous, called *yakudoshi*, during which he was obliged to take the utmost precautions, the chances of accident, of sickness or death being greater then. So as to eliminate the risks of illness likely to occur during these critical periods(twenty-five, forty-two and sixty years of age for a man, nineteen and thirty-three for a woman), it was customary to throw away some personal garment, or to cast it downstream into a river so that it might bear calamities away with it. On the other hand, other ages were thought likely to bring happiness and renown. These *nenga* of Chinese origin were fixed, in the Kamakura epoch, at forty, fifty, sixty, seventy, eighty and ninety years. In the Muromachi epoch, these ages were officially raised to sixty-one, seventy-one and eighty years. The seventieth year was also one of special celebration, the eighth-century Chinese poet, Tu-Fu having written: 'From time immemorial, the age of seventy has always been a remarkable one in the span of human life.' The Japanese had great respect for old age. The imperial court made a point of paying special honour to very old and noble personages by giving them servants and, when they reached the venerable age of ninety (Fujiwara Toshinori in 1203 for instance), presenting them with a stick carved with a pigeon motif (called *Hatozue*), by way of homage. Some lords also made a practice of inviting all villagers over sixty in their domain to a great banquet every year.[43]

When he had reached that age, the head of a family had already, long since, handed over his house, fields, fortunes and cares to his heirs. When he became *inkyo*, that is 'retired', he relinquished all rights over the family, but remained none the less respected and was consulted by his heirs on matters of outstanding importance. In the samurai class, a warrior could, if granted permission by a superior, become *inkyo* even while he was relatively young, and thus leave his properties to his heirs. With the farmers, custom demanded that parents should retire from active life when their eldest son married, but they usually waited until the younger son, who was to inherit the paternal home, was established. It often happened also that parents, on retiring from active life, entered a monastery.

Legends recount that, in days gone by, in certain mountainous and extremely poor regions of Japan, there was a strange custom dictated by dire necessity. When parents had grown old, the eldest son had to carry them on his back to the top of a mountain called Obasute-yama, and there abandon them, thus getting rid of two useless mouths. This action, probably most unusual, and which doubtless only happened in times of famine, gave rise to a number of stories taken up by Buddhist monks who gave them an edifying twist. The same incident provided the theme, superlatively handled, of a short novel by the contemporary writer Fukazawa Shichirô, and entitled *Narayama bushikô* (A study of the songs of Narayama[44]).

DEATH

Death held no terrors for the Japanese of the Middle Ages. The Buddhist doctrine of the impermanence of all things very largely influenced their way of looking at life and death. Nor was there any fear of death in the Shintô mind; rather, it was looked upon as a source of contamination for those who are left behind. The deceased proceeds to a somewhat vague Beyond, a kind of country of the dead, Yomi-nokuni, and, when he has become a spirit or kami, he identifies himself with nature, having the living in his more or less benevolent care, according to whether they venerate him or not: 'Veneration on the part of man renders the divinity all the more exalted while, by the power of Divine Mercy, man's life is doubly blessed . . .' says the *Jôei Shikimoku* (1232) in what, it must be added, is a very syncretic way of thinking.[45] The Japanese, therefore, were quite familiar with the idea of death, regarded it as a universal fate which they knew was inevitable and which, fundamentally, was in conformity with the law of nature. Nor, in the case of the warrior, well used to looking death in the face, was there any room for fear. All things considered, to die was only a way of being born again into a better life.

An ancient Buddhist text[46] gives the necessary instructions for the disposal of the body: 'It is to be washed in warm water, clothed in a white cotton shroud, placed in a gilded coffin, sprinkled with perfumes, covered with sweet-smelling herbs, burned in a fire, then the bones collected and put into an urn (reliquary) . . .'

Generally speaking, clothes and any objects to which the deceased had been attached during his lifetime were buried (or burned) with the body and, so that he could pay for his passage across the river Sanzu, which separates this world from the paradise of Amida, some coins were placed beside him, as were also straw sandals, and a staff, needed for his long journey in the Beyond. The night before the obsequies, custom demanded that relatives and friends should meet together for a funerary vigil (*otsuya*). Sometimes a Buddhist monk came, too, to recite some *sûtra*. Those taking part in the *otsuya* brought presents for the afflicted family: flowers, coins, rice. The family served them a meal without meat or fish. On the evening fixed for the final farewell, the procession of relatives and friends left the house of the deceased to make their way, by torchlight, either to the funeral pyre or to the cemetery.

It was from the fourteenth century onwards that the custom was established of giving a posthumous name (*kaimyô*) to the departed, even when it was a question of someone belonging to the common people. The name was written on a lacquered tablet (*ihai*) which was placed upright on the *butsudan* or small household Buddhist altar. When the deceased was buried, a watch had to be kept over the tomb (for in country districts dogs and wild animals often came during the night to disinter the corpses[47]), then, as soon as it could be afforded, a small memorial stone was erected over it, in the form of either a simple pile of stones, or a *gorintô*, a miniature pagoda symbolizing the five elements (earth, water, fire, air and sky) and the spirit. Lastly, it was essential to leave food intended for the *gaki* (preta or hungry spirits) in order to keep them in the cemetery and prevent them from returning to disturb the living in their homes.[48] Only emperors were buried under great sepulchral mounds planted with trees. As for the nobles, they were the possessors of more modest tombs erected over the urns containing their ashes. Sometimes, instead of burying or burning the effects of the dead man, his personal possessions were taken to the temple or else, later on, they were distributed between his friends as souvenirs (*katami*). Widows, who did not intend to marry again, cut their long hair as a sign that they had renounced the pleasures of life. But in the event of a premature widowhood, the women of the people usually remarried after a few months of mourning.

Every year, from the thirteenth day of the seventh month, and for three days, the feast of the souls of the dead *urabon-e*, or more simply *Bon*, was celebrated. On the evening of the fifteenth day of the same month, the *Bon-odori* were danced for the purpose of entertaining and thanking the souls for their visit; then on the next day, the date fixed for the departure of the souls who during these three days had come to visit their families, torches were lighted to show them the way to their tombs, and strings of light skiffs, decked with lamps, were launched on the waters of the rivers. On that day, all housework ceased and even the cooking was dispensed with.[49] This period was an opportunity for much merry-making and several days holiday. Fireworks were let off in the temple courts, and in the town and village squares huge bonfires were lit, and sometimes there was dancing around them all night long. In this way, the departed were entertained and their souls, having attained a state of bliss, could in future protect the ones they had loved. The dead also became protecting kami; offerings were made to them every morning in the form of *sake* and rice.

At the time of the *higan*, the autumn and spring equinoxes, the head of the family went to the cemetery to pour water over the tomb of his dead and offer a prayer. This custom of *hakamairi*, or the visit to the cemetery, has survived until today.

The period of mourning could vary in length from a year in the event of the decease of a direct ascendant (father or mother), or of the head of the family, to seven days for a distant relative. It was generally fixed by custom at five months for grandparents, at three months for paternal uncles and aunts, wives, brothers and sisters and the eldest son, and at one month for half-brothers and sisters, maternal uncles and aunts, 'inferior mothers', children who would not inherit and the eldest grandson. The period of mourning observed in the event of an emperor's passing was a year for all court nobles.[50] However, as a general rule, mourning was not strictly observed except during the first forty-nine days, the Japanese believing that the soul of the departed did not leave the house it had lived in until the end of that time.

THE FAMILY SYSTEM

The Japanese family, at the time of the samurai and of feudalism, did not differ substantially in its organization from the family as it was during the Heian epoch. It allowed of five degrees of relationship.

This is only theory, for the true Japanese family consists, in effect, of all the individuals who live under the same roof: paternal ascendants in direct line, wives and children. This idea of family unity, put into concrete form by the household, required its own divinities. These, either in the guise of a talisman obtained from a Shintô shrine or of an image of the Buddha, were placed on a high shelf called *kamibako* or *kamidana* to honour the kami, and *butsudan* to honour the *hotoke* or Buddhist divinities. Many homes possessed both at the same time. Held in equal respect in the kitchen (*daidokoro*) were either the gods of the hearth, with sometimes, too, an effigy of Monju Bosatsu (*Manjucri*) hung about with rags, or one of Jizô (*Ksitigarbha*). Authority usually devolved upon the head of the family; from the fourteenth century on, the exercise of this authority was to acquire an absolute character in the samurai class. But, with the common people, if authority was theoretically the father's prerogative, it was the mother who held the casting vote in decisions concerning the well-being of the family: she was both companion and counsellor whose advice was frequently followed, and no important decision whatever could be made without asking her opinion. With the *buke*, however, the head of the family made practically all the decisions and, from the Muromachi epoch onwards, very often without consulting his wife. Members of his family had to obtain his permission before accepting public office, for he was answerable to his overlord for all the relatives in his care. Whoever inherited the paternal name and possessions had to provide for the needs of his brothers and sisters, who thus fell under his domination, the law of primogeniture having become absolute in the samurai class from the thirteenth century onwards.[51]

WOMEN IN THE MIDDLE AGES

The mode of life of women in the Middle Ages allowed of a great deal of variation according to their class and epoch. In aristocratic circles, a woman's life appears, as in the preceding periods, to have been one of intense boredom; most of the novels and intimate diaries written by these women portray this feeling of absolute emptiness in the midst of luxury. According to M. Joüon des Longrais:

'. . . the personal feelings of women do not seem to go beyond submission to duty, because this has been written in the book of destiny from the beginning of time. If any good comes of it, it can only be fleeting in this world where all is transitory. If misfortune results, it is doubtless because some sin committed in a previous existence must be atoned for. It never enters anyone's head to try to evade, by an act of self-will, a doom from which there is no escape. There is neither cowardliness nor stupidity in this state of passivity; the person concerned estimates her chances of good and bad fortune very accurately . . .'[52]

If this is undoubtedly true regarding noblemen's wives, the reality must have been quite different within the other classes. With the samurai as with the ordinary *bushi* (lower-ranking warriors) the woman, although not enjoying absolute authority, held an important position in her family. She often had complete control of household expenditure, and had to manage a staff of servants. It was also up to her to make sure that the very young children and the girls had a sound education. Lastly, and most importantly, she had the task of instilling into the young folk the ideals of their class, with its contempt of death and unquestioning obedience to their lord, and of teaching them the fundamental principles of Buddhism and of Confucian philosophy. However, it can be safely assumed that the lot of the wives of the *bushi* was in the long run a far from enviable one. Their husbands were more often than not either absent on military service, or abroad in attendance on their lord. In wartime, the *buke* were sometimes led by the hazards of battle to defend their own homes, often burnt down in times of strife. In this way misfortunes piled up on these warriors' dwellings; so their womenfolk's lamentations on the harshness of life are understandable:

> I spend my days bewailing
> Wearily so wearily
> The sorrows of this life.
> The longer it lasts
> The more grievous they become.[53]

It has been said that the warriors' wives of this period were neither elegant nor well-read. If it is true that they were a little scornful of the affectations of the court nobles and had a somewhat vague knowledge of the Chinese classics, on the other hand they did not disdain to compose verses in the *Yamato* tongue, that is in pure Japanese, and at least in families of some importance, were interested in all sorts of artistic pursuits. War chronicles, such as the *Azuma Kagami*, tell us of the warlike exploits of samurai wives fighting to defend their hearth and home, handling the halberd, drawing the bow, even following their husbands into battle. It does not necessarily follow that these women had a mannish appearance although they often showed amazing courage. In the lower classes the woman held an extremely strong position and, not infrequently, it was she who controlled the household. But the example set by the *bushi*, especially from the fourteenth century on, was followed increasingly by the common people among whom women began to lose their prestige, at least outwardly. With the ever-growing importance attached to the recognition of the law of primogeniture, with the strengthening of paternal authority, the wife's position tended to become secondary, in contrast to the position of the head of the family's mother.

Both men and women used make-up. It was fitting for a warrior to confront his enemy clean and perfumed. Noblewomen and samurai wives were very mindful of their appearance and liked to have a pale skin. They reddened their lips and blackened their teeth, plucked their eyebrows and took very special care of their long black hair.

LOVE

In the absence of accurate records, it is difficult to describe what the relations were between men and women among the Japanese people, the only texts at our disposal dealing mainly with the feelings and behaviour of individuals belonging to the aristocratic or at least high-ranking warrior classes. The nobles of Kyôto, the majority of them indolent, whose life and constant travel to and fro were hampered by innumerable interdicts regarding their activities and whereabouts (*kataimi*), and who still favoured polygamy, attached great importance to amorous intrigues, which brought distraction from their state of continuous boredom. The men of those days were attracted by details of femininity which would seem trivial to us today: a kimono sleeve hanging elegantly from a carriage door or a beautifully and ornamentally written poem.

Opportunities for casual encounters were fairly frequent, either at the court, during receptions or festivals, or when there were excursions, pilgrimages or ceremonies in the temples and shrines. Narratives often describe noblemen, in the evening or very early in the morning, spying on the women of a house through a garden hedge or a lattice opening: 'Looking closely, he saw that the lady's figure (fleetingly glimpsed at that time) with her dress thrown carelessly about her shoulders, was slender and extremely childlike. The sound of her voice was every whit as charming, though full of dignity. Just as he was thinking how fortunate he had been to set eyes upon her, day began to break so he returned home.'[54]

If the nobles' morals were extremely lax, all their actions were, nevertheless, governed by rigorous rules of etiquette. It was customary for the lover to make known his intentions by sending to his fair one a letter, with a poem to match, which he fastened to a sprig of willow, flowering cherry or plum-tree according to the time of year. There was no need for the lover to compose his own poem: very often he was content to adapt for the occasion one of the many poems contained in the twenty-one imperial anthologies, and which every cultured person was expected to know by heart:

> If the moon and the flowering cherries
> On this lovely night
> Are not alike,
> How I long to show them to the one
> Who perhaps might understand.[55]

In the same way, after the first night, the lover sent a few verses to his mistress: 'Although it was extremely late at night, I went away, for this, it seemed was the fitting thing to do. But how it filled my heart with pain!' He sent her this note with a poem written on a sheet of green paper tied to a sprig of willow:

> Even more than in my days gone by
> When I did not know you,
> Oh! green leaves of willow!
> More than ever, this morning
> Are my thoughts troubled.[56]

The women replied in the same tone, and this poetic correspondence could be prolonged like this for some time, before the outcome of the adventure and quite often afterwards. Generally, the waiting was reduced to a few days, and the lover, often in disguise, found his way each night into the young woman's bedchamber. The lover's main difficulty was to steal, without coming up against too much opposition, behind the screen which hid the object of his desires. Then the rest was easy. At other times, the lover might end by abducting the young girl. In this connection, the *Tsutsumi Chûnagon Monogatari* tells us the highly amusing experience

57

of a young nobleman who proceeded in this way and discovered, when he arrived home, that his beloved's old aunt had taken her place.

'Love affairs began and ended in semi-darkness (apartments being enclosed by heavy hangings and women usually being hidden behind rather high screens called *kichô*) and sometimes lovers were not sure of the identity of their companion.'[57]

Sentiments expressed so poetically (whether they were true or false matters little) were, in the long run, translated into a comparatively ruthless act often without sequel, and it was at times difficult to ascribe the right parentage to children born of these often reckless unions. The novels of the time frequently tell us of lovers being substituted with the help of disguises or of the darkness. What men primarily demanded of women at that time was availability. So, very often, women of the aristocratic classes of Kyôto were, emotionally, extremely unhappy. They could be possessed or deserted at every turn, sometimes even with the complicity of the other women of their household. Their jealousy kept them constantly on the alert, although not in any circumstances might they show it. In the bushi class, the position of women must have been altogether different, since these warriors had adopted the principle of monogamy. Nevertheless, their position was not always enviable, their husbands conceding more loyalty to their lord than to their wives. In the case of the farmers, adolescents were left relatively free, boys and girls could have amorous intrigues as it suited them, and these did not necessarily lead to marriage: for if love was a personal matter, marriage affected the family and, on that account, was a community concern. Even in the event of a child being conceived out of wedlock, the boy married before the birth of the child was not necessarily the real father. But this does not seem to have created any difficulties.

Moreover, the concept of virginity was probably of little importance to men. But after marriage, the wife's faithfulness to her husband was obligatory and, as a general rule, respected. If, in the samurai class, the wife's infidelity was harshly punished, most often either by divorce or repudiation, in the other classes, nobles or farmers, it was of no consequence, so long as the fact was kept secret, so as to prevent the husband from losing face. With sexual matters settled like this, no serious psychological disturbances seem to have developed in Japan at this time; sometimes the act itself was not considered so much a sin as a breach of etiquette (so to speak!). Matters of love appeared as natural as food and drink. Besides, there were numbers of accommodating inns, either in the towns or along the highways, where board and lodging and men's basic needs could easily be satisfied at little cost.

Among the nobles, relations between men and women of the same family were comparatively rare, the sexes being separated at an early age, and sometimes members of the same household had never seen each other since their infancy. In the 'Tale of Genji' (*Genji-monogatari*, written at the beginning of the eleventh century it is true, but customs change very little in aristocratic circles), Yugiri had never had the opportunity of seeing his step-mother, nor Kôbai, his step-daughter:

> 'Kôbai was consumed with curiosity: if only I could see what she looks like! he thought. It really is a pity that she always has to be hidden! . . . One day, when there was no one about, he stole slyly along to the young woman's bedchamber, hoping to catch a glimpse of her, but, peering through the screen which was concealing her, he could not get the least idea of her shape (it was so very dark).
>
> ' "I thought that in your mother's absence, I ought to come and keep you company!" he said to her. "It really makes me very unhappy that you behave so coldly to me . . ."
> 'Because they were separated by heavy hangings, Kôbai could hardly hear her reply, but, from the mellifluent charm of her voice, he pictured to himself how delightful she must be, and was deeply moved by it.'[58]

In this world apart, the feminine sex was sometimes kept socially so remote from men that brothers could grow up knowing nothing at all about their sisters. Male curiosity, thus aroused, incited them to clandestine love affairs. It very often happened that the lover, in accordance with custom having to leave his mistress before daybreak, hardly ever had the opportunity of seeing clearly the face of the one with whom he had been fortunate enough to make love. But it must be added that this only obtained when it was a question of young girls and unmarried women. Women under their husband's control were, as a rule, remarkably faithful to them. With the bushi, monogamy did not allow of very many escapades. The women, although jealously guarded from the outside world, nevertheless

59

enjoyed a relative freedom in their homes; sometimes they even took on the management of the household in the event of the oldest child being unable to undertake this because he was still too young.

As for the farming class, it knew nothing whatever about this game of hide and seek, agricultural labour claiming all available hands and having no time for idle, cloistered women. The noble society of Kyôto (sometimes of the provinces also) therefore led a completely different life from that of the great majority of the Japanese people. Nevertheless, it must not be forgotten that the distinctions we are making here between the classes were not perhaps as clear-cut in actual fact and that there was every grade of society between the poorest farmer and the richest nobleman, and consequently every degree of behaviour, as much from a personal as from a social point of view. When we speak here of classes, it is above all classes considered as guide-marks. For if, during the Heian period, a very clear distinction could still be made between nobles and commoners, during the Kamakura and Muromachi periods, these distinctions became progressively more blurred, society having become simultaneously more complex and more unstable. If, from the point of view of the family and of human intercourse, the aristocratic circles of Kyôto had but little influence on the common people and the bushi caste, on the other hand they did have a great deal of influence culturally, particularly from the time when the Ashikaga bakufu established itself actually in Kyôto, in the Muromachi quarter.

THE FAMILY ECONOMY

In peace time the samurai, who had at their service a large household, comprising members of the family (wife, daughters, daughters-in-law, brothers and sisters) and domestic staff, spent their time managing the administrative, legal and economic affairs of their domains and household. They received the tax or revenue from their lands in kind (rice, silk, hemp, fabrics, land or sea produce), sometimes in money (*kan* or strings of Chinese coins). These possessions were stored not in houses but in *kura*, a kind of granary with a timber frame plastered with mud-mortar and sometimes set on piles, intended to protect the family wealth from fire, a disaster as frequent as it was feared in these wooden houses. The wife controlled the female staff and, in addition to teaching the children, supervised the kitchen and the sewing of the clothing for all the inmates of the house. In all likelihood she had access to the *kura* so that she could help herself, whenever she needed anything – to rice, *sake* or any ingredients for cooking, as well as to lengths of material indispensable for clothing all the people in her charge.

Naturally, a samurai held back for himself a large part of the family income to provide for his military needs, arms, armour, horses, provisions, maintenance and payment of soldiers, etc., or for exceptional needs such as house repairs, extension of buildings, occasionally reconstruction, as well as for works of community interest which could devolve upon him by order of his superiors. In times of public disorders, and if his eldest son was still of tender years, he could instruct one of his close relatives, usually one of his younger brothers, to look after his possessions in his absence but, very often, especially in the case of the bushi whose means were slender, it was his wife who took complete control of everything.

The farmers had less worry on this score. In their case it was the mistress of the house who dealt with the family possessions *de facto* if not *de jure*, the main expenditure, food and clothing falling on her. When important work had to be undertaken (building a new house, mending a roof, digging a well or reconstructing a bridge), the farmer relied upon the community spirit of the men of his village for help. He offered them one or several meals and repaid (in rice or money) the specialists (carpenters, smiths, well-diggers and others), likewise the monks to whom he would appeal for help on such an occasion. In his turn he would have to give help to the other villagers if the need arose. So a highly efficient system of mutual aid was established in each village from very early days; this often went as far as collective cultivation of the fields, rice planting generally requiring far more hands than each family possessed. In this way the village could be almost self-supporting, able to feed the buke and in return be protected by them. Therefore, the farmers were in no way held in contempt by the bushi, even if in time of war they were themselves occasionally cruelly ill-treated, whereas they were, if not ignored, at least despised by the nobles of the capital with whom they never had any direct contact.

Generally speaking, the samurai treated their household servants well; indeed they were often warriors themselves and were liable to accompany their masters to war either as foot-soldiers or simply as servants. Each had his special household duty and fulfilled his task zealously and faithfully. There were grooms in a strange uniform with horizontal stripes which bring to mind our swimming costumes of the nineteen hundreds, gate-keepers armed with bows and halberds, and many other domestic servants. Very often craftsmen settled down for good with rich samurai, to work there as servants, making arrows, bows, armour and different kinds of arms or again dyeing fabrics, or by working as blacksmiths or gold and silversmiths, or with lacqueur or paper. Now and again they left their village by order of the lord of the district and came to take up their abode temporarily under his roof in order to carry out some specific piece of work. They received their pay then in the form of a rice allowance, on occasion in cash, and were often presented with odds and ends of clothing.

Servants, at the beck and call of their masters day and night, had very few holidays: at best they were given permission to visit their relatives at the time of the annual *Bon* festival, so long as their presence was not absolutely indispensable. These retainers were generally extremely faithful and chronicles have preserved for us innumerable instances of servants laying down their lives to ensure the safety of their master or that of his family; this would surely not have been the case if they had felt they were despised or if they had been ill-treated. In some instances, quite frequently, it was the servants who ensured the efficient running of the household and brought prosperity to it while waiting until the orphaned heir was old enough to look after the paternal property. The fidelity of servants of noble houses could not be depended upon in the same way, the relationship between master and servant being very much less a family one than in the bushi caste, and the warrior spirit of faithfulness and loyalty not existing to the same degree among the servants of the *Kuge* (court nobles).

SUCCESSION

Questions of succession and the division of property occasionally led to complicated problems, for the laws of Kyôto and those of the samurai often differed on many points. According to the law in practice at the court, property devolving upon one or several heirs belonged to them unconditionally; whereas, according to the Kamakura laws, the donor could, at any time during his lifetime, give and take back when it suited him and as often as he pleased, the possessions he had distributed between his heirs.[59] We have an account of one of the problems created by this difference in legislation in Lady Abutsu's diary, the *Izayoi Nikki* (Diary of the Sixteenth Moon). This lady undertook the journey from Kyôto to Kamakura in rder to try to recover one of her estates, at that time under the jurisdiction of the samurai, following a transfer of rights (*shiki*) on the death of her husband:

'I believed that my humble person had been forgotten by the gracious government of a wise Head of State, and that the sympathies of his loyal ministers had been denied me; and yet, it was not possible for this state of affairs to continue. However, as there was absolutely nothing I could do about it, I was very depressed. . . .'[60]

And, indeed, Lady Abutsu died shortly afterwards, without her case being resolved, the whole attention of the government being taken up with the Mongol threat.

If the head of the family had the right to choose his heir (heir of the family name or of his property, or both at the same time), the *Jôei Shikimoku* laid down that should the legal heir (the eldest son), be dispossessed, he was entitled to a portion equal to a fifth of the total inheritance.[61] The samurai generally chose as heir whichever of their sons seemed most likely to make a good warrior, on condition, of course, that he supported his brothers and sisters, who were then dependent on him. But in practice, it was always the eldest who inherited. Under the protective Kamakura government, the samurai or the landowner usually split up his wealth among his children when he retired from public life (*inkyo*). However, from the beginning of the fourteenth century, with the spreading of a feeling of unrest and the law of primogeniture becoming general, the division of property was carried out less and less equally. As a result, girls were increasingly debarred from the rights of succession, for fear that when they married they might take their inheritance as a dowry to another family which could become a rival to their own. Added to this, the samurai could not risk giving property to a daughter who could not fight to protect it. In the quite frequent event of a warrior not having a male heir, or else if he judged none of his sons capable of succeeding him, he could adopt some other person, preferably a kinsman, as heir, to carry on the family name.

The decisions of the head of a family were seldom contested, on the one hand because he was entirely free to disinherit any one of his sons he deemed unworthy and because disobedience to parents was severely punished by law (three years' imprisonment for insulting behaviour), the children in consequence could not in any circumstances appeal against their parents;[62] on the other, because it was of supreme importance to preserve the unity of the family, a unity indispensable in the event of defence or attack. The lord of the province or the shôgun himself took particular care that the families of his vassals should not be split up.

The system of adoption or *yôshi* was practised for a very long time in Japan, arising from the necessity of having a male heir who would be able to fulfil the ritual obligations designed to honour the spirits of the ancestors, to look after their tomb and provide for the needs of the family, in the event of their descendants producing nothing but daughters. So it became customary for childless couples or those who had no son to adopt a relative. Later, a man could, if he so wished, adopt adulterine or other children, even if he already had several sons of his own. From the Kamakura epoch on, the custom of adopting a son-in-law or else of marrying a daughter to a man one wanted to adopt, even if he did not belong to the family, became general.

Meanwhile, the ordinances of *Jôei Shikimoku* prescribed the methods of adoption among the bushi. The adoptive father must not have a legitimate heir and he must be at least thirty years old; the adoptee must belong to the same family and be of the same social standing; the shôgun's permission was needed for a samurai to be able to adopt an heir, and the local authority's permission for an adoption by commoners; finally, childless widows were allowed to adopt a male heir. Of course, just as for inheritances, adoption was subject to repeal at any time solely on the decision of the adoptive father or mother.[63] Adoption could then be undertaken for three reasons; for the purpose of succession to the property only, for the purpose of succession to the family name only, or again for the purpose of total succession. It could likewise be effected provisionally or under certain special conditions.

This, at times, stirred up bitter conflicts. One of the most famous caused an appalling civil war in the Ônin era (1467–77), which steeped the country in blood for more than ten years: in 1464 the Shôgun Yoshimasa not having any sons had, on the advice of the Hosokawa family, adopted as heir his young brother Yoshimi.

3 'Storage of rice' from 'Painting of the Four Seasons' by Kanō Yukinobu

But the following year, Yoshimasa's wife, Tomiko, gave birth to a son who was given the personal name of Yoshihisa. Thereupon, the question of succession arose, Tomiko claiming it for her son, the Hosokawa maintaining that Yoshimi must remain the sole heir: war was inevitable.

In the event of a marriage between servants of two different families, at least where the bushi were concerned, the sons had to belong to the father and the daughters to the mother. But in noble families, who still obeyed *ritsuryô*, servants were held in less esteem and their children had to belong not to their parents but to their mother's master.[64]

JUSTICE

Every man or woman was held responsible for his or her own actions, first with regard to his family; and the head of a family had the right to administer punishment to the members of his household and to his servants, without, however, being allowed to beat them in public. Common law varied according to provinces and even to shôen, and the lords enforced it more or less liberally when they had cases to judge. In difficult cases and in the absence of witnesses, a 'soothsayer' was called in, usually a *miko* or Shintô priestess who, after going into a trance and being possessed by the god, was deemed to have established the truth, the kami having expressed themselves through her lips. Nevertheless, the justice which a samurai could dispense had to conform to precepts laid down by the Kamakura government and above all to those contained in both the *Goseibai* (*Jôei*) *Shikimoku* (comprising fifty-one articles) promulgated in 1232, and in the *Einin-no-Tokusei Rei* of 1297 (of which only three articles have come down to us). These 'precepts' considered some typical cases of serious infringement of the law committed by persons belonging to the common people (*bonge*) or by samurai of divers classes, from the *gokenin* or direct vassal of the shôgun to the ordinary bushi or warrior without any official status.

Beating a person in public, for instance, was punished by imprisonment for a fixed period of time when it concerned a commoner, but for the samurai it could go as far as exile or the confiscation of his domain. To this end, article 13 of the *Goseibai Shikimoku* states precisely: 'The person who receives the strokes will, for a certainty, feel the desire to kill or wound his adversary to wipe out his shame, therefore the offence committed by beating a person must not be

65

deemed a trivial one.'[65] Punishments fitted the nature of the crime and the personality of the guilty person or his social status: the higher the standing of the guilty person the more severe was his punishment. Generally a commoner who had committed a very grave offence, such as robbery, flagrant adultery, gross insult, slander or calumny,[66] etc. was branded and was, as a result, excluded from his village community. He became *hinin* (an outcast) in cases of murder, for example, or *murahachibu* (that is, exiled from the village but with liberty to go and settle down somewhere else) in other cases. As for serious offences committed by the samurai, they were generally punished by exile to a distant province (which was tantamount to being forced to transfer rights and possessions to an heir), or to an island (especially in cases of falsifying accounts[67]), or by confiscation of half their lands, or by banishment (in cases of flagrant adultery). For rape committed on a highway outside their own domains, they were debarred from military duty for a hundred days or sentenced to having their head shaved on one side.[68]

The samurai had no right of appeal against the rule that important trials had to be held at Kamakura where the *monchūjo* (a judicial body) attended to the civil procedure concerning senior vassals, and the *samurai-dokoro* to the criminal procedure. The *mandokoro* was responsible for the direction of civil affairs in the city of Kamakura. Complaints recorded at the Rokuhara-Tandai of Kyôto were, after investigation, transferred for final judgement to Kamakura. In this last city, expert judges, called *bugyô*, were charged with the direction of the proceedings. Plaintiff and defendant, after repeating their accusation and defence, not once but three times, were brought face to face. Article 13 of the *Jôei Shikimoku* forbade the samurai, under pain of severe penalties, to insult each other at this juncture.

In cases where it was not possible to pass judgement or if there were no witnesses able to help shôgunal justice to establish the truth, recourse was made to divine judgement or judgement by ordeal. The plaintiff and the defendant, having countersigned their complaints and their pleas, had both to be confined for seven days in a Shintô shrine or a Buddhist monastery. If, during this time, something considered 'extraordinary' happened to one of them, such as bleeding from the nose or some kind of indisposition, if bird-droppings fell on him, if a rat gnawed his clothing, if his horse fell down, or if one of them choked while he was eating, or if some misfortune befell his family, here was the sign by which the gods indicated the guilty one.[69]

It was possible to appeal against a sentence, but once only. Nevertheless, the legal administration of the bakufu being overloaded with appeals, the *Einin-no-Tokusei Rei* from 1297 onwards, decided not to accept any but outstanding ones.[70] Crimes committed by commoners rarely reached Kamakura, or later Muromachi, to be judged. They were usually judged on the spot by the lord of the district where the infringement of the law had been committed. In most cases, however, the villagers, anxious to preserve order in their community, took coercive measures themselves. For on the one hand seigniorial justice was often as harsh for the plaintiff as for the accused, and on the other hand the villagers had their own rules of conduct and their own penal 'code'. As we saw earlier on, two penalties were frequently administered: one, the lighter, was the ostracism of the offender who then became *mura-hachibu* and, in this capacity, was forced to live either on the outskirts of the village or right away from it. No one must ever speak to him again, he no longer asked assistance from the other villagers and was excluded from all the social activities of his fellows. He was generally given a red girdle to wear as a distinguishing mark. This punishment could be revoked if the outcast made honourable amends. Nevertheless, he lost his place within the community, in which he was regarded as the lowest of the low.

The second penalty, banishment, was the punishment for the most serious crimes: murder, arson. In these instances, the guilty person was pronounced *hinin* or *eta* by the council of village elders, and compelled to live in the *tokushu-buraku* (special hamlets, an expression of recent origin) reserved for outcasts, desperately poor people without any civil rights, who had to spend their time doing jobs that were considered unclean: they were grave-diggers, assistants at cremations, tanners, refuse collectors, clearers-out of cesspits. They could not take part either in the ordinary activities or in the festivals of other villages and were shunned by everyone, almost looked upon as 'non-human'. They lived principally by begging, for they were forbidden to till the soil. In their midst were all the outcasts and lepers. In times of famine, they were always the first victims. Their condition was wretched indeed. These *eta*, among whom there sometimes lived wandering monks, possessed no homes, but built themselves temporary shelters of plaited straw, or bits of wood, or sometimes they used shields picked up on the battlefields,[71] which they propped up against posts driven into the ground. A few miserable, worn-out mats served them as furniture and, as a general rule, their sole possession was a bowl which they used both for begging and for eating out of. They were constantly on the move, taking up a position preferably not far from the gateways of temples or towns in the hope of collecting alms, or even of stealing something. To get from place to place, some made themselves a kind of wooden hutch mounted on wheels, which also served as their home.[72] They lived unkempt, in ragged clothing, sometimes even naked or wrapped in skins or straw, in a state of utter destitution and despised by everyone.[73]

CHAPTER THREE

DAILY NEEDS

FOOD

Although the average Japanese of this period does not seem to have been excessively fond of food (at any rate less fond than his contemporary European), he did not despise it for all that. He was fortunate in having at his disposal the very numerous products of land and sea which, in the course of time, he had learned to use to the best advantage. Nevertheless, the eating habits of the Japanese of this era varied considerably according to which class they belonged and, of course, as anywhere else in the world, according to their means. The aristocrats of Kyôto differed from the commoners, the farmers, and above all from the warriors in that they most scrupulously observed the Buddhist prohibitions concerning meat. Howecver, they ate fish. It always filled them with amazement to see the lower classes eating, as if they were beings from a different planet. Sei Shônagon writes in her *Makura-no-Sôshi* (Pillow Book):

'The way in which carpenters eat is truly strange. When the roof of the left wing of the house was under construction, several carpenters sat in a row to have their meal . . . the minute the food arrived, they dived into their bowls of soup and drank up the contents. Next they placed the bowls on one side and attacked the vegetables. . . . A second later, not a single grain of rice remained in their bowls. They all behaved in the same way and I assume that such is the nature of carpenters. . . .'[1]

Although it was not customary for the nobles to eat meat, some of them relished this kind of food, and sometimes secretly indulged this taste. In the *Hyakurenshô*, on the date corresponding to June 24, 1236 it is related that a nobleman was deeply shocked at the sight of warriors eating venison in one of the temples of Kyôto,[2] although this was usual for warriors not bound by Buddhist food restrictions. Obviously, a temple was exposed to defilement if meat was eaten there. Moreover, the *Meigetsuki*, on the dates corresponding to December 10, 1227 and September 30, 1230 states that certain nobles met regularly to eat cranes, quails, various kinds of birds (rumour added rabbits and badgers), despite the complaints of the others.[3] On that account, it became increasingly difficult for these vegetarians, particularly when there was a poor rice crop, owing to wars or drought, to resist the attraction of more substantial fare.

The *kuge* made up for the lack of meat by indulging in reckless drinking bouts and consequently most of them were affected by stomach complaints. Many of them died young and books quote numerous instances of premature deaths due to an excess of alcoholic drink and to illnesses brought about by an over indulgence in *sake*.[4] There were many kinds of *sake*, as a rule with a fairly weak alcoholic content, but since the Japanese at this time were living on a diet that was lacking in fats and proteins, they easily succumbed to drunkeness. '*Sake* parties' were very popular although they had often been prohibited. The women, too, were not averse to drinking.[5]

Nobles and religious bodies ate, in principle, two meals a day (at the beginning of the thirteenth century) and Go-Daigo Tennô's *Nicchûgyôji* shows that the morning meal was taken about midday and the evening meal about four o'clock. But, in imitation of the warriors, the nobles very soon developed the habit of eating three meals a day. The *Ama-no-Mokuzu* (beginning of the fifteenth century) records that they ate little at midday (rice and vegetables) but a great deal more in the evening. The monks who, in theory, were allowed to eat only once a day before midday, were soon following the customs of the day, and had two, then three meals daily. Towards the fourteenth century, the nobles began to acquire the habit of eating a little meat.

They classified most foods as good or bad not so much from preference as from habit and, generally, according to the sound of their name. The Japanese, having at their disposal only a restricted number of syllables (about fifty) to represent the sounds of their language, it follows that the number of similar sounding words was immense. So carp being called *koi*, and this also meaning 'love', was by association of ideas considered excellent; salmon, called

sake, was put in the same category as rice-wine; dorados (*tai*) had
the misfortune to be pronounced like 'evil intent'; as for the name
ayu, a very ordinary little river-fish, it was pronounced in the same
way as 'flattery'. Whereas pheasants and mushrooms were considered good, wild geese enjoyed little favour.[6] It was, therefore,
sometimes relatively complicated for aristocrats to find the kind
of food demanded by etiquette, and their ways of eating were subject to strict rules which, in addition, varied from family to family.

Generally speaking, it was deemed impolite, in the event of a
meal taken in company, to be the first to begin to eat and the last
to finish. According to the *Sezoku Ritsuyôshû* or 'Authoritative Collection of Society Customs', it was good form not to eat the courses
which might be offered when visiting and to take only a little of
the delicacies presented. On the other hand, *sake* could be indulged
in freely. Of course, in the privacy of one's home, these rules were
often ignored. But in some families the rules of etiquette were very
strict, and the 'Book of the Imagawa Family'[7] tells us that when a
meal was eaten in the presence of strangers, a little rice had to be
taken from the bowl with chopsticks, first from the left side, then a
little from the right and finally from the front before lifting the
bowl to the lips. When only the family was present, this gesture had
to be made first from the front, then from the left and afterwards
from the right.[8] The laws of etiquette also demanded that chopsticks should never be placed on the bowl, nor, most importantly,
should rice be offered with chopsticks standing in it (the way o
presenting gifts to the spirits of the dead). Fishbones should never
be put in the corner of the small individual table, nor should soup
be drunk without leaving the chopsticks in the bowl.

According to the *Imagawa Daizôshi*,[9] the best portions of each
course had to be offered to the guests and to those whose rank was
highest. It was the custom for small, individual tables to be carried
in and placed before each guest or table-companion (the Japanese
being unacquainted with large tables, using only these small four-
legged trays). These had to be held as high as possible above the
bearers' heads to prevent the least breath reaching them.[10]

The markets in large towns were generally well stocked and
offered the inhabitants a great variety of products, from the sea
(the most popular), the rivers and mountains, and obviously all
those from the land. But each province had its own specialities,
famous throughout the country. Ice was kept in the mountains

71

where it was collected in the winter and stored in huts sunk into the earth (*himuro*). In summer it was sold at a high price to the noble families who liked to regale themselves with sorbets made with crushed ice and flavoured with herbs.[11]

The *Tsutsumi Chûnagon Monogatari*, which gives us a detailed account of a monk's cravings, gives at the same time a list of the products most appreciated at Kyôto in the thirteenth century:

'It is distasteful for me to talk about it, writes the monk to his benefactress, nevertheless it would also be fitting for me to be provided with food until my brief existence draws to its close: a stock of Shinano pears which smell so good, branches of nuts from Mount Ikaruga, some acorns from the Mikata region, seaweeds from Amanohashidate, *amanori* (a kind of sweet seaweed) from the Izumo coast, round rice cakes from Minohashi, Kôchi turnips from the Wakae region, some rice-paste from Ômi, Yasu and Kurumoto, some of those splendid dried melons from below Komatsu, pineseeds from the summit of Kaketa, some *akebi* from the islands of the North, and some mandarin oranges from Toyama. If, however, you cannot supply all this, give me some simple things such as dried beans from the outskirts of Yamome.'[12]

In addition to these delicacies, which were difficult to obtain and very costly, there were, according to the *Teikin Ôrai*, vegetables: aubergines, cucumbers, *daikon* (a kind of giant radish), *gobô*, potatoes (*imo*), *myôga* (a kind of ginger), thistles, cresses, mushrooms and a variety of salads of different sorts (the *Seiryôki* cites twenty-four kinds of potatoes, nine kinds of *daikon*, sixteen of turnips, fourteen of cucumbers, twelve of aubergines, and three of burdock or *gobô*); fruits: chestnuts, persimmons, nuts, plums, peaches, loquats, apricots, bitter oranges, some kinds of China oranges (mikan, kôji), tart oranges (*yuzu*, *daidai*), pomegranates, strawberries, jujubes, lily-bulbs, acorns, nuts from Ichô (*ginnan*) and, towards the fifteenth century, apples and many kinds of seaweed (at least seven); fish and sea-food: chrysophris, carp, dabs, bonito, trout, various small river-fish (*funa*, *ayu*), flying fish, horned turbot (*sazae*), dolphins, cuttlefish, whale, abalones, octopus, sea-urchins, jelly-fish, cockles, clams, and also fish-pastes (*kamaboko*), leeches and pipe-fish; game: quails, pheasants, wild geese, blackbirds, cranes, sparrows, swans, skylarks, woodcock and falcons, rabbits, deer, *tanuki* (a kind of badger), boars, wild goats, otters, etc.

Many kinds of leguminous plants were likewise used in cooking (about fifty sorts), mainly soya (*daizu*) and red beans (*azuki Sasage*). The red beans called *azuki* were thought to be effective in combating beri-beri, blood and stomach disorders. As for kidney and soya beans, the common people were convinced that they had the power to drive out demons.

Various other products were also on sale according to district and season, as were the specialities to be found chiefly in the Kyôto market: rice from Chikuzen, chestnuts from Dazaifu, seaweeds from Uga, fish (*funa*) from Lake Biwa, carp from the river Yodo,[13] etc.

Mainly under Zen influence, from the fourteenth century on, aristocrats and Buddhist monks (and a few wealthy warriors, too) began to replace meat, which Buddhism prohibited, by food cooked in a great deal of oil (colza, soya, sesame and camellia). This particular method of cooking called *Shôjin Ryôri* (which purifies the blood) included, at least according to the *Teikin Ôrai*, *tôfu* soups, fried *tôfu* (*tôfu* is a paste made from the juice of soya beans crushed and soaked, then hardened by a process of fermentation), soups made from *tororo* (yams) and from various vegetables and seaweeds, rice and wheat-flour cakes and any number of special dishes. Among the last, *suisen* was the most popular: it was made by mixing *kuzu* flour (arrowroot, *curcuma* or amaranthus) with a little water, then heating it. The mixture was left to cool in a flat container and, when it had hardened, was cut into shapes which were fried in a pan. These were eaten dippped in *sake*. If they were to be given to guests they were coloured with gardenia which turned them a beautiful shade of yellow. *Sôkei* was made from the root of the *konnyaku* (*amorphophallus koniak*), a species of arum (reduced to a powder, blended with a little water and lightly salted); it was eaten flavoured with *miso*. *Unsô* was rice soaked in sweet *sake* before eating it. *Manjû* were steamed cakes made from sugar and rice-flour stuffed with meat or vegetables. Finally, towards the end of the fourteenth century, *yokan* appeared, which still remains a much appreciated delicacy today: it is a paste made from red beans (*azuki*) reduced to powder, sweetened with sugar or *ame* (*hydrangea* juice) and mixed with *kuzu* powder (*curcuma*), rice-semolina and steamed. Sugar, known in Japan since the monk Ganjin (688–763) had brought some back from China, was looked upon as medicinal until the Shimazu

73

family from Satsuma had it sent in bulk from the Ryû-Kyû islands.

Custom decreed, probably as a result of various findings, that rice-gruel and *ame* should not be eaten together, nor raw fish and millet, nor should one over-indulge in jujubes, oranges, persimmons or Chinese peaches.[14] In addition to this, there were certain monthly prohibitions, like the one which forbade the eating of raw onions, meat and scraps of food gnawed by rats in January.[15]

The nobles sometimes drank cow's milk, but very seldom, and more as a medicine when they were ill. They ate polished rice whereas the other classes were content to eat just husked rice. There was a variety of flavourings but they were rather mild. These consisted principally of *sake*, rice-vinegar and a fermented condiment of the *miso* type, of salt, powdered dried fruits, ginger and, especially from the fourteenth century, *shôyu* or soya sauce, and imported pepper. Soya sauce, known in aristocratic circles since the sixth century, was not, however, popular before the fourteenth, when it was beginning to be produced in quantity in the Kii province. There were, of course, many varieties of it.

Certain foods, ritual alike for the kuge as for the commoners, had to be eaten on specified dates. Where the nobles and wealthy samurai were concerned, on the first day of the year, seaweeds, cooked chestnuts and abalones were eaten; on January 7th a 'seven herbs' rice soup (*nanakusa*); on March 3rd herb *mochi*; on May 5th *chimaki* (rice-semolina cooked in *sasa* leaves, a kind of reed); on the first day of the Boar of October *mochi* made from young wild boar's flesh meant to drive sickness away; on December 8th rice-soup to keep out the cold. On New Year's Day among the masses and the warriors too, especially from the end of the fourteenth century, it was customary to eat boar and deer so as to live to an old age; likewise *ayu* (river-fish), radishes and cucumbers to drive away evil spirits. On March 3rd *sake* perfumed with iris-root; on July 7th noodles made from wheat-flour were eaten; and on September 9th tea-flowers were put in the 'festal *sake*'.

Tea had been known ever since the Heian period and the *Minamoto Takaoki Day-book* informs us that there was a small plantation of it near the imperial palace, a plantation which flourished under the care of chosen officials. The nobles drank this tea chiefly as a medicine. In the Kamakura era, tea-seeds were brought to Japan by the monk Eisai (who also introduced Zen philosophy in 1187) and planted in the Seburiyama in the province of Chikuzen. The monk Myô-e (Kôben, 1173–1232) planted some at Uji and at Toganoo in the province of Yamashiro (vicinity of Kyôto). Eisai also taught the Japanese the Chinese way of preparing the leaves:[16] gather them early in the morning before dew-fall, then roast them on a sheet of paper over a very gentle heat so that they do not burn, and keep them in a pot with a stopper made from bamboo leaves. Mixed with a little water, it was believed to banish sleep and to be effective against liver and skin complaints, rheumatism and beri-beri. Esai said: 'Tea is the most wonderful medicine for preserving health; it is the secret of long life. It shoots forth its leaves on the hillside like the spirit of the earth. Now, as in the past, it possesses these same extraordinary qualities, and we should make much greater use of it. . . .[17]

From the beginning of the fourteenth century,[18] nobles and high-ranking warriors met together for the purpose of tasting and comparing the merits of seventy to a hundred different kinds of tea. As the number of plantations grew rapidly, tea was adopted more and more widely as a drink, even in the lowest classes. And from the end of the fifteenth century, everyone drank it as a matter of course.

DIET OF THE SAMURAI AND SOLDIERS

At the beginning of the Kamakura period, both high and low grade warriors were an impoverished class who, as a rule, knew nothing of the refined manners of the court and ate the same food as the farmers. They were used to an almost Spartan way of life. The case of the Hôjô Regent Tokiyori is often quoted as an example: welcoming a guest one night, he found he had nothing to offer him but some *sake* and a little sauce in the bottom of a bowl.[19] Ashikaga Yoshiuji, welcoming the same Tokiyori, could only give him some dried abalones, cooked *mochi* (rice-cake), rice and *sake*. The *Azuma Kagami* (*Mirror of the East*) also describes a New Year banquet given to Yoritomo by a high-ranking warrior of the Chiba family, where there was only one course, *sake*, and a bowl of *Ôban* rice: this consisted of a mass of boiled rice so glutinous and piled so high in the bowl as to be three times its height.[20] When the Shôgun visited his longest-serving comrades-in-arms for the New Year it was customary for them to offer him a bowl of *Ôban* as a token of esteem.

This poverty, which occurred in the early stages, soon gave way to a more comfortable way of life as soon as the bakufu was firmly established. Nevertheless, it was a rare thing for warriors to use polished rice, which was reserved for feast days. Indeed, the poorest of them could no more afford to eat rice every day than could the majority of farmers. They lived mainly on wheat, common and red millet, and sometimes on a mixture of rice and wheat. From 1382, following long periods of severe drought, and to make up for the lack of other cereals, they began to develop the cultivation of *soba* (buckwheat) and then this was used to supplement millet and wheat in the commoners' diet.[21] Husked rice (*gemmai*) was eaten boiled or made into soup. Steam-cooking was permissible only on feast days or on ceremonial occasions. The common folk ate little rice: this cereal was not in fact to become their basic food until the middle of the fourteenth century. They lived chiefly on burdocks (*gobô*), aubergines, cucumbers, various kinds of mushrooms and vegetables, wheat and millet, and, if they lived by the sea, fish, shellfish and seaweed. When rice came into more general use among the masses, it was eaten in numerous ways: cooked in a pan, mixed with vegetables or seaweeds, salted, dried, with vinegar, cooked then eaten cold, as a paste, boiled or steamed.[22]

Warriors were enthusiastic hunters; they preserved meat by cutting it up, then salting or drying it, or sometimes by reducing it to a powder or cutting it into thin strips. According to the *Teikin Ôrai*, they particularly enjoyed eating bears' paws, tanuki paws (of the Japanese badger, *viverrinus*) and crackling from wild boars' skin. They also regaled themselves with *mochi* made with herbs or mixed with various vegetables or with meat, and with cakes made from wheat and rice flour (*sembie, yakimochi, chimaki,* etc.).

In wartime their food was less varied: the only pay they received was in rice (*hyôrômai*) and the main problem for them was to have it cooked as and when they needed it, cooked rice keeping badly in summer. One of the simplest methods of cooking rice consisted in wrapping the grains in a cloth. After soaking it in a stream, the package was then buried, not too deeply, in the ground, and a huge fire was lighted over it. If this was not possible and there was no farmer available to cook the rice, they had to eat it as it was – simply steeped in this way. But sometimes they roasted it in bamboo tubes or rolled in leaves.

Army victuals usually consisted of rice, boiled, dried or cooked in a pan, bonito dried and scraped, various kinds of dried and salted fish, seaweed, and occasionally, dried vegetables, salt and *miso*. *Umeboshi* (plums pickled in brine and dried), were much appreciated by the soldiers, especially in summer, for they supplied them with the salt in which they were lacking, and had a certain therapeutic value.

In the fifteenth century and later, when rice had become the main food of warriors and farmers alike, it was reckoned that a man's daily ration equalled five *gô* of rice, that is about 900 grammes of husked rice.[23]

The demand for rice became so considerable in Japan that in 1470 the bakufu was compelled to order from Korea 5000 *koku* (a *koku* of rice is equal to about 180 litres), but could only obtain 500. Dutch ships, at the end of the fifteenth century, also imported some from Java, carried as ballast in the hold. Foreign products (European ones in particular), were also imported at this time. At the end of the sixteenth century, tobacco made its appearance, with pipes of south-east Asian style: a long stem (*rao* from Laos where they probably originated) and a small metal bowl (*kiseru*). Smoking rapidly became very popular and in 1609 the authorities of the Edo bakufu prohibited it on account of the fires caused by the craze and 'because it was not economic'. A year later, the cultivation and sale of tobacco were forbidden. This prohibition was quite ineffective and tobacco continued to be grown and sold under the name of 'life-prolonging tea'.[24]

DRESS OF THE NOBILITY

Both the novels written at the end of the Heian epoch and the chronicles written at the end of the Kamakura era constantly emphasize the style of dress of the people they describe, and their taste in colour. If, for the simple warriors and the commoners, elegance does not appear to have been an absorbing pastime, it was quite a different matter for the nobles and imperial officials who, by extremely strict rules of etiquette, were obliged to attach great importance to their way of dressing and of arranging their hair. Rank and office at that time were reflected in dress. It was also, judging by the quality of the materials used (some were imported from China!) a manifestation of wealth. The nobles vied with each other in elegance, that is in good taste, in accordance with the

77

より、かゝれくあるたあのやうまうゆや。もろひなゆふひこ若ずなの八。

4　Shigenori, a noble of the Fujiwara family, at the end of the
twelfth century　*Drawing by Kikuchi Yôsai (1788–1878)*

criteria dictated, at one and the same time, by their aesthetic sensitivity and by official regulations.

Ranks at court were mainly distinguished by the wearing of a
hat of silken fabric lacquered and stiffened, called *kammuri*. This
was a kind of skull-cap, at the back of which arose a tube about
fifteen centimetres high, enclosing the bunch of hair that was on
the crown of the head. This stiffened tube was tied tightly at its
base and held the tuft of hair securely in place. Finally two flat
pigtails (*ei*) woven with horse-hair or with lacquered silk gauze
hung down the back. Sometimes they were kept from coming un-

plaited by tying them with a piece of cord which attached them to the vertical tube. The colour of these head-dresses had to be dark and pale violet for the highest ranks then, in descending order of rank, dark and pale green, dark and pale wine, and finally black.[25] The lesser nobility could wear only a black head-dress. From the sixth rank downwards, officials and commoners (who had no access to the court) wore an *eboshi*, a kind of tube-shaped head-dress, more or less stiffened.

Court dress consisted essentially of one or several pairs of very full breeches or *hakama* and undergarments with short sleeves (*kosode*), and overgarments (*hô*). Full ceremonial dress, or *sokutai*, a kind of uniform for all high court officials, followed rules laid down in 1212, stipulating the colours of the robes and the length of the train. This train, obligatorily white, and up to three yards long, could be lined with coloured silk. In winter, every article of clothing was lined with silk and quilted. In summer, they were made from lighter materials. Finally came the arms: a sword (*tachi*) held horizontally in the girdle, a small assymetrical bow (about 1·84 metres long) decorated with black and gold lacqueur; on the back a quiver of arrows arranged fan-wise, feathers uppermost, the heads protected by a thick piece of paper held in place by a tie of two-colour silk. So as to move more freely, the train was lifted and the end tucked into the girdle, under the sword.

However, in the thirteenth century this costume was somewhat simplified and the train done away with: it then came to resemble the style of dress called *ikan*, worn by the lesser nobles of the previous century. It consisted, under the outer robe, of full breeches fastened at the ankles by loops but with the baggy part trailing on the ground and almost entirely concealing the shoes. These, a kind of black-lacquered wooden clog with a rounded toe-part and padded inside, were worn without socks. If the colour of the outer garment (*hô*) depended upon the rank and office of the wearer, the colour of the breeches was a matter of individual choice. This was the semi-ceremonial costume adopted for everyday, for visits to holy places and for private ceremonies.

The nobles also wore at times, in place of an over-jacket, a kind of full loose-fitting smock pulled in by a girdle, called *kariginu* or hunting-jacket. When these court officials, dressed in this way, entered a house (*tatami* were not yet in existence), they took off their shoes and drew their feet into the legs of their breeches, walking

5 A noble's court costume, at the beginning of the fourteenth
century *Drawing by Kikuchi Yôsai (1788–1878)*

(or rather sliding) as if in sacks. In the privacy of the family, high-
ranking nobles exchanged their *kammuri* for a high *eboshi* of lacquered
black silk gauze. But when they were on duty at the palace (duty
which sometimes lasted several days and nights running), they
did not even take off their *kammuri* to sleep. Men and women usually went to bed fully dressed, only taking off their outer garments
and brocaded *hakama*. So as not to risk disarranging their hair-
style, they rested their necks on wooden pillows which were sometimes lightly padded (*makura*).

6   A Japanese noblewoman of the fourteenth century: the mother
of Kusunoki Masatsura, an important samurai of the Nanbokucho
period   *Drawing by Kikuchi Yôsai (1788–1878)*

Women of the nobility were sumptuously arrayed in silks. Over a
red *hakama*, they wore numerous *kimono* or very long robes open
down the front and trailing on the ground (their number was
officially reduced to five in the twelfth century), the uppermost
gown richer than the rest, forming a train. These *kimono* were so
arranged as to let each layer of colour be glimpsed. Winter robes
were very thick, lined with swansdown, and the *kosode* (undergarments) were worn in much greater number. In summer, women
wore lighter-weight kimono. Then, when they were at home, over
their *hakama* of light silk, they wore only a *kosode* and a full length
kimono of transparent gauze. For travelling and for pilgrimages,

81

robes and *hakama* were less full. Kimono were then crossed (left over right) and lifted for the ends to be tucked into the girdle so as to hold them well off the ground and give freedom of movement. A very wide hat made of straw or woven rushes (*ichimegasa*), its brim fitted with a long veil, protected them from prying glances and from insects, and hid their faces. They wore straw sandals (*waraji*) or, if the weather was bad, wooden pattens or *geta*.

DRESS OF THE COMMONERS

The dress of the common folk was of the simplest. It mainly consisted of a smock, and a pair of cotton trousers drawn in above the calf, just like knickerbockers. Over the smock, they sometimes wore a very full jacket with wide sleeves split at the shoulders and down the sides, and with a close-fitting collar. Materials were generally dyed some shade of indigo (a dye produced from fermentation of the leaves of a kind of bean called *ai*), or violet (from the crushed root of *murasaki* (bugloss), a wild plant common at that time in Japan, especially in the Kantô), or dark red obtained from the root of the *akane* (madder-wort). When they were on duty, commoners wore a *nae-eboshi*, a soft, black hat, not unlike a night-cap in shape. They went barefoot or, if they had a great deal of walking to do, wore *ashinaka*, straw sandals protecting only the sole of the foot, and not even the heel, and leggings of cloth or straw, sometimes held in place by a piece of string looped around the big toe.

In rainy weather they donned *geta*, wooden clogs made higher by means of two transverse strips, held on to the foot by two straps passing between the toes and over the top of the foot (these *geta* are still worn today by all Japanese, men and women). They protected themselves from bad weather by using either folding or flat umbrellas made of bamboo, or paper or oiled cloth. In winter, they wore a *mino* or loose cloak made of lengths of straw sewn together. In snowy regions, these *mino* were fitted with hoods and farmers also used snow-boots of plaited straw. Hunters, like the ordinary warriors, were often shod in leather. In some families, the servants wore a kind of uniform, generally consisting of a pair of breeches with horizontal stripes and a gaily flowered jacket, whose pattern and colour were more dependent upon the amount of material available than upon a fashion or any definite regulation. In summer, when they were engaged upon domestic or agricultural work, the lower classes paid scant attention to elegance, seeking comfort before everything else. Therefore, they often 'shed' their jackets and worked stripped to the waist or else they removed all their garments and worked in a loin-cloth. Sometimes they wore just a short kimono held in at the waist by a girdle.

Women of the lower ranks dressed in very much the same way as Japanese women do today: a simple kimono with sleeves tapered to the wrists (*kosode*), the folds of the kimono wrapped over and drawn in at the waist by a narrow girldle (*yumaki*), and over it a kind of skirt-cum-apron attached to the girdle served to protect the kimono. The number of kimono worn one on top of another depended upon the weather and above all upon the affluence of the wearer. In the country during summer, women worked in the fields stripped to the waist: exposure of the breasts was accepted in the Japan of this era and, therefore, did not give rise to any unwholesome thoughts. Such is the nature of man that, whatever the country or the epoch, he desires only that which is hidden.

MAKE-UP

It was customary for both men and women of 'good society' (nobles or warriors) to use make-up. Men and women of the aristocracy took great care to avoid the effects of the sun, wind and rain. Confinement in the half-light of their houses conspired to give women a very pale complexion, a sign of beauty much sought after at that time. But this pallor was not always natural and, in the majority of cases, a white skin was acquired artificially by using *nukabukuro*, small cotton bags containing rice-powder; this was moistened with perfumed water before smoothing it over the face during the day or over the whole body after a bath. Women also used a liquid extracted from jalop seeds (*oshiroibana*), a kind of convolvulus, and white lead imported first from China and then, from the sixteenth century, from Europe. The use of this, although highly thought of, must have led to many cases of fatal poisoning (basic carbonate of lead or white lead being an extremely toxic substance); but for all that women did not stop using it. They attached so much importance to a white skin that the *kami konséi*, a phallic deity they often invoked when seeking a husband, was addressed as 'kami the white'.[26]

It was also the fashion for women to make a red spot in the centre

83

of the lower lip by means of a paste obtained by crushing the flower petals of *carthamus tinctoria* (a kind of saffron, called *benibana*); this was done to make the mouth look smaller. It was applied to the centre of the lip with the tip of the middle finger. Sometimes this lip-rouge, laid on thickly, acquired a greeny-gold tint. The red paste was kept in shells or small porcelain cups. Less concentrated and applied with a large, soft brush, this same product was used to rouge the cheek-bones slightly. It is possible, although we have no proof, that noblewomen also reddened their nails.

When young girls reached womanhood, their eyebrows were shaved or plucked, either entirely, or in such a way as to leave just enough to form a very delicate arch. It was considered shocking not to pluck the eyebrows, at least in high society, and the *Tsutsumi Chûnagon Monogatari* gives us a humorous account of a young girl who liked caterpillars, and who refused to use make-up:

'She thought that people's artificial manners were hateful and refused to pluck her eyebrows. She declared that teeth-blacking was even more harmful and dirty . . . and her smile displayed astonishingly white teeth. . . . People were scared and ill at ease before her and shunned her (and another lady of the household said of her): "Even her eyebrows look like caterpillars and her teeth as naked as a skinned animal . . ." '[27]

When eyebrows were shaved, it was usual to paint two black marks called *motomayu* quite high on the forehead. The black paint (*haizumi*) used for this purpose was made from soot obtained by burning oil of sesame or of calza and mixing it with glue. Among the nobility, where polygamy still obtained, only the acknowledged wife would have had the right to make use of this distinguishing mark of her social rank:[28] 'The young girl who was reclining . . . drew her make-up box towards her with the intention of putting a little powder on, but, owing to the darkness, she made a mistake and pulled out (instead of white rice-powder) a bit of paper containing black. Without even looking in the mirror, she rubbed it over her face . . .'[29] The result of this was to put her lover to flight!

Women could boast make-up boxes containing, as well as a polished metal hand-mirror, bamboo or tortoiseshell combs, tweezers of various kinds, shells filled with lip-rouge, packets of black or of white powder, any number of hair or feather brushes for applying make-up, and also sheets of thin paper for removing it. Instead of thick black spots, some women painted very delicate eyebrows quite high on the forehead 'like the antennae of the silk-worm butterfly'. When a woman was widowed or renounced the world, plucked eyebrows were not then replaced by any make-up.

Japanese women used also to blacken their teeth as, it must be added, did the majority of the nobles and many of the warriors. During the war between the Taira and the Genji (1180–5), the combatants recognized each other because the one side (Minamoto) kept their teeth white while the other (Heike) followed the custom of the courtiers and painted theirs black. Later, it became customary for all classes and clans to blacken their teeth, because the Hôjô regents, being members of the Taira family, had theirs black. Even the warriors' children followed this fashion:

'Thereupon, from among those who were watching (the battle) came a young boy of fourteen or fifteen, clad in pale green armour with full breeches lifted up high at the sides, and his hair fastened up in ringlets like a child's. . . . Kajitsu turned round quickly to protect himself from his enemy, but when he noticed the painted eyebrows and blackened teeth of a fifteen-year-old boy, he resolved not to strike him down.'[30]

Beggars, outcasts, *hinin* and *eta* had neither the right to shave their eyebrows nor to use make-up of any kind, not even to blacken their teeth, for they were put on more or less the same footing as animals.

Although the method of blackening the teeth used in the Kamakura epoch is not known for certain, it can be assumed that it resembled (being probably traditional) the one used during the Edo period and described as follows by Casal: 'Blacking was generally obtained from a preparation with an iron acetate base known later by the name of *tesshô* (iron-juice) or *dashigane* (metal extract). Among the lower classes it was simply called *o-kane* (the noble metal) or *o-haguro* (noble teeth-blacking).'[31]

Throughout the Middle Ages, it was customary for men to wear beards and moustaches. The *emakimono* show us nobles, often rather portly, with small pointed beards, in the style of Napoleon III, and small moustaches. However, the warriors who retained these ornaments were few and far between. If it was the custom for young men of the lower orders to pluck their beards, the older men let theirs grow untrimmed. All kinds of beards and moustaches

85

were seen at that time, even side-whiskers.[32] They did not shave the face in those days, or very rarely, but instead plucked their beards and moustaches. Monks took great care to pluck theirs, but shaved their heads.

Men and women tended their hair most carefully. Nobles generally wore theirs fastened up, the ends cut neatly, then gathered into a single knot hidden by a *kammuri* or an *eboshi*. Commoners cut their hair quite short. Women took great pride in their hair. The longer this was, the more lustrous and well-groomed, the more their beauty was enhanced. Therefore, in many instances, noblewomen to whom nature had been a little unjust in this respect, wore wigs (*gihatsu*). As a rule the hair was divided into two: one part, trimmed off neatly at the end, fell over the breast (*kami-no-sagariba*), the other, very long, hung loose down the back.

HYGIENE

In summer, it was customary for the lower classes to bathe frequently in the rivers or lakes or even in the sea, but the nobles, who did not like to expose themselves to the common view, only immersed themselves in cold water when they felt compelled to do so in ritual purification ceremonies. There were at that time two ways of taking a bath, used mainly in the monasteries: the *yu* or hot bath, and the *furo* or steam bath. In the courtyards of temples or wealthy houses, a building was specially reserved for baths. It comprised two small rooms and was situated not far from a well from which water was drawn by lowering a bucket on a rope or by means of a balance-pole (*hanetsurube*). In one room was a beaten-earth hearth on which a huge iron pot full of water stood permanently. The steam thus produced was conducted by a bamboo pipe into the next room where the bather or bathers taking a *furo* were sitting. This same room, called *yuya*, was also used for hot baths, in a huge wooden or stone trough filled with hot water.[33]

Another way of bathing, called *ishiburo*, was sometimes used in certain provinces. A great stone basin, surrounded by beaten earth and surmounted by a small roof to protect it when not in use, was firmly fixed on the ground. First, dry branches were laid in the basin and set alight. When the walls were hot enough, the ashes were shovelled away and water poured into the basin; as soon as it came in contact with the walls, it began to boil. Then everyone entered the bath in turn until the water was cold. The operation was repeated as often as was necessary.

In the *Kemmu Nenchû-Gyôji* (1333–5), the Emperor Go-Daigo relates that, when he lowered himself into the water, he found it too hot and had to cool it with cold water and, he adds, that he had put on for this occasion a *yu-katabira*, a *kosode* of light cotton. Indeed, the nobles bathed like this, whereas the other classes bathed naked. Hot-water baths were deemed a luxury, except in the case of the monks who were obliged to purify themselves by frequent ablutions. As a general rule, the nobles had only steam baths and dried themselves with sheets of paper. The hot bath was mainly looked upon as curative, beneficial for many forms of sickness, especially 'influenza'. The innumerable thermal springs existing in Japan were frequented from time immemorial. They were, as in Europe, regarded as holy places inhabited by gods. For this reason they were called *kamiyu*, or sacred waters. The nobles were particularly fond of visiting them and of spending some time there.

Only the nobles had paper handkerchiefs among their toilet accessories; the lower classes just blew their nose on to the ground, so to speak, by holding their fingers first on one nostril then on the other, as is still done today in country districts. Soap, which was only imported from Europe in the sixteenth century, was unknown: fine ash served as a substitute for it. Fashionable ladies and nobles used pumice-stone to make the texture of their skins more delicate and soft.

As for the needs of nature, they were attended to anywhere at all, at the corner of a street[34] or in the country, wherever one happened to be. For this purpose, people put on *takaashida*, a kind of very high wooden clog, to prevent their clothing trailing on the ground. They wiped themselves clean either with small squares of paper or little wooden sticks (*sutegi*) which they left on the spot. In towns and villages, the *hinin* were given the job of disposing of this refuse. The nobles, however, had small huts erected well away from the living quarters, above a 'latrine'.

Since hands were considered unclean, often rightly so, it was advisable neither to pick up nor carry with bare hands articles intended for the use of a superior. They were usually carried on the sleeves and presented in the same way. The nobles, even in their own homes, avoided touching objects with their hands unless, of course, it was a question of a work of art: 'He came to a house

87

where four or five fair young maidens were bustling about, and where page boys and serving-men were carrying what looked like pretty boxes, coming and going bearing decoratively written letters on their sleeves. . . .'[35] Sometimes objects were placed on fans in like manner before offering them, and it was customary for these fans to be given as a token of esteem.

Just as meal-times were rather capricious, there were no fixed times for sleeping, especially among the nobles who, generally rising very early, often slept the afternoon away in summer because it was excessively hot, in winter because it was very cold. In the lower classes, the family all slept in the same room, and in winter around the hearth. In wealthy households, each slept on his own thick straw mattress: these were spread on the floor, with a simple wooden block for a pillow. In summer, light hangings replaced partitions so that sleep would not be disturbed by insects. As a rule, in the lower classes, husband and wife shared the same bed and slept under the same quilt. There was practically no privacy in the house during the night and everyone was liable to be disturbed at any given moment, at least by those under the same roof. The nobles, who were in the habit of carrying on their love affairs far into the night and, in accordance with established custom, had to leave before dawn, slept mostly in the mornings (unless they had to be on duty at the palace); the commoners, on the other hand, got up and went to bed with the sun. Often, when they visited a distant temple, they stayed the night there, sleeping and praying, and in those days this gave them a rare and unhoped-for opportunity for enjoyment.

TRAVEL

Commoners, warriors and nobles, except when war-time made it necessary, travelled relatively little. Roads were difficult and dangerous, distances very long and methods of travel anything but rapid. However, there were quite regular messengers between Kyôto and Kamakura and the great cities. Mounted military messengers usually had to cover the distance between Kamakura and Kyôto (about 600 km) in seven days. 'Express' messengers took only five. The record was reached by a messenger who, riding night and day, took seventy-two hours to cover the distance![36] But, in the ordinary course the journey took a fortnight, by roads which were at times extremely difficult and bristling with dangers of all kinds, not least among them being bandits. Most often men travelled on horseback or on foot.

Nobles, like invalids, astrologers and doctors, were entitled to a palanquin or a carriage drawn by oxen. These closed carriages, the perquisite of high-ranking personages, ranged from a simple little structure of wooden boards suspended from poles *(koshi)*[37] on the bearers' shoulders, or mounted on huge spoked wheels, for nobles of the fifth rank, to the luxurious closed carriage embellished with lacquer and hung with silken curtains, which was reserved for the nobles. Both kinds were slow and acutely uncomfortable so, for long distances, it was preferable to ride horseback. The ox drawing the carriage was yoked to the two shafts by a curved piece of wood which rested upon its withers. Men and women also travelled on horseback or on foot according to their station. When the road became too difficult, or if there was a ford to cross, servants carried noble lords or gentlewomen on their backs. But this was not always necessary, for there were boats to take them across the most important rivers and, in some places, ferry boats were used to transport passengers and goods. Baggage was carried either on a man's back, by means of a pole resting on his shoulder, by pack-horse or, in the case of goods of any great bulk, on carts. Monks usually carried a huge basket called *oi* strapped on to their backs.

Journeys were made in easy stages, with frequent stops in shrines and temples, where nobles and the wealthy were always welcome. As for the lower classes, they stayed with local farmers, who were always hospitable, or at inns along the highways, or in the villages where they could find rest and food.

CHAPTER FOUR

THE CITY

KYOTO, IMPERIAL CITY

The imperial city of Heian-Kyô (the capital of peace) also called *Miyako*, built in 794 on the same general plan as the capital of the T'ang dynasty of China at Chang'An, and with the same mathematical exactness, had been constructed on a site selected in accordance with the laws of Chinese geomancy; the evil influences believed to come from the north-east were diverted by the river Kamo and rendered ineffective by the setting up of a temple on Mount Hiei, situated exactly to the north-east.

The imperial palace stood at the northern end of the city. A very broad avenue which began at its southern gateway (*Suzaku-Mon*) to link up with the southern gateway (*Rashô-Mon*) of the city divided this into two equal parts, east and west. The city itself was a regular rectangle in shape, measuring some 5,312 metres from north to south by 4,570 metres from east to west, the great central avenue, Suzaku-Oji, being some 90 metres wide. This avenue also had a protective function aimed at restricting damage caused by outbreaks of fire, so frequent in those days since all structures were wooden.

The theoretical city of Heian-Kyô, planned in accordance with the composition of a *mandala* (probably that of the *Kongô-Kai*, the 'Diamond World' of the indestructible spirit, Vajra-dhatu in Sanskrit), was an attempt at the representation of the Buddhist cosmos. 'A *mandala* is a geometrical painting of the universe as an ordered whole, in the dualism of its evolutionary progress from a divine emanation and of its reabsorption into the human, in its dialectic of disintegration and re-integration, a cosmogram which is the paradigm of cosmic evolution and involution.'[1] Although the *Kongô-Kai mandala* does not appear to have been used officially for religious purposes before Kôbô-Daish's return from China in the year 806, it is nevertheless certain that it was known to the Japanese before that date, for it appertained to an esoteric Buddhism now called *Ko-Mikkyô* (old form of esoterism).

The original plan of Heian-Kyô (or Kyôto) tallies with it in every particular, in its perfect regularity of shape as in the position of the *dai-dairi* or enclosure of the imperial palace, in the northern centre of the city, exactly where the statue of *Mahâvairocana* (Dainichi Nyorai), the Great Sun Buddha, is situated in the *mandala*. Nevertheless, although this was placed to the west in the *mandala*, it is possible that the change of orientation may have been motivated by geomantic considerations. However, all this is merely hypothetical.

The city was divided into districts bounded by broad avenues intersecting at right angles, and subdivided by narrower roads surrounding squares measuring 1 square *chô* (about 109 metres along one side). The wide east–west thoroughfares were numbered, reckoning from the northern boundary, from one to nine and consequently called *ichi-jô*, *ni-jô*, *san-jô* etc., up to *Ku-jô*. The north–south avenues, or *ôji*, were given names instead of numbers. The entire city was divided like this into 76 *bô* (approximate equivalent of a district) each measuring 16 *chô*, in all 1,216 *chô*.[2] The palace itself covered a ground space of about 80 *chô* (about 80 hectares). Nevertheless, if this purely theoretical plan determined the location and direction of thoroughfares, it did not, for all that, fix in any decisive way either the boundaries or the outline of the true city.

The Japanese, quick to adopt Chinese or other foreign customs, only made use of them as basic models and hastened, once these were accepted, to change them in accordance with their own way of thinking. Theoretical boundaries were very quickly forgotten and the buildings were laid down rather more in accordance with the shape of this small plan than in accordance with those suggested by the theorists. The many fires which devastated the city between the time it was founded and the thirteenth century (seventeen according to some sources of information, more according to others) gave rise to divers reconstructions and alterations. So, at the beginning of the Kamakura period, the city of Kyôto presented quite a different spectacle from the one it had when it was founded. If the trenches made by the wide thoroughfares remained, areas indispensable for limiting the ravages of fire, the city itself had taken on a most irregular aspect; for, unlike the Chinese city of Chang'An, surrounded by defensive walls six metres high, there were never any fortifications at Heian-Kyô to provide a clear-cut boundary between the city and the surrounding country-side. The roads and avenues were planted with trees among which the willows along the great central thoroughfare were especially famous:

> Stretching as far as eye can see,
> They glitter like jewels,
> Oh! how they glitter, those gently swaying branches
> Of the willows on Suzaku-Oji.[3]

Alongside each road were canals which provided some refreshing coolness and, above all, a ready-made water supply for the inhabitants to draw on whenever fire broke out. Countless little streams flowed from these canals, running from the north-east to the south through the gardens of the great nobles' villas; these were built in Shinden style, and their imposing porticoes could be seen from afar, high above the rows of small 'long houses' lining the roads. These long houses, typical of medieval Japanese towns, were the homes of the lower classes. They presented a single frontage and roof and were divided into a number of apartments. The backs overlooked small gardens, mostly kitchen-gardens. The great nobles' residences, which frequently took up the space of a full *chô*, were situated not far from the palace, in the areas bounded by the first, second and third avenues. The imperial university (*daigaku*) adjoined the southern walls of the palace and faced the imperial storehouses (*kokusô-in*). Provision had been made for the market-places to the east and west, near the seventh avenue, on either side of the *Suzaku-Ôji*; under its noble trees crowds gathered to watch the punishment, usually by bastinado, of minor offenders. The death sentence was carried out on the banks of the river Kamo, generally on a level with the sixth avenue. The prisons stood near the palace walls. As for the merchants' quarters, they were laid out mainly between the fourth and the seventh avenues. The Emperor's extra palaces and the most important temples were dispersed around the city. The To-ji and Sai-ji temples, in their role as guardians of the city, were set up on either side of the *Rashô-Mon*.

The palace itself was completely surrounded by a high wall of wattle and daub, breached by fourteen gateways, chief among them, the *Suzaku-Mon*, at the centre of the south wall. These gateways also served as watch-towers and nobles and military had to man them during specified periods of duty. This guard-duty, called *daiban-yaku*, reduced to three months in 1247, and shortly afterwards rescinded, was generally sought after by the nobles and even more by the warriors, who thereby acquired rank and honours. It was little to the taste of the shôgun who expected to be the only one in a position to reward or punish his samurai.

The imperial family's residence, situated in the centre of the area bounded by walls, occupied comparatively little space; it was surrounded on all sides by courtyards, buildings for the departments of state, various halls designed for official Shintô ceremonies and Buddhist services, and sundry halls reserved for receptions and entertaining of the provincial nobles. The buildings forming the imperial residence were bounded by a wall in the form of a double corridor breached by four gateways with watch-towers on either side. They comprised, besides the emperior's official residence or *seiryôden*, his private living apartments (*ninjuden*) and the residences of various members of his family and of his concubines and ladies-in-waiting. This inner enclosure also contained reception halls (the courtyard of the main one was embellished by blossoming trees of orange and cherry), halls reserved for the archives, for doctors and astrologers, for imperial treasures, for arms and for the housing of the various servants attached to the imperial personage. Access to this interior palace was generally by the southern gateways (*Kenrei-Mon* and *Shômei-Mon*) which opened on to a great courtyard: at the far end was the *shishinden*, which communicated directly with the sovereign's residence; a very wide central staircase led to this. The emperor held audiences in the *seiryôden* which was to the west.

During times of ritual impurity, the emperor and his family were obliged to leave their official residences for one or other of the extra palaces situated outside the enclosure of the main palace, or even for one outside the city enclosure. In the event of fire, they took refuge in one of these 'detached' palaces or else with one of the great nobles where they stayed for the whole time that rebuilding was going on. But, after the great fire of 1227 which destroyed practically the whole palace, this was only partially rebuilt, the imperial treasury being exhausted. The great outer wall gradually fell into ruins, no longer protecting the beautiful *Shinsen-in* gardens from the depredations of the common folk and animals; nothing remains of it now but a small lake to the south of the Ni-jô palace overlooked by a few Shintô shrines, and a small annex of the Tô-ji temple.

Today children come and play on the lake-side. A few buildings of the former palace, rebuilt in 1895 into the new palace (*gosho*) but differently situated, show us how imposing the architecture of the period could be. The roofs were covered with shingles of cyprus-bark or tiles. Pictures on the *Nenjû Gyôji* illuminated scrolls show us what the original buildings looked like and depict certain religious ceremonies and archery contests which were held in front of the palace.

The *Taiheiki*, in its twelfth chapter,[4] gives a description of the palace as it must have been before its destruction:

'At that time the great enclosure of the palace had been built on the same plan as the one bounding the palace of Hien-Yang, the capital of Ts'in-Che houang-ti.[5] It measured 4,280 metres from north to south and 2,308 metres from east to west,[6] the stones of the Dragon's Tail (rear platform of the palace) were laid in the same way. On the four sides were twelve gateways. . . . In addition there was a main eastern gate and a main western one where armed warriors were always on duty. . . . However wonderfully constructed might be the buildings of the great imperial enclosure, they were of no avail against the severity of the elements, even though the phoenixes surmounting the tiled roofs towered into the sky, and the roof tops themselves were hidden in the clouds. They were finally destroyed by innumerable visits from the Fire God so that only their foundation stones remained. . . .'[7]

In spite of constant reconstruction, nothing now remains of these magnificent buildings. The very site of the palace was removed further eastwards so that it was to the north of the true capital. When he returned to the throne in 1333 after his first exile, the Emperor Go-Daigo attempted, on the advice of his nobles, to have the reat enclosure of the palace rebuilt:

'Your Majesty's responsibilities have become extremely heavy and the hundreds of departments of state already in existence no longer function properly (for lack of space). The boundaries of the palace are limited and there is nowhere large enough to hold official ceremonies, for its circumference only measures 475 metres. Even if it were enlarged by at least 120 metres on either side, it could never equal the former imperial residence. A great enclosure must be built . . .'

But this undertaking proved most unpopular, the Emperor having commanded, in order to meet this expense, the appropriation of all the taxes for the year of the provinces of Aki and Suô and, in addition, a twentieth of all the harvest taxes of the country: 'The nation was at the end of its tether and the people suffered intensely' (say the authors of the *Taiheiki*). Taxes and the requisition of materials needed to carry out the work hit the lands of the *jitô* hard as well as landholders in all the provinces. Even the most level-headed showed their concern and declared: 'This is contrary to the will of the gods and is downright arrogance!'[8]

In fact, the reconstruction of this wall had hardly begun before Ashikaga Takauji, setting up his bakufu at Kyôto, forced Go-Daigo to flee. But the misfortunes of the city were by no means at an end: during the centuries which followed, the warriors were to sack the city, leaving nothing but smoking ruins. A succession of wars, riots, attacks by bandits, raids by warrior monks from Mount Hiei, outbreaks of fire and earthquakes were to change the appearance of Kyôto completely.[9]

For eleven years, from 1467 to 1477, the war of the Ônin era witnessed the combatants of the two opposing factions savagely attacking each other in the streets, saw them digging trenches, and setting fire to nearly all the houses still standing. The emperor lived on in a palace in ruins.'

> Miyako that you used to know
> Has now become a wasteland. . . .
> When, at nightfall
> The skylark takes wing
> Your tears flow . . .[10]

The farmers, weary of the demands of the soldiery, formed into defensive bands (*ikki*) and barricaded themselves in the temples, while bandits laid waste the city, setting fire to the few houses still standing so that they could loot them more easily. Deadly strife ensued between the citizens and these lawless, godless marauders. Craftsmen and merchants had fled. But the courage of the inhabitants, although sorely tried, did not fail. Without respite, as the destruction proceeded they rebuilt their city. In spite of overwhelming disasters, the city and its surroundings gloried in the new buildings, temples and exquisite gardens. The shôgun had villas built (Kinkaku or Rokuon-ji, Ginkaku or Jishô-ji), Zen monasteries (Daitoku-ji, Myôshin-ji, Tenryû-ji, Shôkoku-ji, Nanzen-ji) flourished as well as temples and shrines. The emperor, who had deserted the palace, lived at that time in the *Tsuchimikado-Dono*, situated not far from the river Kamo, between the first and second avenue, while the shôgun's residence, the *Muromachi-Dono*, lay to the north of the palace. It was a sign of the times: according to the rules of etiquette, no one had the right to dwell north of the emperor. Ashikaga Takau-ji's villas (Nijô Takakura and Higashi-no-Tô-in) were built in the *Shinden* style of architecture favoured by the nobles living in the capital, but with the addition of buildings, such as stables. And when, in 1379, Ashikaga Yoshimitsu took up his residence at Muro-machi, he had it built on the same plan as the villa of one of the imperial courtesans, Konoe Fusatsugu.[11]

But soon, with peace temporarily restored, the imperial city began to look like a capital city again; once more the streets were lined with merchants' shops and long houses and, as on the morrow of every catastrophe, life was resumed, busier and more luxurious than ever.

KAMAKURA, SHÔGUNAL CITY

At the other end of the country, to the east, Kamakura, capital city of the Minamoto warriors, was only to retain this title until 1333, when the warriors of the Nitta family, acting on behalf of the rebel Emperor, and betraying the last of the Hôjô regents, swept down upon the city and, in the course of a terrible battle, razed it to the ground. The Kamakura shôgunate was destroyed by the same stroke: one of the Shôgun's former vassals established a new shôgunate, this time at Kyôto. Nevertheless, a rebuilt Kamakura was to remain the provincial capital of the Kantô right up to the foundation of the Edo bakufu by Tokugawa Ieyasu in 1603.

Legend has it that in the seventh century the Minister of State, Kamatari, founder of the famous Fujiwara family, in the course of a long pilgrimage arrived one night at a small fishing village called Yui. Thereupon he had a dream: a god commanded him to bury his *kama* (a kind of broad knife similar to a machete) on a nearby hill. In our days this hill is still called *Daijin-Yama* or 'Minister's Hill'. The place then took the name of Kama-kura, holder of the *kama*.

5 'Peasants working on field and elevating water for irrigation of paddy fields' from 'Painting of the Four Seasons' by Kanô Yukinobu

At the foot of this hill, Minamoto Yoriyoshi built a shrine dedicated to the kami of warfare, tutelary god of his family, the Tsurugaoka Hachiman-gû, 'shrine of Hachiman, on the hill of cranes', modern name of the hill originally called Matsugaoka or 'Hill of Pines'. When it was founded (1063), the temple was nearer the sea than it is now. It was Yorimoto who, in 1180, had it rebuilt in the place where it stands today, on the slope of the hill. It then became the heart of the city, which grew up at the foot of a sheltered valley, watered by the Nameri, surrounded on three sides by high hills and bounded in the south by the sea. Seven mountain passes gave access to the city, their entrances guarded by wooden control-posts (*kido*). In the thirteenth century, a woman catching her first glimpse of the city from afar was amazed that it appeared so different from Kyôto, with 'its houses superimposed one upon another (rising in tiers one above another on the slopes of the hills) and looking just like things thrown pell-mell into a bag.'[12] And Lady Abutsu-ni, in her travel diary entitled *Izayoi Nikki*, also finds herself utterly bewildered when she reaches Kamakura: 'The place I stayed at in the east (meaning Kamakura) was called Tsukikage-no-Yatsu (the Valley of Moonlight). It was situated at the foot of a hill by the sea, and was buffeted by the wind. Since it was beside a mountain monastery (the Gokuraku-ji), it was peaceful but bleak and the sound of the waves and of the wind in the pines never ceased . . .'[13] And contemplating the waves of this bay, so different from anything she had previously known, she notes that 'a mist was floating on the waves as they flowed in to and ebbed from the shore, and the innumerable fishing boats were lost to sight'.

> Can there really be small fishing boats
> Hidden away
> In waves so near the coast
> In the mist of early morning . . .[14]

Starting from the great shrine of Hachiman, a broad avenue (the centre section of which was raised by about a metre to form an avenue, the *Wakamiya-Ôji*), connected this heart of the city to the sea. On either side of this main thoroughfare were the residences of great warriors and the most important personages of the bakufu. The shôgun's residence and the government departments were situated slightly to the west of the great shrine. The *Gempei Seisuiki* describes Shôgun Yoritomo's mansion as 'built in the orthodox

97

manner, in imitation of the Kyôto style'. This *Shinden* style of architecture, then in vogue in Kyôto, was, therefore, just as fashionable in Kamakura for the houses of persons of consequence, at least at the beginning of the period. The humbler classes and the ordinary *bushi*, in all probability, lived in houses like the long-houses of Kyôto. Nevertheless, the dimensions of the warriors' residences, like those of their gateways, were regulated in terms of the family's social standing, or more especially of its means.[15]

Traders were restricted to districts concentrated in *Ômachi-Ôji*, between the shore, the *Wakamiya-Ôji* and the hills. A road connected them with the port of Wagae, situated on the coast some distance to the south. A jetty, 200 metres long by 40 wide, enabled Wagae to accommodate large ships. In this very busy port, built in 1232, which traded chiefly with China during the Sung dynasty and was used as a port of entry for such things as rice-taxes, were the centres of powerful guilds, like the timber-merchants' guild (*zaimoku-za*). There the shôgun stored the tax-rice in enormous bonded warehouses. Customs duties levied on cargoes assured considerable revenues for the city of Kamakura.[16] The merchants were only entitled to nine places in the city itself, besides their own districts, where they could set up their stalls, hawking having been prohibited in an attempt to prevent espionage. Choosing the most strategically defensive positions, the great vassals had built fortified houses on the hills surrounding the city. In this way they could easily control the entrances into the city. When Nitta Yoshisada approached Kamakura in 1333, his advance was stopped by these small forts:

'To the north-west he saw a steep road winding through high mountains extending as far as the eye could see up to the pass, and a gateway where some fifty to sixty thousand warriors (this is a literary exaggeration!) were drawn up in formation behind their shields. To the south, at Cape Inamura, the road-way lay along a narrow beach strewn with obstacles right to the edge of the waves. Furthermore, there were boats in line of battle along the water five to six hundred metres away (!) ready to shoot arrows from their towers.'[17]

One would think that the city was easy to defend and that it provided an ideal site for a military government. Nevertheless (miracle or earthquake?), the waters receded from Cape Inamura to free the road, and Nitta's warriors were able to enter the city, to witness its destruction:

'All along the shore the houses of the lower classes were set alight, and those also to the east and west of the River Inase whence the flames spread out under clouds of black smoke, like great wheels, burning down more than twenty different areas up to a distance of 1,000 or 2,000 metres, for just at that moment a howling sea-wind arose. Looming up from behind the flames, and uttering fierce cries, the Genji warriors (Nitta belonged to the Minamoto family) shot down the terrified enemy on all sides with their arrows, hacked them in pieces with their swords, seized and killed them. They captured prisoners, looted, hunted down women and children who were wandering about blinded by the smoke, sending them toppling into the flames or to the bottom of the trenches.'[18]

In the thirteenth century, the population of Kamakura must have been quite considerable, taking into account the small area of the city at that time. No precise figures exist but, in 1252, the bakufu, having forbidden the inhabitants to keep too much *sake* in their houses, organized a search which led to the confiscation of 37,274 jars of *sake*. Out of this number, one jar was left for each house or family, and the rest destroyed. A chronicle of 1293 also tells us that an earthquake resulted in 24,023 dead.[19] It is possible, therefore, that the population may have amounted to about fifty thousand.

Chronicles have left us a description of this city which, despite strict orders to keep the streets clean, must have been somewhat dirty: all kinds of refuse was found on street corners, even dead horses. People there were poor: warriors put in charge of prisoners sometimes let them die of hunger, appropriating the food intended for these unfortunates. Zen temples had set up shelters (*mujô-dô*) for the help of the sick and orphaned. Over a period of twenty years from 1270 to 90 when Ryôkan was Abbot, the monks of the Gokuraku-ji (temple of the Paradise of Amida) thus tended 56,250 sick of whom 46,800 were said to have been cured. Legend has it that this charitable abbot in the same time had 83 temples built or repaired, 189 bridges and 71 roads built, and 33 wells dug, without mentioning many other religious and lay foundations.[20] In 1298 he is also said to have had a hospital for horses built in the court-yard of his monastery.

Biwa players were to be seen at the cross-roads, generally blind monks who chanted traditional epic tales, and also story-tellers and tumblers, showmen with monkeys and puppets. In spite of strict prohibitions and regulations, in spite of night-watches carried out by armed guards carrying torches, there was a widespread feeling of insecurity; one night, even the treasures of the bakufu were stolen. Bandits roamed the streets, young girls and young men were abducted, then sold in the inns along the highways, or as slaves. Life was hard.

However, towards the beginning of the fourteenth century when, as the result of a long period of peace, prosperity had returned, the great samurai gave themselves up to decadent pleasures. Takatoki, the last of the Hôjô regents, delighted in watching dog-fights, and the champions, in rich trappings, were paraded in palanquins. The regent had two companies of actors sent from Kyôto and showered gifts upon them. But Kamakura also lived through moments of intense faith. Zen monks were revered, and legend has it that the famous controversy between Ippen (1239–89), a follower of the Jodo sect, and the Zen monk Dôryû (1213–78) took place there. This dispute is said to have ended when, following an exchange of poems between the two monks, Ippen recanted. Ippen had asked Dôryû whom he accused of useless meditation:

> In this world, even the most arduous exercises
> Yield poor returns.
> So what fruits
> Can one hope to harvest
> From idle drowsing?

And Dôryû had replied:

> The tiny bird on the ground
> Ever scratching about for seeds,
> How can it claim to know
> Where the eagle's eyrie is found?[21]

OTHER CITIES

So little is known of many of the most important cities of the Kamakura era, that they cannot be described in any detail. Ports, like Sakai and Hyôgo (now Kôbe) were already flourishing and engaged in lively commerce. In all probability they hardly differed in appearance from other towns in Japan at that time, except for their enormous granaries or storehouses. Clustered around a temple or a shrine, these cities (apart from the great residences of the nobles) were doubtless limited to straight roads bordered by long-houses, and sometimes by private houses surrounded by vegetable gardens and sheltered by bamboo fences or hedges. The first European travellers and especially the Jesuit missionaries who travelled around the country at the beginning of the sixteenth century have left us but few precise descriptions. However, a change is discernible in the layout of a great number of cities which were built in this period: with the houses grouped around castles, streets become circular, narrow and winding in order to facilitate the defence of the town. Other cities owed their growth to wars, and to the constant traffic of men and merchandise along the main thoroughfares of the country and at the great cross-roads where markets were set up.

At that time, a few hundred houses grouped together constituted a town, generally situated at the entrance of some great temple or shrine, where markets were held on set days. These markets, gaining in importance and developing as the tempo of trade increased, ended up by covering the country with a veritable commercial network. Towards the end of the fifteenth century, the most important of these trading centres became true cities, the most influential traders and guilds (or *za*) having set up centres there, many small merchants, craftsmen and various retainers settled down permanently near them. The *Teikin Ôrai*, written in the middle of the fourteenth century by a Zen monk called Gen-e, and whom we have quoted abundantly in the chapter on food, gives us a detailed account of the products sold in the markets. But, besides these consumer goods, the demand for manufactured goods increased continually, and craftsmen came to establish themselves alongside the shopkeepers, attracted by their clientele. These market men and craftsmen, having placed themselves under the patronage of religious institutions or lords who derived advantage from their trade, started off as seasonal workers, but soon established themselves permanently. These new towns were called *mon-zen-machi* (a group of houses in front of the gates). Following the traders and craftsmen, for their convenience and that of travellers, accommodating inns and places of entertainment multiplied, in their turn attracting an ever more numerous crowd. Towns near a busy cross-roads, especially in the Muromachi period, earned the name of *shukuba-machi* (a group of post-houses).

As for the ports (*minatomachi*), the flow of merchandise and increase of maritime traffic between Japan and China, then with the more distant countries of south-east Asia towards the end of the sixteenth century, brought about their very rapid expansion. The port of Sakai is an outstanding example. Favourably situated at the mouth of the river Yodo, it served as a waterway to the city of Kyôto, and to the great temples and shrines of Nara and Yamato. These ports produced salt, seaweeds and dried fish, which were sent to all the central provinces to be sold to the inhabitants and monasteries, such as the Tenryû-ji, which financed great trading voyages to the China ports. The transport of rice, easier by sea than by land, naturally led to the establishment of huge storehouses at the coastal ports, and to the rise of guilds of wholesale merchants, of carriers, and also of organizations designed for the safeguarding of this vast wealth. Many middlemen and retail dealers settled down there also, and their wealth was an important factor in the development of these cities. In this way, numerous villages, formerly simple fishing ports or pirate hide-outs, become important towns: Hakata, Hirado, Nagasaki in Kyushû; Hyôgo, Sakai, then Ôsaka especially, in Honshû. Father Vilela, a Iesuit Superior, wrote in 1568 that the town of Sakai was a haven of peace and added: 'but, a stone's throw from the city, there is nothing but murder and villainy'.

The building of castles, such as Azuchi erected by Oda Nobunaga or Ôsaka by Hideyoshi (to quote only the most famous), gave birth to new towns. In 1577, Nobunaga granted his city of Azuchi a charter stipulating that in future the town would be a free market, exempt from taxes, and that merchants travelling along the central highway (*nakasendô*) would be obliged by law to stop and put up at an inn for at least one night.[22] In order to attract the greatest possible number of people, and to encourage its development, he even compelled the surrounding monasteries of the Jôdo sect to come and settle down in the new city, where he built the temple of Jôgon-in for them and endowed it most generously.[23] As for Hideyoshi, he ordered all the important personages of his suite to build luxurious residences not far from Osaka, and this obviously contributed to the prosperity of the future city.

Ceremonies in monasteries and shrines generally attracted enormous crowds. It was an opportunity for setting up market and, for the folk of the surrounding countryside, to come and amuse themselves. All the riff-raff took up positions at the monastery gates or in its precincts, hoping to profit from the crowd which never failed to flock there for great festivals (*matsuri*) and celebrations. On either side of the roads leading to them were innumerable hovels belonging to the *hinin*, the blind, paralytics, beggars, lepers, a whole concourse of deformed creatures anxiously hoping for the pity or the generosity of the faithful or of the spectators who came to pay their few coins at the holy place. A motley and picturesque crowd gathered within the temple precincts on feast days: blind *biwa* players, troubadours, showmen with monkeys and trained animals, puppeteers, magicians, jugglers, mountebanks, acrobats, singers and dancers, wandering monks explaining the meaning of holy images or preaching, the faithful praying in loud voices and striking gongs hanging on their breasts. The crowd was dense and pickpockets were busy, ever ready to take advantage of the confusion caused by a quarrel, a scuffle or any disturbance. After every ceremony there were usually performances of *dengaku* and many kinds of dances, religious or otherwise, staged by monks, by *chigo* or by men from neighbouring villages, competitions of 'linked' verse or *renga*, a variety of entertainments in the course of which artists in white and red costumes, both men and women, delighted the crowds in a myriad ways. Prostitutes and thieves did very well on such occasions. Sometimes the crowd was so dense that, to better enjoy the sights, people perched themselves on walls, roofs and branches of trees. Needless to say, small traders and pedlars of every shade and hue did a brisk trade.[24] The *Gikeiki* gives a humorous description of these crowd scenes when it relates the events of the duel which took place in the enclosure of the Kiyomizu-dera at Kyôto:

'When Yoshitsune threw down his cloak, revealing to the common gaze his loose jacket, breeches and under corselet, the startled spectators realized that he was no ordinary person. The excitement reached such a pitch among the nuns, visiting ladies and children that some of them tumbled down from the veranda, while the men hastened to close the doors of the hall so as to leave the duellists outside. Thereupon Yoshitsune and Benkei made their way, still fighting, to the platform reserved for dances. The spectators, who had at first been afraid to draw near, began to move around them, fascinated, like people performing a ritual circumambulation.[25]

HOUSES

The medieval Japanese house, essentially a wooden structure, was planned in accordance with three distinct formulas: houses for nobles, for common citizens and for farmers. The dwellings of lower ranking warriors were like those of citizens and farmers, and varied according to the district and wealth of their owners. We shall take a closer look at them when we deal with the life of the warriors. The nobleman's house hardly differed from that of the Heian period, except perhaps in size, which had depended then upon the social standing of the lord who lived in it. They were still built in the *Shinden* style, but the number of inner buildings had increased with the needs born of the epoch. In Kamakura and in the other towns, persons of consequence generally followed, as we have just seen, the style of the nobles' residences in Kyôto.

Plans of houses, palaces and temples depended primarily on the lie of the land; furthermore, this had to be carefully selected. In this, as in other matters, the Japanese did not feel themselves bound by any rigid set of rules, considering that a strict adherence to them was too limiting. Except as far as the arts are concerned, the Japanese have an intense dislike for this conforming to rule which, they believe, 'fixes' things or renders them static, thereby making it impossible to achieve that harmonious relationship between Man and Nature which is so essential. If rules have been laid down, it is more to advise and guide than to give a definite instruction or an imperative command. It is simply that certain conventions must be respected if the natural order of things is not to be disturbed. Rules, whatever they may be, and they are numerous in Japan in all spheres, were and still are very freely interpreted, not for the satisfaction of a personal whim, but in the pursuit of balance, harmony, beauty – in a word, of 'well-being'.

Once the site was selected, it was first of all essential to determine the size of the building and to work out a ground plan. For this purpose, the Japanese used a unit of measure corresponding to the length of a man lying down, the *ken*, about 1·92 metres in length (see the variations in the appendix): in theory this was the distance between the centres of two adjacent pillars. This basic unit was used to determine, after taking account of the size of the building, the height of the main pillars.

Situated to the rear of a spacious garden, if possible with an ornamental lake fed by a small stream (*yarimizu*), the main house (which was called *shinden*) was roofed with shingles of cyprus or pine bark, or with tiles. The roofs of outbuildings were generally thatched or covered with planks of wood. The steeply sloping roof of the *shinden*, projecting far out over a veranda which surrounded the building, was supported by massive round pillars of plain wood with superimposed corbels whose component units gave sufficient play to allow the entire structure to resist the wind and slight earthquake tremors. These pillars rested on 'foundation stones' set flush with the ground. The whole structure owed its stability solely to the weight of the roof. It is one reason why these were so immense.

The floor was raised, sometimes by more than a metre, to provide a 'hygienic space' between it and the ground as a protection against humidity during the rainy seasons. Up to the fifteenth century, the floors of houses were made of polished wooden boards just placed edge to edge so that they could be taken up easily to clean the ground under the house. Usually, round straw cushions of varying sizes, called *en-za*, were placed on the floor. Towards the end of the fifteenth century, rectangular mattresses of thick straw covered with finely woven rush (*tatami*) on which the master of the house used both to sit and to sleep, were made in standard sizes (one *ken* by half a *ken*); since they covered the entire floor of the house, they ended by determining the exact area of it, the length of each *tatami* being necessarily the same as the distance between two pillars, that is one *ken*. A *tatami* always being twice as long as it was broad, two *tatami* placed together made up a square each side measuring one *ken*, determining a floor space of one *tsubo* (about 4 sq. yds.). But if one counted in *tsubo* to estimate the entire ground-space of a house, it was still customary to calculate the area of a room in *tatami*. It would be said that a room measured four and a half *tatami*, eight, ten, or twelve *tatami*. They never built one of just four *tatami*, this number being considered unlucky, for the number four is pronounced the same as *shi*, the word for 'death'.

The size of a room could be altered as circumstances required by means of sliding partitions (*fusuma*). Before the fifteenth century, these were often replaced by multiple-folding screens or by upright screens mounted on feet; their purpose was to provide a little individual privacy. Most of the fixed partitions and outer walls of buildings were of light masonry, consisting of a framework of bamboo coated with plaster or daub, or whitewashed and the surface smoothed over. The wooden framework and brickwork were left showing on both sides of the exterior walls, thus giving them a half-timbered appearance. If need be, they could be pulled down without in any way weakening the solidity of the structure, for they were not supports but merely 'screens' filling in the gaps. From the fifteenth century, when tea and incense ceremonies were beginning to assume great importance in the lives of nobles and samurai, it became fashionable to display *kakemono* (upright picture scrolls), flowers or precious porcelain in the room for receiving guests. It was, therefore, essential to take into account, in the ground plan of the living quarters of a house, room for the *tokonoma*, without which a dwelling would not be considered truly noble. This was the name given to an alcove, measuring one *ken* or a *ken* and a half in length by a depth which could vary from a quarter to a half-*ken*, raised by about fifteen centimetres and not furnished with *tatami*. The *tokonoma* was always built in the most open and finest room in the house, as a general rule the room used for receiving guests.

GARDENS

A Japanese dwelling-place worthy of the name would have been inconceivable without a garden. In those days this was not looked upon as a separate entity, set apart from the house: on the contrary, it was one of its essential components. The Japanese garden did not adjoin the house, rather did the house form an integral part of the garden. The veranda surrounding every *Shinden* residence provided the indispensable link between it and nature, like the hedge leading from the house towards the garden designed to draw attention to the landscape. We know the characteristic Japanese love of nature, of its lakes, mountains, rivers, stones and trees. It was against the temperament of a Japanese to want to alter nature: all he dared venture to do was re-create her in miniature, to rearrange her components in order to obtain an overall effect reminiscent of nature, so as to have some of her manifold wonders always under his eyes.

A Japanese garden holds a special charm for Westerners who are used to the regular outlines of a garden *à la française*, or to the cool shadiness of English gardens, first by its tranquil beauty, then by the careful arrangement of its stones, islands, and bridges which seem to have been distributed as if by some marvellous accident. Next, it enchants us by its variety: there is always some nook to discover, some new aspect. Finally, we are filled with wonder at the gardener's handiwork. For it takes some time to realize that the hand of man has a part in it: that Japanese hand so discreet in its elegance that it delights in not being noticed.

A Japanese garden is at the same time a place for strolling, a picture to contemplate from the terrace of the house, a subject for meditation, a veritable prayer. It is not designed to distract attention, but on the contrary to urge it in the right direction, to turn it towards the heart of things, towards the heart of man. And it is no coincidence that one of the gardens most visited in Japan, the garden of the temple of Saihô-ji at Kyôto, created in the Muromachi era,[26] should have as its living centre a lake made in the form of the Chinese character *shin* meaning 'Heart' or 'Feeling'. The Japanese garden is also a screen. Its final role is to conceal the house, to make both it and its inmates one with sovereign nature, alone worthy of admiration. For the dwelling place begins in the garden and the door of a house is not really this wooden shutter drawn from its box-cover at nightfall to block the *shôji* [translucent screen], but rather it is the entrance gate into the garden, the true waiting-room leading to the real dwelling place.

COMMONERS' HOUSES IN THE TOWNS

As more and more people flocked to the towns, less building space was allotted to the 'gentry' and court officials. The commoners' houses lining the streets assumed an elongated look. The façade of town houses, not enclosed in large gardens and inhabited by minor officials, generally presented three bays (between-pillars), one of them being the door. The only garden space was the plot of land at the rear of the house. The roofs were covered with thatch or wood shingles, and the walls more often than not made of thick layers of rush or of bamboo lathing, sometimes covered with daub. The standard town dwelling, considered separately, was not basically different from its rural counterpart: it possessed the same component units, was built in the same way, and served practically the same purposes. Instead of a living-cum-reception room and one or several extra rooms, it usually comprised a fairly large number of rooms, and a kitchen situated out of sight of visitors. The entrance hall formed a separate room generally accommodating the large square hearth or *irori*. When the garden was in front, the way leading from the gate to the entrance hall of the house had to be winding and to pass around at least one bush, so that the house could not be seen in its entirety the moment one came in sight of it. As regards the common folk's dwellings, laid out at street level, they very rarely allowed of a wooden floor. Most of them had an entrance-hall with a beaten earth floor where the kitchen was also situated. The main room, however, was always raised and sometimes had a wooden floor.

Apart from these long-houses, there were many private dwellings. Generally of the same kind as the farmers', often not as fine, they looked like plank huts surrounded by a minute fenced-in garden, and were indeed no more than simple boxes provided with a roof. This roof had a double slope and was usually made from overlapping wooden planks which were held in place either by transverse beams, or by huge stones fastened by cords of woven straw. A small ditch, plumb with the edge of the roofs, was crossed by means of a plank or a flat stone placed in front of the door, and was used to catch the rainwater. The gate in the hedge or fence was an ordinary wooden wicket. A *mon-mamori* was hung on it; this was a sheet of paper or a small wooden plate with writing on it indicating that this was private property. Sometimes *shinren*, small protective cords against evil influences, were hung on the gate.[27] Because of the almost 'temporary' character of their construction and their primitive style, these houses contrasted sharply with the nobles' residences. Nothing is easier to understand if one thinks of the incredible number of times they were liable to be destroyed. They had to be made so that they could easily and at little cost be rebuilt from their ruins. Indeed, and by reason of the precariousness of the times, they were more shelters than real houses. But it is just their temporary character which makes it possible for these cities to survive all storms.

DOMESTIC LIFE

It cannot honestly be said that Japanese houses at the time of the samurai, and throughout the Middle Ages, were comfortable, even according to other than European standards. At the beginning of

108

this century, this lack of comfort led Basil Hall Chamberlin to write: 'Nothing to sit on, nothing but a brazier to warm oneself by, yet considerable risk of fire, no solidity, no privacy . . . insidious draughts piercing through innumerable lattice-openings and chinks, darkness whenever heavy rainfall necessitates the shutting down of one or more sides of the house . . .' And what was valid for the first years of this century was even more so during the Middle Ages. It was only possible to live in comfort in a Japanese house, even if it were a palace, in summer when it was hot and extremely humid.

As for the other seasons, they were almost unbearable in these dwellings with thin walls open to all the winds, enormous roof surfaces, flimsy floor boards and practically no heating. During the cold season, while country and ordinary town families could, whenever necessary, huddle together around the square sunken hearth (*irori*), nobles and samurai living in much more spacious houses could only try to warm themselves by small wooden braziers, lined with clay or metal, in which glowed a few live coals occasionally stirred by an iron poker (*hibashi*). Until the fourteenth century, charcoal, while not unknown, was deemed a luxury; because it was so expensive, the only people who could afford to use it were the nobles or the monks of wealthy monasteries. People of modest means fed the fire of their *irori* with faggots. During winter, the nobles donned layer after layer of clothing and, shivering with cold even in their cocoons of quilted coverings, had no alternative but to wait for warmer days. In the Kanto and the northern provinces, life during winter was even more difficult, owing to frequent and extremely heavy snowfalls. The only solution was to lead a very active life. This is one reason why the northern provinces produced the finest warriors.

Since furniture was practically unknown, Japanese houses in those days were almost empty, except for a few lacquered, bamboo chests which were easy to move and were used for storing clothes, armour and things for everyday use. These chests were of varying sizes. The commonest, called *nagamochi*, were of woven bamboo, about two metres long by one metre in height and width. Sometimes they were made of light *kiri* wood (paulownia). Some were fitted with small castors for easier movement. In some houses, light shelves set on feet (*zushidana*) made it possible to keep within easy reach boxes and writing equipment, as well as articles essential for an official's work such as bowls, boxes, writing brushes, paper, waterpots,[28] etc. A few small, low tables, *chôdai* or *tatami*, which were movable, round straw cushions for sitting on (*en-za*), and upright or folding screens made up the main furnishings. *Chôdai*, which people of quality generally used as a sort of bed-chamber-cum-sitting-room, were enclosed by curtains. A rhinoceros horn was suspended over them at one end to ward off illness and, at the other hung two round mirrors to drive away evil spirits. These *chôdai* could be very thick, their thickness being dependent upon the social rank of the one for whom they were intended. The one the Emperor used to sleep on is said to have measured sixty centimetres in depth and to have taken up the area of two *tatami*. In noblemen's houses there would also be concave elbow-rests (*kyôsoku*) enabling them to relax when they were sitting.

Small, individual tables were kept in the kitchen: these were for the use of guests and were only brought out on special occasions, except in the houses of the high-ranking and wealthy. Generally speaking, it was customary to use the floor as a table, food being placed on sheets of paper[29] or trays. In well-to-do houses, there was always an abundance of screens. They were used for cutting off a section of a room and as a protection from prying eyes, or from the wind coming through an open door. They were always decorated, either by verses written with a calligrapher's brush, or by a very delicately drawn landscape, or again by portraits or varied scenes. They varied in size and if, as a general rule, they were no longer than a *tatami*, they could measure up to 1·84 metres in height.

Light hangings or paper screens were also used, especially during summer. The material hung from the cross-bar of a frame, the bar being upheld by two slender little columns driven into a large block of ornamented wood. These screens were known as *kichô-dai*.[30] At night-time, clothes were hung on an upright wooden frame (*misokake*),[31] or else they were thrown over the top of upright or folding screens (*byôbu*) which were used to secure partial privacy for any member of the household.

For lighting, the nobles used oil-lamps of the most primitive kind (a shallow basin filled with oil of sesame with a cotton or hempen wick floating in it), and placed on tall stands (*kikutôdai*). A kind of taper made of resin was also used, and shed an extremely poor light. After sunset, the nobles lived in a semi-obscurity which favoured the amorous escapades of the younger element amongst them. As for the lower classes, they rarely used lamps and went to bed with the sun. Whenever light was needed outside during the night, long torches of pine wood smeared with resin were either held in the hand or driven into the ground (*kagaribi*).

Although there was little variety in the furnishing of wealthy households, it was of rare quality as regards both material and ornamentation. Even in those days, an interest was taken in the production of hand-made goods: certain craftsmen were renowned for their skill. In the *Tsutsumi Chûnagon Monogatari*, the waggish monk whom we have already met demanding food from his benefactress also requests some indispensable articles, which he would obviously like to be as fine as possible:

'If you have no *tatami* with brocade borders, with Korean borders (broad with a black pattern on a white ground), with rainbow coloured or crimson borders, at least find me some worn *komo* (coarse rush mats) edged with hempen cloth. Concerning worn *mushiro* (rough, thin rush mats easy to roll up for carrying), please give me whatever you have. If you have no sound ones, I beg of you at least give me some used *mushiro*. It would be a good thing too if I could have some folding screens; upright screens with Chinese or Japanese paintings on them, or even hempen ones; gold framed Chinese screens; or screens encrusted with Korean stones. If you have none of these things, then give me a worn wicker-work screen (the kind the poor make for their own use). Have you a toilet basin? Please send me one, either round or a carved wooden one. If you have none of this description, then give me another, even if it is broken. Although there are Noto tripods (on which to rest the basin) smelted in Keburigasaki: although there are Sanuki kettles made in Matsuchigawara; although there are pans from the province of Yamato made in Isonokami, and Ômi saucepans stacked up during the festival of Tsukuma . . . please send me some of them. I also need a brazier, one of those made at Oku and a low table on which to put my food. . . . An umbrella from Shigaraki and a rain cloak of stitched straw are equally important. I would also like a portable box from Iyo and a leather box from Tsukushi. At least let me have a small Urashima box (legendary magic box) or a leather bag to place in my sleeve . . .'[32]

Kitchen equipment was more important and often included, apart from one or more clay hearths, wooden chests on feet for storing provisions, oil or *sake* jars, a variety of kitchen utensils such as cauldrons, buckets and trays, eating bowls, and also a great number of baskets and boxes. In a corner there were sometimes large wooden mortars and pestles used either to crush seeds or pound rice for making *mochi*, and small kitchen mortars. Buckets (*oke*) were made of thin layers of turned wood or, for drawing water from the well, of boards adjusted to the shape of the square well-seats.

Valuables, go-boards or *sugoroku* boards, paintings, statuary, musical instruments and chests full of clothes which were not in daily use, were kept in a *kura* adjoining the house. This *kura* or storehouse was a building made of stone and clay with heavy doors also covered with clay and which, in the event of fire, ensured the salvaging of the most precious possessions. If misfortune befell the house, the inmates took out of the *kura* upright and folding screens which they placed around the entrance of this *kura* (being fire-proof it generally withstood the flames) and this then served as a temporary shelter while the house was being rebuilt.

The use of these clay *kura* (*dozô*) became widespread, especially during the Muromachi period. They often had a double door, the inside one, of wood, being protected by another outside door covered with loam or plaster.[33] And it must be admitted that it is thanks to these *kura* and *dozô* that we are still able to enjoy writings, art treasures and paintings of these dark days, fires having completely destroyed everything that could not be fitted into them. In fact not a single house of this period, be it of noble or commoner, remains. The only things that have survived are a few surpassingly beautiful temples.

CHAPTER FIVE

THE COUNTRY

FARMER AND SETTING

Japan, by the very nature of her soil which is arable over so small an area of her islands, cannot farm on a very large scale. Therefore, the system of small-holdings, adopted in the seventh century remained the basis of land development throughout Japanese history. Even if the land belonged to *shôen*, or to great landowners, the farmer cultivated the small plot allotted to him as he pleased, since the kind of farming he undertook then was not included in any general scheme of production. Farmers, working the soil for generations, considered themselves the rightful owners of the land, at the same time paying taxes to an overlord. Whether this was a *kuge* living in Kyôto or a bakufu samurai, made little difference to their way of living; in either case they were subject to taxes and duties.

The main problem facing the Kamakura military government from the start was the problem of the registration, distribution and development of land. It was also essential to restrict the loss of manpower through abscondence without, however, turning farmers into slaves. Last but not least, there was the problem of the collection of taxes. It can be said, therefore, that the social changes which came about in Japan between the end of the twelfth century and the beginning of the seventeenth, a period of time when society was virtually 'frozen' to a standstill by the dictatorial methods of the Tokugwa, all arose from the innumerable regulations laid down by the governments and from the edicts issued by the dictator-administrators in order to control the peasant masses. Since this peasantry constituted ninety-nine per cent of the population, it was in the long run the only class which, by its continuous labour, enabled the country to survive and the ruling classes to live in comfort.

It would be difficult to understand what a farmer's life was like at the time of the samurai without recalling the development of its legal framework. We have already seen that economic conditions in Japan were based on the distribution of land. The man who owned rights to the land held, at the same time, the elements of power. And if whoever owned these rights wanted to enjoy them and be powerful too, he had to see that the land was cultivated and made productive: he was, therefore, forced to rely on the farmer, upon whom he depended, while at the same time dictating to him. The way in which he depended on him, coercing or chastising him through the instrumentality of the law, had its effect, on the one side, on the production and life of the farmer, and on the other on the authority of the holder of these rights. However, it must not be forgotten that it was difficult, in Japan at that time, to predict the results of harvests, these being at the mercy of a variable climate and recurring calamities: periods of severe drought, floods, typhoons, earthquakes, tidal waves, and sometimes incredibly hard winters, took such toll of harvests that famine years were only too frequent. Drought and natural calamities affected the farmers' lives all the more in that, as there was no general system of irrigation, even in the ordinary course of things, it was only possible to have a third or a quarter of the fields under permanent cultivation. The average harvest at that time yielded only a quarter of what the same fields can produce today.[1]

A much more serious matter was the difficulty of communication between the various parts of the country, on the one hand because of the very mountainous nature of the terrain, and on the other because the provinces (in theory sixty-six) were in the hands of lords who were often on bad terms with one another, and who levied heavy taxes on men and merchandise at the barriers they had set up on the highways. But these very difficulties and shortages made it necessary to look for compensations elsewhere. Arable lands had to be won from forest, waste land and marsh.

Peasants as a body, the country folk, were called *bonge* or *kôot-sunin*, that is 'nobodies'; it was they whom the *kuge* of Kyôto looked upon as 'grotesque creatures'. They were also known as the *hyaku-shônin* 'men of a hundred names'[2] for, lacking family names, they were referred to by nicknames of every kind. They were divided into several classes, apart from the *eta* or *hinin* of whom we have already spoken. First of all, at the bottom of the social scale, were those who at worst could be compared with serfs or slaves, although these names give a rather misleading notion of their true status. They were the *zômin*, the people engaged in lowly tasks, those who had no special function and who could be called farm-workers or farm-hands, and the *nuhi*[3] or *genin* (base people). The latter were usually either foreigners, Chinese, Koreans, Ainu or their descendants, or cultivators of a high grade overburdened with debts and reduced to a state of penury, or again regular farmers who, because of their wretched condition, had voluntarily sold themselves to other people (as had happened especially during the appalling famine of 1231[4]). These *nuhi* were not slow in leaving the land to offer their services to overlords and warriors. Some took up the profession of arms. Others became craftsmen. To encourage them to continue farming, the government sometimes granted them tax-free lands.[5] From the end of the Kamakura era, that is from the beginning of the fourteenth century, the majority of the *nuhi* had become warriors in the entourage (*shojû*) of a samurai, or freed men. The law, according to which their master had the right to recapture them up to ten years after they had absconded, had been modified.

Above these very low classes were farmers who were tenants of lands belonging to a farmer owner. These low-grade cultivators (*gesakunin*) were very often private warriors who, in peace time devoted themselves to farming to make a living. They rented lands, on which they settled down with their families, from *ryôke* (high-ranking landowners) or from ordinary farmer landowners,[6] or again from samurai who held land that was worth reclaiming. Finally, came the cultivators and farmers who owned lands which they in actual fact developed and who kept about half the harvests[7] for their own use.

Class distinctions among the peasantry were not, however, as cut and dried as it may seem here: in Japan, where nothing can be too clearly defined, there is always room for some ambiguity, especially in matters concerning human relationships. Class distinctions were based on actual conditions rather than on strict rules. Consequently the Kamakura government, rather than attempting to enforce a way of life, merely improved upon what, in its eyes, appeared to be deficient. There was never in medieval Japan any policy, agrarian or other, which followed a predetermined course: policy was formed from day to day, meeting the needs of the time, rather like a piece of cloth that is mended every time a hole appears, or has a piece added or replaced as occasion demands. The Hôjô regent

Yasutoki, one of the authors of the *Formulary of the Jôei Era* (*Jôei Shikimoku*), wrote in 1232: this legal compendium 'has been drawn up in response to practical requirements'.[8] The *jitô* or military administrators sometimes acted in excess of their rights, and the government was forced to restrain them. When peoople made a practice of selling themselves, it became uneasy again. In 1240, the *Azuma Kagami* recorded this mandate from the Kantô:

'The prohibition against the transfer of individuals has been repeated many times, either in the new laws (*shinsei*) promulgated from generation to generation (by the Emperors), or in the Kantô mandates. Nevertheless, during the famine that raged in the Kanki era (1229–32) there were men who sold their children, others who surrendered their rights (*hôken*) of allegiance (*shojû*)[9] in order to save their own persons. To prohibit such transactions would, at that time, have had no effect except to cause further suffering to the people concerned, so no action was taken. Now that the condition of the country has returned to its former state, there are some who flout this prohibition. It is truly iniquitous and in future this practice must be checked.'

In 1261 the Hôjô regent Tokimune ordered the culprits to be punished: they had, from 1290[10] on, to be branded on the face.

We have already seen that, on his accession to power, Yoritomo had divided among his faithful followers lands previously held by nobles of the Taira family and their allies, and had set up in each *shôen* a warrior-administrator or (*jitô*) entrusted with preserving order and levying taxes. Some of these *jitô* had the right to claim for their own personal use about an eleventh share of the harvest and a tax for military purposes (*kachômai*) amounting to five *shô* of rice per cultivated *tan* (nine litres of rice per approximately one tenth of a hectare).[11] In addition the *jitô* were given a piece of land (*kyûden*) very nearly equal in value to a tenth of the area of the *shôen* they administered; and they shared with the *ryôke* the revenues from common waste lands, from rivers or from produce of the sea if their estates lay along either of these. They also had the right to deduct a third of the fines they had imposed and of the goods which they themselves had confiscated,[12] and they made the most of this right to satisfy their greed. They taxed dwelling-houses unlawfully and they prescribed levies (*fuyaku*).[13]

The farmers were forced to make a direct appeal to Kamakura

or to Kyôto to denounce the abuses of the *jitô* who, they maintained, sometimes even threatened to abduct their wives or children, or to cut off their noses or ears. In some *shôen*, the *ryôke* came to an understanding with the *jitô* and generally received a half-share of their lands, thus enabling these jitô to become the true overlords, owing their allegiance solely to the shôgun. If the *jitô* were all powerful in their domains, they were none the less expected to abide by the laws of the Kantô. The articles of the *Goseibai Shikimoku* (1232) ordered temples and shrines to be revered (articles 1 and 2), they dealt with arrears concerning payment of tax by the *jitô* and forbade them to intervene in legal conflicts between *shôen* (articles 3 to 6). Article 8 laid down that if an administrator (*shugo* or *jitô*) neglected his lands for more than twenty years, his rights or *chigyô* (his actual ownership and exercise of this right, or ownership based on the claim to exercise the right) would be forfeited. On the other hand, if a man devoted himself conscientiously to a piece of land for more than twenty years without having any legal right to it, his rights to this land would be deemed his due.[14] Later on, these twenty years became three generations. The *Einin-no-Tokusei-rei* of 1297 (of which only three articles are extant) confirms this last provision and prohibits the sale and mortgage of lands (article 2).[15]

At the beginning of the fourteenth century, the land was therefore divided into benefices shared among the *honke* (shôgun, lord, or powerful monastery), the true master of the land (*ryôke, ryôbu* or *jitô*), warriors and officials who had received grants of land (*onkyû*) of which they could not dispose as they pleased, farmers granted lands in their own name (*myôshu*)[16] and those who had leased lands.[17]

But after the downfall of the Kamakura bakufu in 1333, many more rights were granted to warriors. The country having been split up into fiefs and *shôen*, the *buke* (warrior families) tended to live as parasites on the lands of farmer owners so as to be able to exercise the profession of arms more freely. The *jitô* and *shugo* (stewards), grown all-powerful on their lands, were not slow to absorb the possessions of the *ryôke* by buying or appropriating their rights (*shiki*). From 1368, all lands (with the exception of those belonging to the emperor and his family, the shôgun and privileged temples or shrines) were theirs in actual fact.[18] The farmer who, under the Kamakura government had enjoyed a life of comparative freedom, very quickly found himself downtrodden and despised. Soon there were only two definite classes among the country people:

the *buke* or warrior families and the *hyaku-shônin* or cultivators. The latter preserved their traditional right to farm the land (in theory not transferable, but in fact hereditary) provided that they none the less paid tax to an overlord.

Feudalism, which was purely nominal in the thirteenth century, was gradually to become an established fact from the middle of the fourteenth century and the farmer was, of course, the first to suffer from this state of affairs which, unfortunately, only worsened as time went on. Rice-taxes (*nengu*) could absorb up to two-thirds of the harvest in some instances. In addition the farmer was forced to hand over a certain quantity of silk and hempen cloth, and to do his fair share of forced labours where matters of community interest were concerned (*kuji*) such as the reconstruction of roads and bridges, irrigation works, and the building of dykes.[19] In times of famine, the country folk were in a desperate plight; numbers of starving farmers revolted or joined forces with gangs of bandits. The houses of wholesale dealers, of usurers and distillers of rice alcohol were attacked, monasteries looted and officials murdered. When these revolts spread even to the warrior farmers (*ji-samurai*), the government was compelled to grant the farmers a remission of their debts by means of 'Acts of Grace' or *tokusei-rei*. There were at least thirteen of these edicts during the shôgunate of Yoshimasa alone (1435–90).[20] During the period called *sengoku* ('country-at-war', 1460 to about 1500) the villagers were forced to look to their own defence and sometimes to arm, so as to prevent wandering bands of warriors from laying waste their possessions. Sometimes they secured a pledge of non-devastation against payment (*yazeni*, arrow-money).[21]

As a rule, the war only affected one district at a time, which explains why it was possible for the general economic situation of the country to improve. The war-leaders divided the lands and shared them out between themselves, the authority of the Muromachi government being virtually non-existent. As the villages were well organized, they were able, in spite of everything, to resist demands and sometimes to buy their way out of levies, with the exception of those which involved the building of castles.[22] For want of shôgunal or imperial laws designed to maintain peace in their lands, some of the great lords, from 1440 on, prescribed a number of rules applicable to their own domains. The best known of these family edicts was the one the Azekura family issued in 1490 in the province of Echizen and which was entitled *Toshikage Jûshichi-ka-*

jô or *Injunction in seventeen articles*.[23] These edicts show that the new feudal chiefs were to some extent anxious to put down abuses, to govern well, and to promote the development of their province by seeing that work was carried out, especially in the matter of irrigation. This did not prevent them from showing savage cruelty on many occasions, from recruiting farmers for their wars and even, as did Takeda de Kai in 1577, from mobilizing all men between the ages of fifteen and sixty. Punishments were harsh and the principle of collective responsibility, until then reserved for noble families accused of high treason, was applied to all farmers.

Hideyoshi's rise to power in 1583 was to bring about some small alteration in the despotic authority of the provincial lords (*daimyô*), but it was only to grind down the farmer class even more, at the same time assuring it of relative security. Hideyoshi attempted to bring in a tax-reform; he undertook to have a survey carried out, known since then by the name of *Taikô Kenchi*. It appears that Oda Nobunaga had already had this notion but had been unable to put it into execution owing to the complexity of rights attaching to certain domains and to the defectiveness of investigations (by means of questionnaires) upon which he relied to make his new assessment. Hideyoshi, therefore, resumed the working out of the plan at once: each parcel of land was measured, valued and allotted to a single individual who was to be responsible for the collection of tax. It was all the more important for him to call this in, in that the upkeep of immense armies, intended as much to preserve peace as to attempt an invasion of Korea and China, called for vast resources; in 1590, when the survey had still not been completed, Hideyoshi was already demanding for his own needs two-thirds of all agricultural produce, which left the farmer with little above the minimum needed to stay alive. To prevent rebellions, he had previously taken the precaution of forbidding the monks and anyone not of the bushi caste by birth to carry arms (1587): 'Regarding the farmers, said the edict known under the name of *katanagari* (sword-hunt), the sons and grandsons of farmers must devote themselves solely to agriculture and possess only agricultural tools.'[24]

Three years later, in 1591, the *rônin*, or masterless, landless men, were driven out of the villages and a new census of houses and inhabitants taken. In future, farmers were forbidden to leave their land, to become tradesmen or craftsmen and to harbour strangers in their village. Each family had to have a separate house. Finally the farmers were rendered jointly responsible in groups of ten (*jûnin-gumi*). Samurai and ordinary warriors were grouped in the same way but in fives (*gonin-gumi*), with one of them as headman answerable to the village or the authorities:

> 'If a farmer leaves his fields, either to engage in trade, or to work for hire, not only must he be punished, but the whole village must be indicted with him. All those who are not employed in military service or in cultivating the land must also submit to an investigation by the local authorities and be expelled. . . . In the event of anyone hiding farmers who have engaged in trade, the whole village or town will be held responsible for this infringement of the law. (Signed: Hideyoshi, Tenshô 19 – 1591 – 8th month, 21st day.[25])

The farmer thus restricted, overburdened with taxes, petrified at the thought of offences others might commit and for which he would have to pay the penalty, forced to inform against his fellows, more wretched than ever, and condemned to forced labour or death by starvation, was in future to lead the life of a slave, a situation unchanged until the end of the nineteenth century.

THE VILLAGE

We have very little information about the planning and setting up of villages before the sixteenth century. They appear to have shown considerable variation, depending not so much upon the times as upon districts and upon how much defence would be needed. Roughly speaking, they could be reduced to two categories which we could call 'peace-time villages' and 'war-time villages', the latter perhaps having sprung up in the north of Honshû where the farmers were constrained to band together to withstand pressure from the Ainu.

'Peace-time villages', up to the beginning of the fourteenth century, were still planned in accordance with the old-time distribution of land: small groups of at most six or seven houses were spread over a considerable stretch of land, among fields. Only the administrative division of land, where a certain number of lots of the same size adjoined one another, allowed of these houses to aspire to the title of a definite 'estate'. Each of these settlements included at least one temple and a number of shrines: the block of houses it took in could at a pinch be regarded as an administrative unit equivalent to a village. Actually, there was no such thing as a real village: it was merely a collection of groups of houses or hamlets,[26] an arrangement which, under different names (*buraku, mura*), was still in existence on the eve of the last war.[27] During a civil war, which steeped the country in blood and made rural areas unsafe, a regrouping of houses took place, either near shrines or temples, or near a wood, a lake, a hill or crag. Nor was the administrative division of land, from 1340, made up of a great number of hamlets, but of a few groups of comparatively important houses (*sô*) the most important being the houses of the leading representatives of authority.[28]

In certain districts, north of Honshû, Kantô and Yamato, where war raged almost continuously, and where the villagers were forced to protect their harvests and possessions, groups of considerable size then came into being around the house of the *dôgo*, the wealthiest local landowner, who was at the same time a kind of village 'mayor'. This house (or rather the land on which it was built, the *yashiki*) was usually surrounded by mud walls or at least by solid fencing, for the *dôgo*, often a *ji-samurai* or warrior farmer, needed to guard against possible attacks from other warriors, from *rônin* (vagrants) or quite simply from bandits. The richest *yashiki* at that time covered an area of about one *chô* (a hectare). Access to it was by one or two gates guarded by watch-towers (*yagura*) made of wood planks. Inside the walls were the storehouses (*kura*) and places for storing arms and farming implements. Sometimes it was surrounded by a moat fed by water from a stream running through the village. On occasions, this moat encircled the whole cluster of dwellings. All round the *yashiki* were houses belonging to the relatives of the *dôgo* and the houses of the more affluent farmers (those who owned their land), sometimes the holy ground of a small temple or a shrine, stables, cowsheds, and the huts and cabins of small farmers. These often extended beyond the boundary made by the moat and formed a group with the farm workers' dwellings (*nago* or *hikan*) just where the foot bridges across the moat gave entry to the village.[29] The social status of the farmer was, therefore, obvious at a glance from the distance which separated his house from the *dôgo*'s, and from its position inside or outside the boundary of the village.

The residences of the *yashiki* and rustic buildings such as sheds, granaries and shelters differed so much according to village and district that they would require a special study. They had only one common characteristic: all were wooden structures. Nevertheless, the design of both kinds was governed by the same principles, and the same methods of construction were used as for town houses, palaces and temples. Obviously, the framework was not as costly nor were the buildings as elegant, but the love of fine workmanship was apparent everywhere. The village carpenter was a master of his craft.

The building of a rustic house began, as in the case of the noblest edifice, with the assembling of the roof-truss avove the main pillars. Once the constituent elements of the house had been made ready, a day's work was enough to set it up. All that remained was to lay the floor-boards, build the square hearth (*irori*) and fit up the kitchen. A wooden plate (*monmamori*) bearing the owner's name was fastened over the door, indicating that he had taken possession, and charms were hung from the edge of the roof to keep evil spirits at bay. The building of a house, or even the simple restoration of a roof, being a communal effort, was an excuse for merry-making in which the whole village (or hamlet) took part. The carpenter and his assistants climbed on to the roof-ridge and set out *mochi* (cakes made from rice-paste) and salt on the main girder, fixed an arrow there pointing towards the north-east to ward off demons, then, after an exchange of cups of *sake* with the owner, threw to the four winds pieces of *mochi* which the children, laughing and jostling one another, tried to catch. Next, all those who had taken part in the building met together for a feast, with the carpenter sitting in the seat of honour. While this was going on, the new owner's family sat down to a special meal. The owner, in his turn, had to be willing to help whenever a neighbour had a house built or repaired.

The living or reception room usually opened on to a small outside veranda sheltered by a porch-roof. The entrance-lobby where shoes were left, was only separated from the large kitchen-cum-living-room (*daidokoro*) by either a folding screen or a light partition. In the courtyard of the house stood one or several storehouses (*kura*), raised on massive piles and surrounded by a low wall made of mud or of loose stones, a well with a wooden lip protected by a small roof, or a pump-well, and various utilitarian buildings of simple shape for keeping straw, hay, animals farm implements and carts under cover. In the houses of the well-to-do, one corner of the courtyard was laid out as a garden, with a small pool, a few rocks and a tree-lined path.

As for the houses of the common peasants, they varied from a wood cabin to a hut made of branches. They were dark and dirty inside, and the beaten-earth floor was more than likely to be flooded whenever there were heavy rainfalls. The interior was divided into two or three compartments by screens of bamboo or plaited rush. At the entrance, near the door, was the earthen fireplace on which the peasants cooked their food and, at the far end, the room where they slept, often a simple alcove. Needless to say, the main room was the largest and here the family usually sat. At nightfall, the peasants slept on straw with which the rooms were provided; as a rule they had neither coverings nor warm clothes. Having no means of lighting, the peasants rose and went to bed with the sun, after putting the fire out, for economy's sake and for fear of setting the place alight.

Some small farmers possessed larger cabins, with thatched roofs and sometimes the rooms were fitted with wooden floor-boards. Others, less fortunate, lived in huts made of branches daubed with mud. The excessive frugality of these peasants filled the more leisured classes with amazement. On her journey to Kamakura, Lady Abut-su-ni, noticing a peasant's house, marvelled:

'In a place where bamboos were growing round about a hillside, appeared a cabin with a thatched roof. The sight of it made me wonder how and on what they could live like this:

> Who ever can be master of this hut
> Clinging to the mountain slopes
> His sole neighbour
> A solitary bamboo grove?[30]

RURAL LIFE

The most important villages, of about twenty houses or more, and situated not far from the capital or from Kamakura, profited by being so near these cities. They generally consisted of one or a number of streets on either side of which stood houses, more or less in a straight line; they were either built very close together or separated by small gardens. Sometimes a canal ran through the village streets which were, as a rule, very wide and this was bridged by means of one or two tree trunks thrown across it.[31] Many villages were closed at night by barriers placed at either end of the street.

The houses were of wood-frame construction roofed with planks and shielded from inquisitive eyes by a high fence made of bamboo trellis. Some had windows fitted with sliding shutters. Not far off stood the temple, surrounded by mud walls and including at least one *hondô*, that is a building in which a statue of the divinity is set up, most often a likeness of Kannon the *Bodhisattva* of mercy, or of Amida Butsu, he who welcomes souls into his Western Paradise. Other buildings contained a bell and a water-trough for ablutions. One or two lesser buildings were set around a courtyard. Sometimes beside the temple, also surrounded by a little low wall, there was a plain roofed structure sheltering a boarded platform reserved for the dances of the *Nembutsu* (*-Odori*) by Amida's faithful followers. Farther on, hidden among trees, there might be a very simple, rather remote Shintô shrine, only the *torii* or wooden portico rising up at the beginning of the pathway betokening its presence.

Villages were often established along the highways and near rivers with embankments deep enough to prevent overflowing when there were floods. The bridges across the rivers were kept in good repair by the villagers, but Yearly floods swept them away. Then the peasants gathered together; everyone brought wood, lianas, ropes of thickly plaited straw, or loam, and the bridge was rebuilt. Because of this, not one of these old structures still stands. These fragile fabrications were replaced almost everywhere at the end of the last century and at the beginning of the twentieth by stronger and more modern bridges of iron or concrete. Big bridges were a rarity. They were generally of the Chinese style, either with multiple wooden piles (the Arashiyama bridge in Kyôto, and the Uji bridge) or with several wooden arches resting on stone piles, or suspended. These suspension bridges, *tsuribashi*, known in Europe as 'monkey-bridges', were very common in mountainous districts where they enabled people to cross torrents and gorges.

A wide, gently flowing river (as a rule near the coast), was crossed by means of boats alongside each other and connected by planks (*funabashi*). The *emakimono* have handed down to us pictures of these pontoon bridges which seem to have been in general use at that time. The usual way of crossing a river was by means of a ferry, for which the ferryman had to be paid with a few coins or, failing that, with rice or a length of cloth. Monks, on account of their sacred office, generally did not pay.[32]

There was always a stable near important houses. This was essential in the very frequent event of a farmer being also a samurai. The stables were made of wood, open at the front and, contrary to European custom, the horses faced the entrance. Their owner took the greatest care of them; he loved to ride out so as to make an inspection of his territories, when he was not abroad waging war on behalf of his lord. In the evening after work, horses and oxen were brought back and given fodder.

Here and there in villages and in the courtyards of great houses, wells were dug, protected by plain wooden rims, wells that always had muddy surroundings and where there was an everlasting crowd of gossiping women, with naked children splashing about in pools of water. When it rained or when a tornado threatened, the mouth of the well was covered over with wooden planks held in place by huge stones. In some districts, fresh water springs served the same purpose as wells, and in summer, the women went there to wash both themselves and their linen, trampling this underfoot on flat stones.

The men did not engage in hunting to any great extent because of Buddhist food prohibitions, except in times of famine. If the warriors hunted with the bow – this was a form of enjoyment and training for them – the farmers were content to use snares to catch small game. Great landowners had carts with enormous wheels for carrying wood and rice; these were drawn by an ox straining under the yoke of incurved wood.

Around the dwellings grew vegetables which the farmers cultivated either for their own use, or for selling in the nearest market on fair-days. Some farmers held, in their own right, tiny plots o land hidden in waste land or forest, which they had patiently cleared for cultivation whenever they had time to spare, in an effort to better their condition a little. All around the village stretched fields and rice plantations, small squares of land bordered by low embankments, dark or light green according to the time of year, and dotted with scarecrows made out of sticks heaped with rags or hung with threads bearing thin plaques of rattling wood.[33] There was little fallow land close to the houses. Farmers cultivated for their own use all the small plots of arable land not registered for taxation, which just about enabled them to keep body and soul together when the daimyô proved too greedy or when the harvest had been a poor one. But these small plots which belonged to them in their own right were pitifully few for they had to be won and cultivated in addition to doing their ordinary work. Sometimes the poorest farmers' sole fortune was no more than a half-*tan* of ground (five ares), on which they grew sweet potatoes (*yamaimo*), hemp and soya-beans. When they were not labouring on this poor field, they hired out their services to more well-to-do farmers and, as well as submitting to ordinary levies, they were often compelled to cultivate the fields belonging to the shogun's officials. Their free time was taken up with cutting grass in the mountains as fodder for their animals and in collecting wood for cooking and heating.

Village life was monotonous. During the day only the old men, the children who had been left in their care and the dogs which swarmed everywhere in Japan, trailed around on the outskirts of the dwelling houses. Every able-bodied person available in the village worked from dawn to dusk in the fields or at some forced labour. From time to time, a monk might pass, offering his prayers in exchange for a hospitality that was always generous (although villagers often steered clear of monks because they were a reminder of death). Sometimes, too, on festival days, the arrival of a *biwa* (a kind of lute) player, or of mountebanks exhibiting trained monkeys, drew a great crowd.

On market days the men loaded on to their backs bales of hemp or sacks of some other produce and left before daybreak to be certain of finding a sheltered position. The markets, at times some distance from the villages, were held at regular intervals near a great temple, a shrine, the residence of a *jitô* or of a great landowner. The nearest market might be set up on another *shôem*. There, in a great open space, stood thatched shelters set in long rows where the *hyakushônin* displayed their wares. Some farmers had set up permanent booths where their wives or children plied their small trade, while they were at work in the fields. Then the owner of the ground made them pay, through an official called *ichiba-satanin*, a yearly tax which could amount to 200 or 300 *mon* (coins). The farmers themselves sold their produce to customers or to the holders of these small shops.

When he had disposed of all he had brought to market, the farmer sometimes bought grain (millet at that time was worth thirty-eight *mon* per *to*, that is eighteen litres[34]), cloth, iron hoes, or large knives for clearing undergrowth (*kama*). The wealthiest farmers sold indigo, wheat, millet, fruits, chestnuts, sesame and sweet potatoes. Others offered articles they had patiently fashioned during the winter months: *waraji, ashinaka* (straw sandals), *geta*, rakes, buckets, troughs, manure shovels, ropes, mats. Thread, salt, dried fish, and a few more scarce and costly products were also on sale in these small markets. In the big ones, which were set up in important towns, or at the great cross-roads of main highways, as well as cloth, swords were sold, and armour, lacquered boxes, ornamented bows, decorated fans, or luxury foodstuffs such as *sake* of many qualities, seasonings and sometimes game. On his way home, late in the afternoon, the farmer was likely to stop at one of the inns bordering the highways, to drink a cup of *sake* as he joked with the girls who were there to offer him some distraction from the tedium of his life.

Winter was the hardest season for the farmer, especially in the villages of the north, where it was harsh and prolonged. It was a time of enforced rest, a time for doing the work the lord of the district required in his house as well as jobs in the home. The smith came and set up his forge under a shelter in the village and mended ploughshares and hoes, surrounded by farmers who took advantage of this opportunity to warm themselves for a short time. Free time was needed for making straw boots and cloaks, for plaiting ropes of straw, for mending clothes, thrashing skins, repairing a hearth or a low wall, for pounding rice, and, in addition, for giving the children a little schooling. It was the time for gatherings at one house or another. Classes were organized in order of age, generation by generation. The oldest took precedence over the youngest, as it should be. The questions which arose when these meetings took place turned on the demands of the *jitô*, or of the tax-collectors, or ways of withstanding abuses and avoiding levies, on communal labour still to be done. The question of festivals was also discussed. In the event of ceremonies in the temple or shrine, the inhabitants of neighbouring villages had to share in the expenses: therefore, the contribution of each village had to be agreed. For example, in 1272, for the rebuilding of the shrine of Taka-jinja belonging to three villages to the south of the city of Uji (near Kyôto), twenty-seven rich men (*tonobara*) had supplied two horses, three *koku* of rice (five hundred and forty litres), a *tan* of white cloth (about nine metres by thirty centimetres wide), twenty *kan* and a hundred *mon* of coins.[35]

Thus, in spite of their exceedingly hard way of life, the country folk had created their own unwritten law determining the rights and duties of every man and enabling all to live in harmony.

SEASONS AND OCCUPATIONS

The Japanese farmer's whole life was regulated by the seasons which prescribed the course of his activities. The calendar in use in the Middle Ages, closely copied from the fiftieth Chinese calendar,[36] had been adopted in 861 and then adhered to without alteration. This calendar was far from accurate and, the months being lunar, some years a thirteenth or intercalary month had to be added in order to catch up with the sun. Whereas the court was able to regulate its ceremonies by an almanac written in Chinese and calculated by the *Ommyô-ryô* or Bureau of Astrologers, the farmers could only regulate their activities by very much simpler almanacs, written in the *kana* syllabary and issued by shrines and monasteries. The most famous of these calendars were those made at the shrines of Ise, Mishina (Shizuoka), Omiya, Saitama, Yamato, etc.

However, the majority of the farmers, not having access either directly or indirectly to these calendars, relied solely on the moon and the changing of the seasons. In those days, these did not quite tally with the seasons as we know them, and spring began on the first day of the year, called *risshun*, which roughly corresponded to February 4th or 5th by our present day calendar. Every change of season was called *setsubun*. There were no months (as we understand them) only lunar months numbering from one to twelve or thirteen according to the year, the thirteenth being then styled 'intercalary'. Theoretically, the seasons were divided into six parts or 'short seasons', called *ki*. These *ki* (breaths) were in their turn divided into three parts or *zassetsu*, these also being more theoretical than serving any actual purpose. There was also a catalogue of days, very commonly used, which gave each day the name of an animal, rat, ox, tiger, hare, dragon, snake, horse, sheep, monkey, cock, dog and boar, corresponding to the symbols of the yearly Chinese zodiac: the day of the dog nearest to the spring equinox was, for instance, thought propitious for sowing seeds. Indeed, legend has it that Kôbô Daishi, the founder of the Shingon sect, bringing back some grains of rice from China in 806 was attacked by a dog which shook the precious seed out of his sleeve; it germinated and produced a bumper harvest. The hours of the day were announced by the sound of temple bells. Day and night were divided into six parts of unequal length according to season, and called *koku*. But as a rule farmers relied above all on the height of the sun and in actual fact acknow-

7 'The great Buddha Amida' at Kamakura. Cast in bronze in
1252, it is fifteen metres high

ledged three parts in a day: dawn, midday and dusk, which was adequate for their needs.

Farmers, as we have seen, not only cultivated rice but also many kinds of cereals, in order to make use of the rice-plantations between harvesting and sowing. In fact, in 1264, a law laid down by the Kamakura bakufu ordained that 'farmers must sow wheat after the rice harvest, and this wheat will not be taxed'.[37] Already, in 1189, Yoritomo had impressed the *rônin* (this was the name given at that time to absconding farmers or those without land of their own) so that they could put dry fields and waste lands under cultivation, and sow cereals and vegetables there. Rice production improved continually throughout this period with the arrival of new varieties of seeds from time to time from south-east Asia and southern China; rice growing could thus be adapted to the varying climates of the Japanese islands. The *Seiryôki* (middle of the sixteenth century) describes ninety-six varieties of rice, twelve of wheat and as many of barley, as well as fifty kinds of leguminous plants.[38] Rice had become the staple diet, whereas until the fifteenth century it only represented an occasional food for farmers. They lived mostly on the vegetables they grew, leguminous plants and cereals such as wheat, barley and rye.[39]

Fields and rice-plantations at the beginning of the Kamakura era were mainly cultivated by hand but, later, the use of oxen for ploughing became general and the same *Seiryôki* states that: 'the use of at least one ox or one horse was required to cultivate a field of one *chô* (about one hectare)'. The implements in most general use at that time were the plough (a wooden ploughshare hardened in the fire or strengthened with metal), the hoe and reaping hooks, besides rakes, buckets and wooden flails made by the farmers themselves. The wheelbarrow seems to have been unknown (whereas it was used in China) and earth was carried either in baskets, or thrown on to a screen made of straw or rushes drawn by hand and slid along the ground.[40] Production varied according to the district and the year. In the fourteenth century in the Yamashiro region (outskirts of Kyôto) the yield from top-grade rice plantations was estimated at about one *koku* and three or four *to* per *tan* (that is, almost 240 litres of rice for ten ares) and, from less productive plantations at about 150 litres for the same area.[41] As for vegetable produce, it was especially important in the Kantô which, in the sixteenth century, exported it to other provinces by special boats.

Farmers did not enjoy many days of rest, and Sunday obviously did not exist. Nevertheless, there were *harebi* or 'shining days' – looked upon as holy and which consequently were days of rest from work – when the seasonal feasts came round indicating important stages in agricultural labours: ploughing, sowing, planting out, prayers for rain in periods of drought, etc., or when there were important religious festivals. These days were solemnized by the preparation of food only eaten on occasions like this (generally dried fish, rice cooked with red beans, *sekihan*, or again *mochi*). Those who could manage it dressed in their finest clothes on such days as these. Farmers also believed in all kinds of superstitions in connection with their work in the fields: lightning without thunder (*inazuma*) was for instance thought to betoken a fine harvest, lightning being, traditionally, the spouse of rice.[42] A full moon was always eagerly awaited: children saw in it a hare pounding rice in a mortar for making *mochi*.

SPRING

It corresponded to our months of February, March and April. The first day of the year (*tarotsuitachi*) was a festival day. On that day the spirits of mountains and rivers (*taro*) were supposed to change their abodes as a token of the New Year: then none dared wander in the mountains, and everyone kept clear of the water. This belief still holds today in many districts.[43] At the beginning of spring, taro roots and lotus bulbs were gathered in and towards *higan*, at the approach of the spring equinox, the first beans (*soramame*) and wild honey were brought in. Fresh water crabs and edible snails from the rice fields were also much appreciated at this time of year. Finally, at the end of the third lunar month, the wheat and rye were harvested.

The first day of the horse of the first lunar month was a *harebi*, for at that time the kami of harvests, Inari, was worshipped, and it was most unusual for a village not to have at least one shrine consecrated to this kami and his guardians, the *kitsune* (foxes). The ceremony was merely a matter of visiting a shrine and offering the kami a few grains of rice and a cup of *sake*. On that day (from 1371 onwards), there were always crowds flocking to the shrine of Fushimi, near Kyôto: nobles, townsfolk and farmers came to pay homage to Inari and to beseech him to grant them abundant harvests and prosperity.

The third day of the second lunar month was the time for manuring mulberry trees and sowing barley. The equinoctial week witnessed neighbours paying each other short visits and exchanging gifts: this was deemed a propitious time for social gatherings. The fifteenth day of the first lunar month was the anniversary of Buddha's death, but there was little celebration of this except by the monks, the same as for the anniversary day of Kôbô Daishi's death on the twenty-first day of the second lunar month, in the first quarter of the moon. The fourth day of the third lunar month was also a festival day: this time prayers were offered to the kami of the wind to spare the crops. Four days later the birth of Buddha was celebrated. In the temple courtyards a *hanami-dô* was erected, a small building decorated from top to bottom with flowers, and inside a statue of Buddha as a child was placed in the middle of a small ornamental pool. The faithful came to pour *amacha* over the statuette. This was sweet water made from an extract of the hydrangea which they drew from the basin. This potion, after flowing over the statue, was believed to have healing virtues: therefore every member of the faithful took a little away with him. Bouts of *sumô* (wrestling) were sometimes organized on this occasion, and young villagers delighted in trying their strength. At the end of spring, the wheat and rye were harvested and a small patch of the rice field was dug over in preparation for sowing rice grains. In the farmyards women energetically pounded camellia seeds with their mallets on the edges of the oil-press, seeds whose oil would make their hair lustrous and black.

SUMMER

This season comprised the months of May, June and July, and it was one of the most important in the year. At the beginning of the season the farmers, especially from the Muromachi period onwards, erected grotesque effigies in the fields to scare off insects and so ensure the successful outcome of their harvests. The first day of the dog of the fourth lunar month (the beginning of May), rice mixed with seeds saved from the last year's crop was planted, then the preparation of the rice-fields for planting out began, by ploughing up the earth, flooding it, removing the wooden plaques which were used as water-gates for the irrigation channels, and by breaking up the clods of earth so as to transform the rice-field into a muddy lake. Time was filled in by making the first collection of silk-worms, for about forty days were required for the rice seedlings to grow to sufficient size for planting out.

Then the young rice plants were taken from the seed-beds (a painful task for the young leaves are sharp edged and great care must be taken not to break the roots), and tied into bundles. When it was time to plant out, right at the beginning of the rainy season, the bundles were carried into the fields and placed on the narrow embankments of dry ground. This arduous task, requiring many hands, was generally undertaken as a communal operation, all the inhabitants of a hamlet working one field at a time. The bundles were undone; men and women in lines across the entire width of the field, up to their knees in mud, with bent backs, planted the young shoots at regular intervals of about a half-*shaku* (15 cm) row by row; moving back a pace as each seedling was planted, they sang to give themselves courage for this work. When the field was planted out, the peasants rested awhile to exchange coarse jests about fertility and the sexual act. After they had washed the thick mud off their legs, they set to work again on another plantation.

The work had to be completely finished before the summer solstice. Then a general holiday was observed and the peasants met together to sample some kind of delicacy, to drink *sake* and to watch frequently licentious dances performed by the married women. Sometimes a monk was asked to read *sûtra* in memory of the insects killed during the planting out. The essential tasks immediately after this were tea-picking, the making of garments from mulberry bark fibre (*kôzo*) and the preparation of frames for the silkworms' cocoons. Then homage was paid to Yakushi Butsu, the Buddha of healing, Amida Butsu, Kannon the Merciful and Jizô, the Patron of souls fallen into hell and of children (the evening of the twenty-third day of the fifth lunar month). *Sake* was prepared, the rice then requiring three months to ferment.

Then came the day when the souls of the dead left their heavenly abode to come down and visit their relatives. A few days later, the *bon* festival was held, the greatest festival of the year. Graves were cleared of weeds and covered with flowers if they were recent ones. Carved stone statues of Jizô, which stood at the cross-roads of highways were washed and decked out with flowers. Houses were cleaned, the family altars (*butsudan*) adorned and in some provinces, the souls of the departed were accompanied on their return journey by little straw skiffs decked with oil lamps and entrusted to the waters of the nearest river. During the three days the *Bon* festival lasted, there was much merry-making, exchanges of visits and dancing. On the last day no cooking was done. Then came the season for gathering beans, cucumbers, aubergines, for cutting the grass known as *kaya* which was used for thatching roofs, for picking peaches and plums which, pickled and dried (*umeboshi*) will keep for a long time, for stripping oil-plants, for weeding and hoeing rice plantations and for collecting silkworms for the second time.

AUTUMN

It corresponded to our months of August, September and October. At the beginning of the seventh lunar month, buckwheat and millet were sown, then *miso* was prepared, a fermented soya-bean paste used for making soups and mixed with salt and rice-yeast, a popular seasoning. The fifteenth day was the festival of the moon and, on this occasion, young villagers met for a tug-of-war, each group tugging with all its might on a thick rope of rice-straw. Since, according to tradition, the losing side was bound to have a bad harvest, the players kept changing ends as soon as one side began to weaken, with the result that neither could win or lose, and finally the rope broke before a decision could be reached. It was also the fishing season for eel, trout and carp. Prayers were offered for the souls of silkworms killed during the year. Towards the end of the seventh lunar month (August), the rice was ready for harvesting to begin: it usually ended about the time of the autumn equinox. Sickles were used for reaping; the stalks were cut and tied into small sheaves put to dry in the sun on dry ground, on hedges, hung from branches of trees or even on roofs. In the evening, the grain was covered with straw to prevent the dew from wetting it. It was turned and aired every day for three weeks. During this time, nuts, mushrooms, sweet chestnuts, horse-chestnuts, and camellia seeds were gathered; also vegetables were brought in, taro, *konnyaku*, *gobô*, beans, ginger, and barley was mowed while a start was made on storing the rice harvest.

WINTER

This season, which corresponds to our months of November, December and January, witnessed the ploughing of rice fields for wheat to be sown on them, the threshing of rice with flail or beater on the bare earth of the courtyards, and the drying of grain in the sun. Then this was measured out, sometimes in the presence of the representatives of authority, of the tax-collector or the overlord by means of a *masu* or square wooden measure. It was put into sacks made from woven straw (*tawara*) each holding 4 *to*, that is about sixty kilos of rice. Taxable rice was loaded on to carts and transported straight to the overlord, *jitô* or *daimyô*.

With the drawing in of the days, operations slowed down a little. Sticks were gathered for firewood, time was devoted to the felling of trees and the sowing of vegetables, to the spinning of hemp and silk, and sometimes the men went hunting. In some regions, rye was planted or onions and rape gathered in. Finally came the last day of the year, *setsubun*, when it was customary to scatter soya-bear~ in the corners of the rooms and outside the house (to drive awa/ demons and attract good fortune) at the same time shouting lustily: 'Oni wa Soto! Fuku wa Uchi!' (Out with you, demons! Come in Good-fortune!) Children were given wooden dolls believed to have propitiatory virtues, and sometimes the last night of the year was spent on visits to friends or the temple.

So the cycle was complete and the year began again, the same in every respect as the one that had just gone by, with certain variations depending on regions and eras, the monotony only enlivened by the appearance of an itinerant healer, a horse doctor, or pedlars, or by the possibility of visits or pilgrimages to the near-by temples, by a marriage or a birth. Occasionally processions of monks came to the village chanting and dancing the *Nembutsu-odori* (in the name of the Buddha Amida), beggars too, and people who, especially in winter, were making pilgrimages to the thirty-three shrines of Kannon.

Disasters came only too often to disturb the course of the seasons: typhoons, outbreaks of fire, wars, banditry. And life was lived under the constant threat of taxes and additional levies. The most dreaded calamities were prolonged periods of drought and an over-abundant rainfall. These two abnormal weather conditions made famine inevitable, villages having no reserve supplies of food whatever. However, famines were never very general in Japan, since the country was split up by mountain ranges with deep valleys differing widely one from another. Therefore, fishing villages were very little affected by famines. But inland provinces were hard hit.

Roads being either bad or non-existent, the inhabitants of an entire province could die of starvation while its neighbours were hardly touched by it.

But, even more than the difficulty of communications, both road barriers and the absence of a sense of national unity were stumbling blocks to any effectual mutual aid. There were even instances of famine being advantageous to some provinces. The defeat of the Taira clan in 1185 was, without any doubt, much more the result of a famine from which only the west had suffered than the result of the military disaster of Dan-no-ura; an army of 20,000 starving men of the Taira clan had gone over to the enemy which, in the east, had not had to endure starvation. In times of famine, people living in country districts were reduced to eating roots and, in some extreme cases, even resorted to cannibalism.

Kyôto itself was witness to this in 1259.[44] According to the *Hôjô-ki*, the famine was so dreadful that year in Kyôto that the streets were strewn with corpses. A monk of the temple of Ninna-ji who, to ensure the salvation of souls and their rebirth in the Paradise of Amida, went about tirelessly signing the foreheads of the dead with the first letter of the holy name of Amida, maintained that he alone counted 42,300 corpses[45] in this way. In the countryside, corpses were thrown pell mell into the fields, the survivors no longer having the strength to bury or cremate them. Consequently, every famine was followed by frightful epidemics. And Ippen (1239–89) the singing monk, surveying the Owari plain exclaimed, at the sight of the corpses scattered over the fields:

> Alas! to end like this.
> See them strewn across the wasteland.
> Ah! how fleeting
> Is the life of man![46]

FISHERMEN

Fishing techniques seemed to have made but little progress during the early part of the Middle Ages compared with the techniques in use before the twelfth century. It was pretty nearly the end of the sixteenth century before the invention (or introduction) of the drag-net, which resulted in a more efficient method of fishing, by using boats modelled on Korean fishing-boats (a minor result of Hide-yoshi's desire for conquest), which held the sea better. There were two kinds of fishing villages at that time: villages inhabited by farmers who became fishermen during the fishing season, and villages whose men were engaged in activities connected with the sea all the year round while their wives spent their days cultivating the fields.

Fish, as plentiful in rivers and lakes as in the sea encircling Japan, included many different species: sardines at Matsuura, dorades and tunny-fish in the Pacific, sole, mullet, bream, mackerel, carp, trout, turbot and also sea-bream, sleeve-fish, seaweeds, etc. Salt also formed the basis of an important industry. So it is that an official report dated January 2, 1445 showed that, out of sixty-one trading vessels arriving at Hyôgo, about half were laden with salt, the cargo of the others being chiefly rice and wood.[47] There were various methods of salt production. When Lady Abutsu-ni undertook her journey to Kamakura (1277), she spoke about the 'harvesting of seaweeds and burning of salt'.[48] At that time a kind of seaweed called *moshiogusa*[49] was sprinkled with water a number of times, then dried in the sun. These seaweeds, impregnated with salt, were burned. The residue was put into water so that the ashes could then be easily separated from the brine. This method of simple evaporation produced pure salt. Another method, said to have originated in the Matsushima region, consisted in simply boiling sea-water in large cauldrons, but this was a rather laborious method, for it demanded a great quantity of firing, so poor fishermen were hardly ever able to use it. Salt was in great demand, not only for culinary use, but also for ritual purification, salt being thought to keep both baleful influences and sickness at bay.

Seaweeds also made up a good part of the fisherman's income: dried, they were a very popular item of food. River fishing was done either with casting-nets or line, the fishermen using small fishing-smacks, or monoxylons. On some rivers, particularly on the banks of Lake Biwa, cormorants were specially trained for fishing. In the *Masu Kagami* at the time of the first lunar month of 1277, the emperor Go-Uda watched cormorant fishing on the river Oi and, in the *Gofuka Shin-in Kampaku-Ki* on the thirtieth day of the third lunar month of the year 1373, there was also a reference to this particular way of fishing.[50] Fish-dams were set up on some of the shallower rivers at the appropriate season. At sea, larger boats, with sails, made it possible, thanks to ground-lines, dragnets (*hiki-ami*) or to dipping-nets (*sade-ami*) to fish some distance out from the coast. However, net-fishing did not really develop in Japan until the fifteen century. As for whale-fishing, it was carried on in the sixteenth century with the harpoon (*mori*) off the coasts of the province of Awa in the island of Shikoku. Nevertheless, the majority of catches were made close to the coast.

CHAPTER SIX

OCCUPATIONS AND CRAFTS

DOCTORS AND CRAFTSMEN

No society can develop or prosper unless it includes men who are specialists in an art, a handicraft, a science or a trade, men by their very nature being dependent on each other not only for their subsistence but also for everything affecting their creature comforts. Therefore, there usually sprang up, in every type of society, what one might almost call 'guilds' grouping together men with the same skill, either because they felt the need to exchange or to transmit the secrets of their art, or because they wanted to guard these secrets more closely in order to ensure their own livelihood and to discourage competition. There were also some occupations which were the prerogative of certain families, so there was no need for them to form guilds. From the beginning of Japanese history, family groupings of craftsmen are to be found, 'men of a common art' known as *be*, whose secrets and tricks of the trade were handed down from father to son. The same must have been true of certain occupations which, strictly speaking, did not belong to a real craft, but which had none the less some of the characteristics of an art, like medicine.

Real doctors were a rarity in medieval Japan. Apart from court physicians, there were many quacks who wandered from village to village, offering their services, or on market days placed themselves at the disposal of their customers. But these itinerant doctors, or rather healers and pedlars, merely sold drugs and magic cures. Some town doctors, enamoured of the Chinese classicists, followed the teachings of specialized treatises dating from the T'ang era, and of Japanese treatises like Tamba Yasuyori's (928–84), entitled *Ishinhô*. In 1592, Hideyoshi brought back from Korea Chinese books dealing with medicine and plants, in particular the *Chao-hing kiao-ting king-che tcheng-lei pei-ki pen-ts'ao*, a herbarium which appeared in China in 1159, the work of several doctors, the only remaining

138

copy of which can be found in the botanical gardens in Kyôto.[1] Doctors practised acupuncture (*hari-ryôyi*) and *moxa* (cauterisation by means of cones of herbs dried and burned), in accordance with methods imported from China as far back as the seventh century and developed by the Japanese. From the Muromachi era onwards, the techniques of massage (*amma*) and medicinal baths were also used.

Chinese medicine was comparatively well known to the Japanese and they made full use of its methods. Treatises describing plants and their pharmaceutical use had long been published in Japan. Some *emakimono* refer to them and moreover give very accurate reproductions of medicinal plants (as in the *Bai Sôshi Emaki* of the thirteenth century, more particularly intended for veterinary use). Certain diseases, hitherto unknown in Japan (syphilis, for instance), having made their appearance towards the middle of the sixteenth century, were described in detail and the appropriate treatments sought. It was not, however, until 1557 that Western medicine appeared on the scene in the form of a hospital founded by Luis de Almeida (1525–83) with the help of several other Portuguese missionaries. A one-time Portuguese Jesuit priest, who took the name of Sawano Chûan, translated certain scientific books into the Japanese language; he even wrote a treatise on surgery called *Nambanryû Geka Hidensho (Secret Treatise of the surgical methods employed by the Barbarians of the South)*. But the most famous Japanese doctor of the sixteenth century was Manase Dôsan who, having become a Christian in 1548, none the less professed Chinese medicine. According to tradition, his 800 pupils became Christians as well.[2]

An *emakimono* of the beginning of the thirteenth century, the *Yamai-no-Sôshi* (picture-scroll of illnesses), portrays the commonest complaints at that time; one of its pictures show us a doctor treating an eye complaint by lancing (or puncture). The blood is spurting from the patient's eyes into a pan held by a woman. The text adds that after this operation, the sick man gradually lost his sight! There was, of course, no question of asepsis as yet (treatises on acupuncture did, however, advocate boiling the needles and some-times wounds were cleansed with vinegar), and both medicines and treatments had varying results. But as much could be said about medicine in Europe in the same era.

In country districts much more notice was taken of 'old wives' remedies' and magical invocations than of the doctor, who was only called in (by rich families) when more ordinary methods of healing had proved ineffectual. The peasants were used to looking after themselves in their own way; they had recourse to plants, to infusions or decoctions, or to remedies made according to recipes that had been handed down to them. In cases of serious illness, they sometimes bought medicines from the patent medicine vendor: bear's gall-bladder (*kuma-no-i*) for curing stomach disorders, Gin-seng roots for prolonging life and curing anaemia, oil of toad (*gama-no-abura*) for skin complaints, etc. As a rule, they were satisfied to apply leeches and to make use of the healing virtues of herbs. Some of the following recipes were in general use at that time: for burns, an application of the white of an egg or soya sauce; for insect bites an application of crushed convolvulus leaf; for stomach disorders, drink the ash of bamboo leaves in hot water; for diabetes, eat seaweeds; for fever, drink the juice of willow wood boiled; a decoction of peony roots was believed to be a sovereign remedy for diarrhoea; for toothache, apply the ash of pine needles to the gum; and so on. The most commonly used remedies were obtained from various roots, from orange peel, mushrooms and ginger. A number of 'teas' were made with the leaves or flowers of the following plants, *kuko, cassia, hydrangea*,[3] to which many healing properties were attributed. They also made use of the juice of the *hechima* (*luffa cylindrica*) particularly as toilet-water, of *daikon* (a kind of rape containing pepsin) to help digestion, of *gobô* roots, of the nuts of the *ichô* tree (*ginko*) known as *ginnan*, for a cough, and of the roots of the *konnyaku* (*amorphophallus*). These remedies were not without merit, their use generally being the result of prolonged observation.

Treatment by *moxa* was recommended for nervous disorders and for regulating the circulation of the blood. In many cases, a *miko*, a priestess of a Shintô shrine, was called in; something of a sorceress, her business was to drive away the evil spirits (*oni*) deemed responsible for the illness by means of incantations. The illustrations of the *Kasuga Gongen Kenki-E* (1309) show us ceremonies of this kind. The *miko*, having set down beside her a tray on which sand or rice was placed, recited invocations to induce the protecting kami (whose mark will be seen on the sand or rice) to 'descend'; she beat a tambourine or twanged a bow-string, while a *yamabushi* (sorcerer-monk) cut the air with mighty sword-strokes as he exorcized the evil spirits of sickness by his chanting. Outside a 'sacred place' had been set up, in the form of a rock serving as a 'seat' for the divinity, and in front of which was planted a wand to which *hei* or purifying paper strips were attached and a lock of hair from a woman's head (this hair had the power to put demons to flight). Offerings were laid on the ground and these objects encircled with a straw rope twisted 'to the left' (*nawa*) betokening the sacred character of the whole. A purifying fire was lighted in front of this shrine. When the *miko* was possessed by the kami she had invoked, she danced as she recited magic formulas and translated the kami's words. If the divinity had granted the prayer, he set his sign on the sand. The ceremony was then complete.

Wandering monks might also be called to the bedside of a sick person, to recite prayers for a speedy recovery:

' "The wife of the master of the house is tormented by an evil spirit. Will you not pray for her?"

'Genson answered: ' "As I am only a monk of inferior rank, my prayers will not be of great use. But our leader, who is this moment resting in the temple at the cross-roads, is someone whose efficacy in this respect is very great. If I speak to him about it, he will certainly want to help your mistress."

'Hearing Genson's words, the mistress of the house took heart, saying: "If this is so, I beg of you, bring this august monk, your abbot, here." And she rejoiced mightily.

'When Genson had hastened back with this news, the prince (Morinaga, disguised as a wandering monk) and his entourage made their way to this house. The prince went into the sick woman's room to pray that her sickness might leave her, and recited the invocation to Kannon of the thousand arms (*Senju Kannon Darani*) several times in a loud voice, with a great rattling of rosary beads. The sick woman's mind began to wander, meaningless phrases escaped her . . . and she was bathed in perspiration. Then indeed the evil spirit left her, and from that very moment she was cured. The master of the house, her husband, was filled with joy and said: "I cannot make you any particular offering for I have nothing in reserve, but I beg of you to stay here and rest for at least ten days." '

However, apart from professional doctors, quacks and medicine-men, the temple priests often gave much of their time to alleviating the distress of the common people and to tending the sick. Moreover many doctors were priests.

Treatment of the sick was practically the same for animals and especially for horses. The 'horse-doctor' (*bai*) was of considerable importance, for these animals were the object of the samurai's greatest concern. Their horses were regularly currycombed with warm metal combs and their gums bled. They were not shod and consequently had to be rested frequently. When they covered long distances, their hooves were wrapped around with straw to protect them from injury.

The raw material of which the Japanese made most use and which was most readily available was wood. They made such good use of it that innumerable handicrafts came into being. Living in the forests, the woodcutters (*somabito*) were as a rule very poor folk. They felled the timber required for the building of temples, houses and palaces, and – this perhaps was their main job – cut up timber for firewood. Some of them spent their time making charcoal. Tree-trunks were cut down, assembled in rafts and set afloat on the rivers; then they were taken to the places where the building was to be done, or at least close by.[7] There they were stripped of their bark, dried and finished by the carpenters.

The timber-trade was one of the most prosperous, and boats carrying undressed timber from all over the country, especially from the north, called regularly at certain ports like Wagae near Kamakura. Carpenters' guilds had an enormous membership. Fires, typhoons and earthquakes, by destroying buildings of every kind, kept them fully employed at all times. The massive tree-trunks, tied with ropes, were dragged along either by hand or by oxen; they were slid on to logs which assistants levered into position. Perched on tree-trunk or beam, the overseer, with *eboshi* on head and fan in hand, directed the work of his men[8] by word and gesture. The tree-trunks were squared and sawn into planks by the use of metal or hard-wood wedges driven into them with mallets. The job was finished off by axe and adze. Finally, the planks were cut to the required length by means of short saws with convex blades. The marking was done with a line soaked in ink, and with an instrument like the one present-day carpenters still use (*suminawa*). The foreman handled the square and the measuring instruments, rods one *ken* in length divided into six *shaku* (about 30 cm) into *sun* (3 cm) and *bu* (3 mm) On rainy days, carpenters used a shelter made of planks which served as a workshop.[9] Their basic set of tools, limited to a few saws, hatchets, broad-axes, chisels, knives and adzes of various kinds did not prevent them from achieving amazing results, which were at times incredibly accurate. Woods were skilfully selected, carefully cut and polished before being transported on ox-carts and assembled.

Often each carpenter had his own specialized job to do, whatever the work undertaken. Some were solely responsible for roof-brackets (*tokyô*), very complicated at that time, others for flooring, still others for pillars. Indeed many village carpenters built, single-handed, simple houses, or carts and palanquins. There were also men who specialized in boat-building. The monk Chôgen, known as *Dai-Kanjin* or Great Architect, and entrusted with the restoration of the great temple of Tôdai-ji, burnt down in 1181 by Taira troops, had brought back from China during the Sung dynasty new building techniques and assembly methods which enabled him, by the strict specialization of carpenters working for him, to erect imposing buildings speedily.

Working together with the carpenters, there were many joiners, numbering among them sculptors in wood. These were often priests or artists attached to monasteries, working for them by carving images of divinities which the various cults worshipped.

Japanese paper, with such varied textures and now greatly appreciated in other countries, was made entirely by hand. It was, according to tradition, the Korean monk Donchô who, in 610, introduced into Japan the techniques of both paper- and brush-making. However, it would seem that paper was known there, if not made, before that date. It continued to be a peasant and family craft until the Muromachi era during which, the demand increasing rapidly in proportion to the development of *shôji* (window-frames covered with paper) and above all of the administration, there was a notable extension of the craft of paper-making.

Paper was made chiefly from the barks of various kinds of mulberry trees called *kôzo* (*Broussonetia kajinoki*), *mitsumata* (*Edgeworthia papyrifera*) and *gampi* (*Lychnis coronata*). Each district developed its own techniques and papers of different types were earmarked for specific purposes, for *sumi-e* and calligraphy, painting, letter-writing *shôji*, fans or official documents. It was said that paper from *gambi* was noble, from *kôzo* masculine, and if it was made from *mitsumata* bark, feminine. The wood was first of all boiled so that the bark could be more easily separated. The bark, scraped and carefully washed, was afterwards boiled with potash taken from the ashes on the hearth, then washed in running water to eliminate this potash. After this, it was beaten to reduce it to a pulp. This was then mixed with vegetable glue extracted from the root of the *tororo*, a plant similar to the taro. Supreme importance was attached to the cleanliness of the water used as well as to the temperature, which had to be as low as possible: paper made in winter was considered the best. After they had been 'shaped to the tank' the sheets were put to dry in the sun on polished wooden planks so as to extract the excess water. The beauty of the various kinds of paper lay in their texture and in the way the fibres were interwoven. Ordinary paper was used for innumerable purposes – ribbons, linens, handkerchiefs – which our modern twentieth century has only just discovered.

A handicraft that was a corollary to that of wood- or paper-making was lacquer-work. In Japan techniques of lacquer-work (*urushi*), used throughout Asia, reached a degree of perfection rarely equalled in other countries.[10] The marvellous manual dexterity and patience of the Japanese craftsmen enabled them, thanks to the co-operation of famous painters, to create masterpieces. From pre-Buddhist times, lacquer had been used in Japan to waterproof wicker-work or to decorate combs and bows. Lacquered objects have been found associated with late *Jômon* pottery, or placed in sepulchres of the *Kofun* period (fourth to seventh century). The Lacquer-workers' Guild (*Urushi-Be*) was one of the oldest guilds in Japan; tradition holds that it was a certain Mimi-no-Sukune, living in the days of the emperor of the mythical Koan era, who was its first leader. Lacquer-work was greatly favoured during the Nara period; it was used either to decorate religious objects or those in daily use in the nobles' houses, or to make sculptures with clay or wood as the core. The Shôsô-in Museum in Nara has preserved many objects, such as bowls, boxes and musical instruments, ornamented with this virtually indestructible material. Up to the Heian period, ornamental motifs and lacquer-work techniques had been brought over from China and Korea. Leather, hempen cloths, wood and wicker-work were widely used as foundations for lacquer, embellished at that time with inlaid mother-of-pearl, with precious metals or with patterns made from colours ground in oil.

The technique known as *makie*, in which gold and silver-leaf were replaced by gold-dust mixed with lacquer, was to take the place of other techniques from the Heian period on, and to enable lacquer workers to attain a truly Japanese style. Lacquer seemed to have become so indispensable in the Nara period that the government had encouraged the cultivation of the lacquer-tree, *urushi-no-ki* (*Rhus vernicifera*) whose sap produces the basis of lacquer. This process was in such high favour in Japan at that time that it was perhaps one reason for the relatively late development of the art of glazed pottery. During the Heian period many techniques in lacquer-work disappeared in favour, almost exclusively, of *makie*. Gold-dust, silver-dust and *aokin* or 'pale gold' (a mixture of gold and silver dust) were used instead, either applied thickly or lightly dusted on, and inlaid mother-of-pearl was sometimes used in conjunction with coloured crystals.

Japanese products were at that time highly thought of on the Korean and Chinese markets both for their masterly execution and their elegant ornamentation. During the Muromachi period, the art of lacquer-work followed the tendency towards realism seen in painting. Metal-dust was practically given up in favour of fretted gold (*kirikane*), resulting in more vigorous effects. Decorations in relief (*taka-Makie*) made their appearance and workmanship of fantastic skilfulness was executed on saddles, toilet-boxes and writing-cabinets. At the same time a more popular school evolved, like the one known as the Negoro, in which red and black lacquers were used exclusively on articles for everyday use, bowls, plates and a variety of boxes. During the Muromachi period, painters of repute at that time were asked to decorate lacquer-ware, artists like Nôami, Sôami, or painters of the Tosa family. But soon Chinese products began to compete with Japanese lacquer-work which, for its part, was exported in large quantities to the continent. The two countries then exchanged techniques and styles; but perhaps also with the growth of ceramic art, Japanese lacquer-ware, influenced by modes of the Ming dynasty, lost its originality by resorting to new shapes and methods of decoration. Lacquer-ware then became overloaded with ornamentation of sometimes dubious taste. The Momoyama period here, as in other arts, evinced a tendency often exaggerated to the point of lavishness. The painters of the Kanô school collaborated in the decoration of some pieces. But these were expensive products which were only within reach of the extremely wealthy.

On the other hand pottery was more available to the common people. Ceramic art had been known in Japan from time immemorial and some pottery can be dated at nearly 7,000 years before our time. During the whole of the Nara and Heian periods, hardly any advance was made in ceramics, the nobles importing the pieces they needed from southern China. The Japanese kilns at Bizen, Tamba (near Kyôto), and at Seto in Owari continued to work solely for local needs (mainly tiles with a cobalt glaze), reverting at times to primitive methods which made use of the mould in place of the potter's wheel. In the Kamakura epoch, the Seto kilns began to extend their range and produced glazed stoneware in greens and yellows, then blacks and browns, fired at a very high temperature. Vessels made like this were always decorated with incised or printed, stylized floral patterns. During the Muromachi period, after the resumption of official relations with China, an enormous amount of Chinese pottery was imported into Japan, chiefly for use in the tea-ceremony and for the interior decoration of palaces. The shôgun and nobles often presented their favourites with a piece of Chinese pottery. It was then that Japanese potters began to design pieces especially for this tea-ceremony, introducing into the plastic arts the *wabi* or rustic style inspired by Korean models. Products from the kilns at Bizen and Shigaraki contrasted with the ornate Chinese products and were more in keeping with the taste for simplicity of the followers of Zen philosophy. When the cult of the tea-ceremony spread to the warrior-class, the demand for pottery that was both beautiful and rustic led to the re-opening of old kilns and the founding of new ones. Numerous kinds of ceramics then made their appearances, *Rakuyaki*, *Shino*, *Oribe*, etc. In Kyûshû, Korean potters established by Hideyoshi on his return from Korea, then produced ware known as *Karatsu*, sometimes simply decorated with a design in black on a grey ground, the brush strokes heavily applied, and with a white glaze that was incised.[11]

As for the art of metal-work, which was accountable for the employment of a great number of craftsmen, this also flourished throughout this medieval period. Born of a long tradition, it developed rapidly, with the ever increasing demand for weapons required by the warrior-class. Metal craft found its purest expression in the forging of sword-blades (*tachi*, *katana* or others depending on their shape or purpose) and sword-guards or *tsuba*. Apart from the casting of gigantic bronze statues like the Daibutsu of Kamakura, erected in 1252 (nearly 15 metres high), the art of metal-work from the end of the twelfth century, concentrated principally on the making of swords and various weapons, on armour, mirrors (*ekagami*), anchors, sewing needles, pieces of harness, agricultural tools, cooking utensils, locks, metal fittings for buildings, bells, fishhooks and nails. There were several kinds of swords: the most ancient called *ken* or *tsurugi*, were straight, double-edged and had a hilt with a pommel. It is only towards the eighth century that these blades of the old type were gradually replaced by the ones on slightly curved swords, with a single cutting-edge. The Japanese usually call sword-blades made before 1530 *kotô*, and those fashioned after that date *shintô*, when the technique of forging was at its highest. The infinite care taken by silver and goldsmiths in the ornamentation of sword fittings, particularly of guards (*tsuba*), was only equalled by the pride of their owners. Swords were things of great value which were handed down like heirlooms.[12]

To obtain the ore required for the manufacture of cast or forged articles, it was essential to work the mines. But in this field, the technique was far less advanced than that employed in the purifying processes, in the refining and forging of metal. Until the fifteenth century, only the working of surface-ore, or that found near the surface, was known. Fortunately, Japan was blessed with a fair number of open mines and great quantities of ferriferous sand. It was only towards the end of the sixteenth century that *kôdô-bori* or mine-working by means of horizontal roads was used. Gold was found in the gravel of rivers, iron in the sands and silver at Tsushima. Besides gold and iron, copper, tin, mercury, lead and sulphur were worked, the last being exported in large quantities. Pits were often dug to get iron-ore, but these pits could not be very deep, owing to the hazardous nature of the methods employed and above all because of the seepage of water which was bailed out with metal buckets. Methods of assaying silver and refining copper were only imported from China in the sixteenth century. Miners were generally people belonging to the lowest classes; they were recruited particularly from the *hinin* and the *eta*. On the other hand, smiths and sword-makers enjoyed a very high social status. They were often attached to Shintô shrines.

Among other professions and handicrafts which played their part in the progress of Japanese civilization, mention must obviously be made of the makers[13] of fans, those indispensable accessories of everyday ceremonial, of the weavers, basket-workers, umbrella-makers, tanners and cottage industries of an almost infinite variety.

SCIENCE

Contact with Europeans was to enable the Japanese to improve their techniques and to begin to make progress in all fields – those relating to crafts as well as to science. The first firearms were introduced in 1543 and the first cannon appeared about 1550. Following Hideyoshi's expedition to Korea, at the end of the sixteenth century, there was an advance in printing techniques by the use of Korean metal types and by the importation into Japan of a European printing-press using movable metal type. It was during this epoch that missionaries and traders brought in new techniques, like those concerning the weaving of wool and the manufacture of glass (already long known in Japan but seldom made). At the end of the sixteenth century, Japan was to enter into a new technological era.

Nevertheless, except in medicine, it cannot be claimed that science had made any progress throughout the Middle Ages. Scientific concepts had in fact remained the same, or very nearly so, as those held in the twelfth century. The exact sciences continued to be an aristocratic pastime. Only, or almost only, the monks could calculate. They still used a somewhat primitive method, called *sangi*, consisting of small wooden rods which were placed in such a way as to form numbers and which when moved enabled them to carry out simple mathematical operations. The use of the *soroban*, or Chinese beaded abacus, was not to spread to Japan until the end of the sixteenth century, coinciding with the development of commerce. But until then the use of mathematics was limited to the practice of the four operations and the rule of three. It was of little use except to traders and sometimes to fortune-tellers.[14]

Astronomy and astrology had made no progress and the few outstanding men of letters who could read Chinese books were more interested in the processes of divination or the exorcizing of evil influences than in scientific observations.

TRADE

The period of constant warfare which followed the downfall of the Kamakura bakufu, far from hindering the rapid progress of trade and barter, on the contrary only gave them a great impetus. Wars, begetters of needs, nearly always further the development, if not of trade itself, at least of a certain class of merchant. During the Kamakura period, merchants had tried, while supplying commodities to temples, monasteries, wealthy shrines and people of importance, to keep for themselves exclusive rights in their clientele and to obtain certain privileges. These merchants, the better to resist the demands of the lords of the *shôen* and the ravages of war, eventually formed themselves into kinds of guilds known as *za*. These guilds then made sure of the protection of their most powerful clients who, for their part, benefited from the transactions carried out by the *zashû* or traders, merchants and various money-lenders, members of the *za*.

These associations first came into operation in Kyôto itself, where many merchants had to satisfy the needs of a wealthy clientele, especially after the Ashikaga bakufu had finally established itself in the Muromachi district. These organizations claimed great privileges: exemptions from town dues demanded at the barriers set up by the *jitô* and by the *shugo* on the borders of their *shôen*, the monopoly of the sale of their goods in a specific district, immunity from taxes on their trade and on markets belonging to them. Thus powerful guilds were formed, connected with the monasteries or influential lords; the monasteries of Mount Hiei were patrons of warehouse keepers and wholesale merchants, the Shinano shrine protected the brewers and vendors of *sake*, the Gion shrine looked after the interests of the raw cotton merchants, the Hachiman-gû monasteries at Oyamazaki were patrons of the oil merchants (who enjoyed exclusive rights not only in Kyôto but at Ise, Tamba, Omi, Izumi, Kawachi, Mino, Owari, Awa, Higa, etc.) There was also a very important *za* in Kamakura, a joint guild of timber merchants and carriers.

The affairs of these *za* were generally managed by lower orders of priests called *jinin*. These *za* saw to the distribution of commodities whose manufacturers they represented, and to the transport of these goods, either by boat, or by means of the many pedlars who travelled through the countryside from year's end to year's end. In the ports, merchants became warehousemen and carriers (*toi-maru*) of the commodities paid by the various shôen as tax. Some of these middlemen who, by way of payment, deducted a large share of the merchandise carried or stocked, in a few years amassed considerable fortunes which they augmented by lending money or rice at exhorbitant rates of interest.[15] In times of famine, since farmers and poor samurai were unable to pay their debts, this system, especially from 1428 on, gave rise to many revolts which the bakufu could only quell by cancelling the debts of the penniless. At the same time, the number of *za* increased and soon every trade or craft was an excuse for forming corporations obviously comprising recognized 'patrons' and 'clients'. The peasant-farmers were the only ones to suffer from this state of affairs and to endure hardship as a result of the practices of this system, the number of barriers having multiplied to such an extent that the cost of transport was doubled by the countless town dues levied on merchandise.[16] Certain towns and ports like Sakai or Hakata were able to obtain so many privileges, their population being almost entirely composed of merchants, that they became more or less self-governing. Sakai in particular had become so wealthy that it loaned money to the Muromachi bakufu in 1543.

This intense commercial activity contributed to the formation of a new social class half way between the farmers and the samurai and priests, a class of townsfolk engaged in a craft or trade; this formation was further facilitated by the ever increasing use of copper coins called *mon* and imported from China in considerable quantities.

The great temples owned entire ports (Hyôgo, now Kôbe, belonged to the Kôfuku-ji monastery of Nara, Sakai to the Sumiyoshi shrine); in the same way some of the great *daimyô* owned lands along the sea-coast. These last named made enormous profits from foreign trade as much by exports (Japanese goods were sold in China at more than four times their value on the Japanese market) as by imports. The most important Japanese ports at that time were on the north coast of Kyûshu, at Hirado, Hakata, Imazu, and on the island of Tsushima, and also on the shores of the inland sea, at Sakai, Hyôgo, Itsukushima. In these ports there lived a mixed population of Japanese merchants and traders, Koreans, Chinese, interpreters, middlemen, ships' crews, masterless and landless samurai (*rônin*), a bustling, lively population of jacks-of-all-trades, women of easy virtue and all kinds of dubious characters.

Ships sailed regularly from the Japanese ports from June to February and March, avoiding, however, the typhoon months of August and September, making either for Korea, then China, or straight for the port of Nimpô, near Shanghai. The passage took from five days to a fortnight by the northern route and from three to six or seven days by the southern one which, although more direct, was considered more dangerous. The return voyage to Japan was made towards the month of June so as to take advantage of the most favourable winds. Japanese ships were poorly constructed and generally small, being unable to carry more than 60 to 100 passengers and crew. The largest vessels (able to hold up to 300 people), lacking in manoeuvrability, could not venture into the open sea and were content to make short runs from harbour to harbour along the Japanese coasts.

Merchant ships were generally built of camphor wood, a wood that is rot-proof and stands up well to the effects of sea-water. The *Kegon Engi Emaki* depicts such a ship, a two-master with bows and stern standing very high out of the water; studying this picture, it is obvious that the ships of this epoch were shallow-draft ones. Below deck, forward, were the armoury, water supplies and kitchen. Amidships were four compartments intended to accommodate both freight and passengers. Between the main mast and the quarter-deck stood a tiny, square cabin, fitted with windows, for the use of important passengers. The look-out men kept watch from the roof of this cabin. Two stone anchors were suspended from the bows, held in place by a horizontal winch on which were coiled cables made from the twisted creepers of Fuji wistaria (*Wistaria sinensis*). These ships required two rudders forward and sometimes three aft. When the winds were favourable, the sails were hoisted (which, once they were taut, revolved round the mast) in order to catch the wind. In a dead calm, the crew put out long oars through port-holes set along the bulwarks. Ships' crew and merchandise shared the deck.[17]

Despite the discomfort and lack of security these ships offered, about fifty of them were reckoned to reach Nimpô every year. Japanese exports consisted mainly of gold from Ôshû, silver from Tsushima, pearls, sulphur, mercury, wood (pine and cedar), either in the form of trunks or planks, and of objects of artistic value and handicraft: lacquer-ware, screens of all kinds, fans, articles in gold and silver and weapons (bows, arrows, armour, swords and hal-berds). Japanese weapons were in great demand in China where they were looked upon as *objects d'art*. In the year 1483 alone, 37,000 swords were exported there.[18]

On their homeward passage, the ships were laden with copper coins, perfumes, medicaments, birds (peacocks, parrots), sheep (very rare in Japan), and Chinese dogs and cats, horses, textiles cotton, silk, precious woods (sandal), bamboo for making flutes, books printed in southern China, particularly religious and, philosophical treatises, porcelains, paper, ink stones (*suzuri*), sticks of Chinaink, tiger and panther skins, jade, paintings, tea and spices.

Japanese ships brought back so many coins that the Ming government was alarmed and, in 1432, sent an envoy to ask the bakufu to reduce the number of merchant vessels trading with Chinese ports in order to arrest the flood of copper coins, China being in danger of not having enough for her needs. The only form of currency in Japan was, as a matter of fact, Chinese *sen* until Hideyoshi had coins minted, issuing silver and gold *tenshô-tsûhô* in 1587 and silver *bunraku-tsûhô* in 1592. However, it appears that paper money was sometimes used, especially during the restoration in the Kemmu era (1333–6). The *Taiheiki*, indeed records that 'paper money was made of a kind which had never yet been used in our country from ancient times until the present day . . .', without adding precise details (Chapter XII).

But there were not only traders at sea. Many Japanese pirates, the *wakô*, roved the coasts of Korea and China to the supreme advantage of the *daimyô* who took a lively interest in this profitable pursuit. The Ming emperor had even been compelled to fortify his coasts to enable him to defend himself against these *wakô* who operated in groups of ten to twenty ships. At the request of the Chinese rulers, the bakufu was forced to prohibit these practices, until then deemed highly respectable. In 1587, Hideyoshi presented the merchant marine with a kind of charter comprising nineteen articles, after taking steps to ensure that quarrels between Japanese and foreigners in the ports should not hamper maritime relations with other countries; and he issued an edict under his 'Vermilion Seal' (*shuin*) which authorized approved merchant ships to trade as far as Cambodia and Siam. Consequently, the first Europeans to land in Japan found people who were fully prepared to trade with them and to make use of them as agents between the Asian countries and themselves. The priests from the monasteries who had been the first, in 1342, to freight trading vessels to finance the building of the temple of Tenryû-ji, had found dangerous competitors in the Catholic priests and Portuguese merchants. And this is perhaps one of the reasons which later on led to the expulsion of European priests.

Inland, trade came up against serious obstacles: an ever increasing number of tax barriers and bad road conditions, where practically the only ways of transporting goods were by porters or pack-horses. These barriers were generally guarded by soldiers. The legendary story of Yoshitsune (*Gikeiki*) relates in great detail how the hero, disguised as a monk, succeeded in getting past the Mitsuno-kuchi barrier:

'On the northern slope of the mountain, at a place called Mitsuno-kuchi, where the road branches off to Wakasa in one direction and Nomiyama in the other, two local lords, Tsuruga Hiyôe of Echizen and Ineou Saemon of Kaga, had built a toll-house protected by forbidding-looking control posts. Night and day, three hundred guards were constantly on the alert to detain and question all travellers.

' "Monks or not, you must pay your tax. . . . Pay and pass. By command of the Lord of Kamakura we have to provide for our own needs by collecting tolls from all travellers without exception," said one of the guards.

' "This is outrageous!" cried Benkei. "Since when have the monks of Haguro had to pay toll? No one else has ever done sò, and neither shall we!" '[19]

Although these barriers had been officially done away with by Go-Daigo in 1334, they continued to be set up all over the country:

'The barriers in the four directions and on the seven circuits were places where important prohibitions relating to the provinces were proclaimed and where warning notices were posted up in abnormal times (of famine or serious public disturbances). The emperor (Go-Daigo) however ordered the closing down of all barriers in all districts except those of Otsu and Kuzuha. For (because of their numbers) things had come to such a pitch that they were preventing the arrival of the yearly tax and, by their right of exclusive control, were submitting merchants to too many expenses during the long journeys.[20]

Bridges were practically non-existent; precarious pontoon bridges were used instead. Highways were narrow, difficult and hazardous: gangs of bandits robbed travellers less well armed than themselves, or ruthlessly fought them and boasted of their exploits at the inns. These brigands spread terror throughout the land. So, transport of goods by boat along the coasts was much more profitable. On land, pedlars and merchants joined forces and hired the services of a few fighting men to escort them and defend them if necessary. They stayed the night in the temples or else at the inns which stood at the cross-roads, and where they were sure to find board and lodging and, if they were so inclined and had the means, other diversions.

In this way they were able to reach, with the minimum of risk, the market-towns for which they were heading. At Kyôto, however, after Go-Daigo had ordered the suppression of the barriers, 'he commanded the police superintendents . . . to inspect the cereal reserves hoarded by rich merchants in the hope of making sizeable profits (during a famine), and to set up markets near the second gate, where inspectors were to weigh and fix the price of grain. Thus, in actual fact, the merchants were able to enjoy their profits while the common people thought it possessed enough reserves for nine years.'[21]

But in this matter the *Taiheiki*, biased as it is, distorts the truth somewhat: if the abolition of barriers benefited the merchants, the farmer noticed little change, for he hardly ever travelled. Whatever changes might take place in the country, his lot could only worsen. The establishment and gradual rise of the merchant class, during the Muromachi and Momoyama periods, far from alleviating his wretchedness, only further increased his state of subjection.

CHAPTER SEVEN

WAR AND WARRIORS

THE WARRIOR OF THE MIDDLE AGES

At the beginning of the Kamakura period, a period that could almost be termed 'pre-feudal' (true feudalism not being established in Japan until the clan leaders were completely freed from the tutelage of a centralized government and no longer owed it anything but nominal allegiance, that is until the fourteenth century), the warriors formed but a small part of society, at least in the central provinces. In the Kantô and more northerly provinces, it was different, the warriors of the northern clans being nearly all sprung from farming stock. Their leaders, at that time called *saburai*, were quite naturally those who governed them in their capacity as territorial rulers. These *saburai* were, therefore, mainly *gokenin*, direct vassals of the shôgun, and *kenin* or immediate vassals of the latter, or else fighting-men holding some important office in the bakufu administration. They had their own troops and servants, and they had the right to ride into battle. The other warriors, or *bushi*, belonged to the *kôotsunin* classes or *bonge* (ordinary folk). From the fourteenth century on, the name *saburai* only applied to 'war leaders' obeying the Muromachi bakufu and also to certain warrior nobles in the service of the imperial household, these last being given the more particular name *goshozamurai*.[1] It is because of a phonetic development that this was later pronounced 'samurai' and it is this last designation we shall use here.

The warriors from the eastern provinces, styled 'barbarians' by the court, experienced in the practices of 'the Way of the Horse and the Bow' (*Kyûba-no-Michi*), must have been uncouth fellows, in a way analogous to our medieval 'barons'; the affectations of the Heian-Kyô court had not yet had a softening effect upon them. Yoritomo's victory over the Taira, if it was largely due to the famine which had weakened the Heike troops, was equally the result of the soft life these men had led in Kyôto. The warriors of the east and the north, split up into numerous clans, only understood the meaning of unity on the battlefield,[2] a temporary unit which Yoritomo, far-seeing as he was, was able to use cleverly to the advantage of his military government and to make more or less permanent by encouraging the relationship of interdependence between his vassals and himself. The way of 'The Bow and the Horse' was preserved by forbidding the samurai any intercourse with the aristocracy of the capital, and a tacit agreement was formulated, strengthened by laws like those of the *Goseibai Shikimoku* of 1232 which gave actual sanction to a customary law already in force in the provinces.

But with the weakening of the bakufu's authority, the result of the disastrous 'state of war without recompense', consequent upon the defence of the country against the attempted Mongol invasions of 1274 and 1281, and with the resumption of relations with Kyôto, the warrior way of thinking, so evident in the days of Yoritomo and of the first Hôjô regents, soon began to change. Most certainly a number of moral principles remained, strengthened by the philosophies of the Zen sect and of Chu-Hsi's neo-Confucianism, both recently introduced, but moral strictness had disappeared: war became accidental and no longer a *raison d'être*, an opportunity for reaping rewards and winning titles to fame or riches. Already at the beginning of the fourteenth century, when Ashikaga Takauji established his bakufu at Kyôto, it was a far cry from the spirit which prompted Yoritomo to say when addressing Toshikane, vice-governor of the province of Chikugo, who had appeared before him richly clad:

'Why do you not practise economy? Look at Chiba Tsunetane or Dohi Sanehira, they are *shugo* (military constables) and their domains are much more extensive than yours. Yet they do not wear such rich clothing. So they can put aside the surplus of their incomes and enlist in their service many vassals who will help them, when required, to perform feats of arms for which they will be rewarded. You, on the contrary, do not know how to make use of your resources, your dress is too lavish: do you not think it is extravagant to wear clothing like this?'[3]

The warriors vied with each other in elegance and luxury. The *Taiheiki*, a warrior chronicle of the Emperor Go-Daigo's time, conjures up the picture of a march-past of armed men:

'The magnificence of this procession was truly a splendid sight! First of all, behind the bannerman, appeared eight hundred warriors all accoutred in like manner, riding huge, powerful horses decked with lofty plumes. Two hundred and fifty metres behind them rode the great Marshal, Nagasaki himself, clad in crimson armour deepening in colour towards the surcoat, with a speckled under-dress and wide short breeches of heavy silk. Eight golden dragons crested his silver-starred helmet with a neck-shield in five pieces curving outwards behind: likewise his iron greaves were silver-plated and his two swords decorated with gold. His horse, Ichi-no-heguro, was the finest in the eastern provinces. It was sixteen hands high, decked with fine plumes of bright yellow and its saddle was embellished with a picture of a ship aground on a beach at low tide, a picture drawn in pure gold-leaf on spangled gold lacquer. The thirty-six arrows in Nagasaki's quiver were white, with broad black spots in the middle and notches of silver, and he held a rush-bound bow by the centre. In truth the streets (of Kyôto) seemed narrow as Ichi-no-heguro advanced. In two lines in front and behind marched five hundred soldiers of middle rank wearing breast-plates and protective gauntlets (for drawing the bow). And about a hundred thousand (!) horsemen rode five or six hundred metres behind, each in armour of his own choice, with glittering helmets, in serried ranks, filling the roadway, like nails in the sole of a shoe, while five or six leagues . . .'⁴

The frugality, the Spartan ways of the warriors at the beginning of the Kamakura era, their very poverty, could not long withstand the temptations of every kind that assailed them. The last Hôjô regents themselves had not scorned extravagance and the majority of their vassals eagerly followed their example:

'About this time, the people living in the capital took a great fancy to a dance called *dengaku* (a rustic dance) which became extremely popular with high and low classes alike. Hearing of this, the monk of Sagami (the Hôjô regent Takatoki) summoned both the old and the new style troops of dancers to Kamakura, where he gave himself up to enjoyment morning, noon and night, and could think of nothing else. . . . When he was drinking one night, he became merry on *sake*, so up he rose and danced (it was the futile dance of an old drunken monk of more than forty years of age). On one occasion some dogs happened to gather in the courtyard of his house and started fighting; thereupon he issued orders to the provinces, demanding that dogs be supplied to him as tax, or requesting them as gifts from powerful families of high rank and people in positions of importance. . . . This led to very great expense for he fed them on fish and game and hung gold- and silver-plated chains around their necks. On the days these dogs travelled in their palanquins, travellers hastily dismounted to kneel before them, and villagers working in the fields received orders to carry them on their shoulders. . . . Kamakura was full of strange-looking animals, to the number of four or five thousand, surfeited with meat and resplendent in brocade. Twelve days each month were set aside for dog-fights, during which the Hôjô's attendants, great lords with their hereditary vassals and others, sat in the halls and courtyard to watch the fights. Two packs of dogs, with from a hundred to two hundred animals in each, were released and savagely pursued each other, leaping and rolling on top of one another, and the sky re-echoed to the cries of battle and the earth was shaken with them.'[5]

FOOT-SOLDIERS

Besides these leaders and powerful lords who could lend their aid to the party of their choice as it suited them (at least after the Muromachi period), there were numbers of foot-soldiers (*zusa*), more lightly armed and generally bare-foot, whose role in wartime was, strictly speaking, more that of assistants and servants to the samurai than of regular fighters. From the end of the fourteenth century, many foot-soldiers, called *ashigaru* (fleet of foot), enlisted by unimportant war-leaders, made their appearance; these soldiers fought more for the sake of loot than for the glory of their leader.

Not only professional or part-time warriors engaged in warfare, but also a whole host of humble folk, inexperienced in the profession of arms, who attended on the armies, undertaking maintenance and supply jobs. These *chûgen* or *komono* (people of small account) or again *arashiko*, who had a hard life, were generally more farmers than soldiers.[6] Finally came the *fudai*, warriors attached as more or less hereditary vassals to a great family of the *bushi* caste to whom they were in a way higher-class servants.[7] Among all the warriors, the *ashigaru* formed the lowest class, somewhat despised by the others. But with the advent and development of fire-arms in Japan, these infantrymen proved to be increasingly necessary and eventually became indispensable. The majority of these foot-soldiers were warriors or farmers whom the hazards of war, alliances and politics (especially during the *Sengoku* period or the civil wars of the fifteenth century) had deprived of their means of livelihood. Their numbers often included bandits and *hinin* who in this way had managed to escape from their wretched way of life. These mercenaries, who hired their services to whom they pleased, had in fact been in existence for a long time, but they were not actually used systematically and in great number until nearly the end of the Muromachi epoch, completely changing the character of campaigns which, from cavalry skirmishes between ordinary lords or samurai, turned into pitched battles. And it was the son of a poverty-striken *ashigaru* who, known by the name of Hideyoshi, became dictator and ruler of the entire country.

Warriors, samurai and others, from the eastern provinces were, as a rule, rather illiterate. The majority were, in fact, completely ignorant. Very few of them were able to read and understand the Sino-Japanese characters. During the campaign conducted by Go-Daigo's faithful followers against the Samurai of the Kamakura bakufu, the warriors of the watch found a message written in verse on a piece of cherry bark and intended for the captive emperor. When they saw this poem, they did not know what it meant: 'What is it?' they asked.[8] Nevertheless, there were, of course, a few well-read men amongst them. The Ashikaga shôgun knew how to surround themselves with learned men and aesthetes, and themselves became learned, and great admirers of Chinese culture. In fact, no one knows just what the degree of learning was among ordinary warriors. Although they were styled illiterates in the chronicles of the period, it is nevertheless likely that a good number of them, perhaps even among the humblest, could read and write their own tongue with the help of the *kana* syllabary, which was taught by the monks throughout the country.

Most of the warriors made up their faces and perfumed themselves before going into battle, as indeed they did in peace time. We have seen that at the beginning of the Kamakura period, the Taira warriors, having adopted the customs of Kyôto, blackened their teeth, contrary to the Genji fighting-men. The custom soon spread among all warriors and was kept up for quite a long time.[9] It was not abolished by imperial decree until 1870.

THE SHÔGUN AND HIS VASSALS

The shôgun, being the emperor's official deputy (a deputy often more powerful than his majesty), treated his warriors more like subjects than vassals, and demanded an unswerving loyalty from them.[10] At first, there was no code governing the relationship between lord and vassal but the principle of dependence was deep-rooted in these rough warriors who, in as much as they had freely chosen their master, expected everything from him – lands, glory, justice and recompense.

The Kamakura bakufu demanded from military officials and provincial vassals, a written oath (*kishômon*) which was sealed by affixing a finger-print made with blood from the finger (*keppan*) and before a divinity, usually Hachiman, the kami of warfare and the tutelary god of the Minamoto family. The vassal owed numerous services to his overlord. In the first place, of course, he owed him loyalty; then guard-duty at Kamakura or at the shôgun's residence, at Kyûshû on the coastal defences (until the beginning of the fourteenth century), at the tax-barriers or on the frontiers of provinces, or again in Kyôto, either at the emperor's palace, or at the Rokuhara, the residence of the Kamakura shôgun's deputy in the capital. Furthermore, it was compulsory for senior vassals (*gokenin*) to have a dwelling-place near to the bakufu, first in Kamakura then later in Kyôto, where they had to leave their families as hostages when they returned to their fiefs. The vassal had, in addition, to answer for the loyalty as well as the good behaviour of his relatives. Depending upon his income, he was in duty bound to contribute towards the expenses incurred by the bakufu and, on a mere command, to report at the place appointed by his lord with his men equipped for battle. A written receipt acknowledged the total strength of his fighting force.

At the beginning of the Kamakura era, there was no fixed number of men required from each vassal. Later, in particular in the sixteenth century, the *daimyô*, for every *chô* of land they owned, were compelled to supply the army with at least one fighting man and his servant and food supplies for thirty days. But this crushing requisition was an exceptional one, Hideyoshi at that time needing

9 *Nanban Byōbu*—Portuguese fathers visiting a port in Kyūshū (southern Japan). Screen painting by an unknown Japanese painter, sixteenth century

many men for his planned invasion of Korea. For his part, the lord (*shôgun, gokenin*) owed his vassals help and protection and they expected him to reward them for their feats of arms. In the course of battle, he might make a gift of a horse, a sword or a banner to those he wished to honour. The *Gikeiki* tells us that when Tadanobu was ready to sacrifice his life to save his lord Yoshitsune's, the latter made him a present of a valuable sword:

' "A tired man is handicapped by a long sword. Fight to the end with this . . . " He handed him a weapon ornamented with gold, two and a half feet long, with a narrow groove running the whole length of the finely forged blade.

' "It is short but the blade is of the best. I have treasured it almost as much as my own life." '11

The overlord also granted his vassals a charter (*jô*) which confirmed them in their rights over the lands they had been given, so that there might not be any claim whatsoever on the part of the previous owner or lord. On the other hand, the shôgun could revoke his gifts whenever he thought fit, and there was no appeal against his decisions.12

After the downfall of the Kamakura bakufu and the wars which followed the coming of the Ashikaga, the strictness of this system was modified. In point of fact, after 1336, the only leader acknowledged by the warriors was no longer the shôgun nor the emperor but the war-lord who had managed to set himself up as ruler in his province. At this time, it was not unusual for warriors to shift their allegiance, attracted by the hope of a greater reward, or sometimes simply for sentimental or family reasons. The war leaders or *daimyô*, who were legally 'mandated' by the emperor, by a prince of the imperial family (in the emperor's name) or by the shôgun, witnessed an immediate increase in the number of their vassals, so great was the respect still paid to the principle of legality. This resulted in considerable rivalry between the war lords who, in order to try to win a legal 'mandate', determined to prove their might by overthrowing their rivals. For ultimately only the daimyô who was the strongest was 'mandated' by the emperor.

THE WARRIOR CODE

Despite the crumbling of the feudal system resulting from this constant rivalry the warriors, samurai and others, retained strong feelings of loyalty and fidelity towards their leaders, and respect for customs and laws. As M. Joüon des Longrais so rightly states, the samurai believed above everything else that their first duty was 'a military duty. The warrior must do his duty as a warrior for the honour of his family and of his class, so as not to be despised by them. . . . The *bushi's* contempt of death is closely bound up with his conception of the future. All the same, he is not enamoured of death. His life of self-sacrifice in the execution of his duty as a warrior is without any doubt for the *bushi*[13] the highest ideal of "nobility".' This contempt of death, this absolute devotion of the warrior to duty, this regard for the plighted word were on a par with the filial piety extolled by Confucian philosophy. And the contemporary 'gestes' constantly alluded to the paragons of virtue of ancient China or to the doughty deeds, which had become almost legendary, of the epic struggle engaged in by the Heike and Genji clans. Since the warriors believed in *karma*, the retribution in a future life for deeds performed in this, they did not shrink from death in order to accompany their lord or their father into the Beyond: 'Nevertheless, said one of them, I am sure that he (my father) will lose his way on the road which leads from death to reincarnation, and that is why I have come here alone in order to die like him, to fulfil my filial duty even after death. . . .'[14]

To prevent this young warrior from sacrificing himself uselessly, a monk had previously admonished him in these terms:

'What is your purpose? Your father would undoubtedly have taken you with him (into battle to die with him) if he had left before the others just to win glory. His intention was to offer his life to the monk of Sagami (the Kamakura regent) in such a way that his reward might bring some little prosperity to his descendants. If you are in such reckless haste to seek death at the hands of the enemy, who is there to succeed you? Who will reap the reward? It is said that descendants show their filial piety to their ancestors by prospering mightily. It is natural for you to wish to die with him, for there is grief in your heart at present, but stop and consider, I beg of you!' [15]

These fine sentiments so highly praised, professed by so many samurai and by ordinary *bushi* as well as by the women of their household, were not however universal, and history records a good number of examples of cowardliness, treachery, perfidy and useless cruelty. The ideal warrior has never existed, even in Japan, except in novels, neither has the ideal samurai pictured in contemporary epics, nor the Yoshitsune of the ballads sung by the *biwa* players for the edification of their listeners. Harsh men, inured to suffering, resigned to the blows of fortune, the samurai of the Middle Ages were none the less men with all the human frailties that this condition implies. These men were deeply religious. There were many who placed pious images beneath their armour before going into battle. The most hardened samurai, after a grim battle which had won them material benefits for their descendants, took the tonsure, adopted a religious name and retired to a monastery, to pray there for the souls of those they had slain. And such a warrior who had all his life devoted himself to some cult peculiar to the kami saw nothing at all heretical, in those days of religious syncretism, in becoming a Buddhist monk.

The most important vassals, the wealthy samurai and the shôgun were liberal in their financial support of monasteries and shrines; they had chapels built to the memory of the gallant warriors who had fallen in their service and who had virtually become kami in their turn. If the conduct of these warriors was not inspired by religious fervour (contrary to our European knights in the Middle Ages) nor excused by it, it was religion that enabled them to mitigate the effects of their failure to live up to their precepts, and to seek shelter from the troubles of this world. In certain more exceptional cases, it enabled warriors to escape capture and death, a monk being considered to some extent a sacred person. The whole life of the samurai, like that of the simplest of the *bushi*, was based on the deep feeling, essentially Buddhist, of the impermanence of all things: 'The colours of the flowers bear witness to this truth that all that blooms must fade . . .'[16] But these melancholy sentiments of resignation in no way prevented the men, when they had the opportunity, from enjoying life, from feasting and celebrating in the euphoria engendered by their success in battle with its gains and rewards.

In this sense, the samurai of medieval Japan were very like our knights of old. If the epic tales sometimes reveal what seems to be savage cruelty, cruelty which was dictated to them more by what they believed to be their duty as a warrior than by their nature, they also describe them in moments when, freed from their social responsibility, they are filled with tenderness, even towards their enemies. For the spirit, the *raison d'être* of the samurai of the Middle Ages, is the sense of duty which can still be seen in the Japan of the twentieth century.

THE SETTING OF THE WARRIOR'S LIFE

During the Kamakura period, the strict customs and the adoption of Buddhist philosophy by the samurai class were even reflected in their dwelling places: the place they lived in had to be a combination of fortress and monastery. When the power of the shôgun and their vassals increased, the lords of Kyôto, poorer now, tried to work out for their use a compromise between the severe style of the warriors' houses (*bukezukuri*) and the old style still favoured by the nobles (*shindenzukuri*). But this hybrid style had only a limited success. From about the year 1400 and under the influence of Zen monks, it was replaced by a more elegant style, simpler although spacious, called *shoinzukuri*, a style which drew its inspiration from both the severe style of the *bushi* houses and that of the *shinden*, and which was soon adopted by wealthy samurai and *daimyô*.

The samurai were compelled to live in dwellings that were easy to defend, with well guarded approaches. The residence had, therefore, to be of modest size and to possess, as well as the dwelling house proper, at least one stable for the horses (*umaya*) and a few outbuildings to lodge vassals and ordinary warriors. The wealthiest samurai also had to provide for open spaces which would allow their warriors to practise archery, horsemanship and the handling of weapons. Some residences belonging to clan leaders or great families, modelled on the *shinden* style, enclosed within their walls reception or state rooms, courtyards and gardens, and also quarters for lodging guests, should the occasion arise. Other residences took on the appearance of fortified palaces, surrounded by fences (*hataito*) or proper walls made of lath and clay (*tsuiji*). Buildings set aside for foot-soldiers were called *toozamurai*. Sometimes there was a small Buddhist chapel inside the enclosure (*jibutsudô*). The guard-houses were generally placed near gates above which rose either defence towers (*yagura*) or watch-towers.

But the warriors and ordinary samurai did not boast such elaborate residences, which only the most well-to-do could afford to build. These samurai and *bushi* lived in the mansion of a great

eader or high-ranking samurai, or had a house of their own on
ands belonging to them. In this case, they were often farmers
ji-samurai) as well. To facilitate its defence, their house was then
urrounded by wooden fences covered with a protective layer of
oam (to help guard against danger from incendiary arrows) and
ometimes by trenches or ditches filled with water, or by areas
strewn with obstacles.[17] The way into these enclosures was by a
simple gate surmounted by a yagura or turret with a balcony,
also of wood, and intended to house the archers. The main house
differed little from those of the rich farmers, except in size and by
the fact that it was surrounded by a roofed veranda; sometimes also
by the presence of wooden flooring, although many samurai had
rooms with mud floors only. The master's house was roofed with
thatch, the outbuildings with planks. In wartime, the roofs were
covered witha a layer of mud which protected them from incendiary
arrows. Stones, sometimes with a rope tied around them to fix
them to the roofing, made sure that the whole structure was secure.[18]
Lower-ranking *bushi* were lodged inside the enclosure walls in *sajiki*,
types of cabin-shelters of limited size, with walls of rush or woven
bamboo or, in summer, merely made of folding screens. These
huts were divided into rooms by curtains; cooking was done outside or under open sheds put up for this purpose. In this way the
bushi were always ready to answer a summons from their lord.
There were always warriors on duty at the gates, responsible for
checking the comings-and-goings. In wartime, kinds of watch-
towers were erected inside the enclosure, so that the cluster of
houses in the neighbouring village could be kept under observation
and notice given of the enemy's approach.

Until the building of castles began, fortresses were in no way
permanent dwelling-places. In times of public disorder, they were
set up in places likely to provide the armies in the field with a base
of operations or of resistance. Very often, the buildings of a temple,
fortified by barriers, felled trees or other improvised methods of
defence, were enough to constitute a fortress: 'when they had left
the river Ishi behind them, they caught sight of the fort. It had
certainly been built in extreme haste! The moat was strictly speaking not a real moat, and there was only a simple wooden wall overlaid with mud. Furthermore, this stronghold was scarcely more
than a hundred or two hundred metres in circumference, with only
twenty or thirty hastily erected towers (!) inside it. . . .'[19] These

forts were often erected on mountain tops, in places that were difficult of access: in this case they no longer served as a base for operations but for entrenchment. The wooden walls that had been put up on the crag were made fast by ropes to heavy stones which, by their weight, held them firm. The value of these fortresses depended primarily upon the possibilities of provisioning with water and victuals:

' "It will be impossible to demolish this fort easily by force alone. It will likewise be a long time before its reserves are likely to run out; Kusunoki is sure to have built up a plentiful stock of food, for during these last years he has held the provinces of Izumi and Kawachi in the palm of his hand. But there does not appear to be any place there from which water can be obtained for the fort, for on three sides there are deep gorges and on the fourth, flat ground. And the mountains are a long way off. Nevertheless, they are using water to put out the fires started by our arrows. They have obviously managed to bring the water from one of the rivers of the southern hills by means of underground pipes, for they have water in abundance, although it is a long time since rain fell. . . . My lord, would it not be as well to gather some workmen together and get them to dig up the ground at the foot of the hill?"

' When the workmen had dug straight down through the hillside in the direction leading to the fort, they did in fact discover a trench six metres beneath the surface, with walls reinforced by stones and a roof made of cyprus planks, which conducted the water from a place more than a thousand metres away. And the attackers dammed up the water. . . .'[20]

In the open country or on the seashore, fortresses were mainly defended by very wide moats fed by the waters of a near-by river. They could shelter not only villages, but also a large number of soldiers. Many of them were originally castles or towns like Ôsaka or Edo (the modern Tôkyô), whose citadel was erected on the site of a small entrenched fort built in 1457 by Ôta Dôkan, a samurai in the service of the Uesugi family. But in the sixteenth century, after the introduction of fire-arms, the temporary fortresses erected in wartime no longer seemed adequate; the *daimyô* and the war leaders felt the need, in order to have better control over their provinces, to own operational bases placed in strategic positions (mountains or cross-roads on main highways) able to withstand musket balls and projectiles from small cannon, and yet spacious and comfortable enough to serve at the same time as permanent residences. One of the first castles to be built, perhaps under European influences in 1576, was that of Azuchi, erected on the shores of lake Biwa by Oda Nobunaga. Other small castles, somewhat older, did not allow of a keep (*tenshu*) raised above the rest of the building. Azuchi's keep comprised many floors, the rooms of which had been decorated by the best artists of the time. A great number of captains and *Daimyô* imitated Oda Nobunaga and had keeps, fortified in the same way, built in the provinces.

These castles underwent little change until the nineteenth century. The base was sharply inclined, constructed by a skilful stacking of huge stones and surmounted by a high timber structure with thick walls of mud and plaster. The keeps had several floors, offset one on another, each with its own roof. The only way of getting into the castle was by crossing movable bridges easily drawn up in case of danger, and by passing through a series of gateways arranged in zigzag fashion. Fortified castles at the beginning of this period were built on easily defensible heights. At that time they were known as *yamajiro*. Later, they were more likely to be set up in open country, where a better watch could be kept on the main highways, which was also of importance for trade in peace time. These fortresses were called *hirajô*. As in Europe during the Middle Ages, these castles were big enough to hold and shelter a very large number of people. It often happened that castle and village became merged, the one containing the other.

However, between the temporary entrenchments of the thirteenth and fourteenth centuries and the great castles of Nobunaga and Hideyoshi, fortresses well-defended by moats had been built, like the one the Jôdo-Shinshû sect (Ikkô) of the Hongan-ji of Ôsaka had put up in 1477 at Yamashina. This stronghold 'took in a fortified area of 33,000 m², including three walled enclosures with moats. In 1496 the same sect had a fortified monastery built at Ishiyama which served as a refuge against the Hosokawa. Attacked later by Nobunaga in 1572, fifty-one small forts were erected around the main castle.'[21] Meanwhile 'a sudden development and a transformation from top to bottom . . . came about during the fifty years when fortune favoured first Nobunaga, then Hideyoshi.'[22]

'The celebrated castle of the Hôjô at Odawara was colossal. It comprised an inner enclosure of 430 metres, a second of 870 metres and a third one 70 metres outside this. Finally an exterior rampart incorporated a part of the town. The whole had a circumference of ten kilometres. It was flanked by twenty towers. A shopping street had been laid out inside the ramparts and merchants had been compelled to build up enough reserves of rice to feed refugees and soldiers for a whole year. Sixty-six forts and fortesses surrounded the main castle.'[23]

Japanese castle enclosures were seldom regular in shape; they generally followed the contours of the piece of land on which the castle was built. However, fortresses of the *Hirajô* type tended to be more or less rectangular. Ornamentation was mostly exterior: roofs with glazed tiles, decorated with *shibi* or 'sea monsters', curved entrance gables, hipped roofs with gently tapering lines. But if the keep was, at least in the beginning, severe looking and designed for wartime needs (except perhaps in certain very large castles), the buildings seen in later enclosures were more attractive in style. The *ni-no-maru* was generally reserved for the residences of the lord of the district and his court: the buildings in the *Shoin* style were sometimes richly decorated. The castle which Hideyoshi had built for him at Osaka was magnificent beyond imagining and contemporary descriptions speak of gilded pillars and ceilings, nail heads and locks of solid gold, and a table service made entirely of precious metal. There was a succession of gardens and temples inside these enclosures, as can still be seen today in the *ni-no-maru* of the Nijô castle in Kyôto. Nearly all the castles built in that epoch have now disappeared, either burned down when the *daimyô* were warring among themselves, or destroyed by order of the shôgun, or else victims of the disastrous bombings of the Second World War. Those we can still admire today are only reconstructions.

In wartime, the camps where samurai and various armies assembled were very hastily set up. In order to split up the groups belonging to different lords or provinces, simple bands of cloth called *jinmaku* were stretched between posts, marking out the space in squares. Holes were cut at regular intervals in the cloth to enable the men to see what was going on on the other side. These bands of cloth were sometimes decorated with *mon* or samurai 'emblems', so that the place where they were stationed could be easily picked

ut. These 'roofless tents' were grouped according to district or
army.[24] They were only used in wartime, especially in time of siege.
t may well be imagined that discipline in these camps had been quite
trict at the beginning of the Kamakura era, but the *Taiheiki*
nforms us that it was an entirely different matter in 1333, when the
pirit which had actuated the troops of the Hôjô regents had to a
great extent disappeared.

'Then the great war-lords had prostitutes brought in from Eguchi
and Kanzaki to the encampment to entertain the soldiers in
various ways for they were weary of guarding the fortress without fighting. It happened that two great captains, the lay-monk of
Tôtômi and his nephew Hyôgo-no-Suke, of the Nagoya family,
had their camps near the point of attack. One day, in the course
of a game of *Sugoroku* (a kind of backgammon), they cut each other
down with their swords in front of some members of their suite
(for they had probably quarrelled about a throw of the dice).
And, following their example, their warriors in their turn began
to slaughter each other so indiscriminately that in no time the
ground was strewn with two hundred dead.'[25]

The strength of the army was certainly not founded on discipline
at this time, when every man was out to win glory and rewards for
himself or his descendants, without bothering himself too much
about any ideal. Furthermore, the samurai made no attempt to
find out whether the cause their leaders were upholding was good or
bad.

EQUIPMENT

The Japanese warrior's equipment, like that of our steel-clad knights
of medieval Europe, although it might be suitable if need be for
single combat, was utterly unfitted to combined troop movements
or to rapid changes of station of a single troop. That is why, from
the time the armies were equipped with arquebuses, foot-soldiers or
ashigaru assumed a much greater importance in hand-to-hand fighting than the heavily clad samurai on their prancing steeds. In peace-
time, the samurai was only distinguishable from civilians of equal
rank by the wearing of a *samurai-eboshi* or head-dress of black stiffened cloth triangular in shape, worn on the top of the head and
secured by ribbons fastened under the chin. In normal times,

7　A warrior, at the end of the twelfth century　*Drawing by Kikuchi Yôsai (1788–1878)*

high-ranking Samurai were dressed like members of the nobility o
the imperial court, in a *kariginu* or hunting-cloak.

　In wartime, they wore armour made of lacquered steel plate
jointed and overlapping each other, and tied together with coloured
cords. Ordinary samurai wore the *hitatare*, a kind of long coat
under their armour, or else the *suikan* of the lower classes, slipped or
over it. They only donned this armour if it was necessary however
for it was heavy. In normal times, it remained locked away in a

chest. The upper samurai's war-dress was composed of a leather or lacquered steel breastplate made up of several sections protecting chest, back and sides, and fastened down the back by cords, and of matching, jointed sections forming a kind of square-shaped shirt. Their arms were encased in long gauntlets made of fabric covered with lacquered steel plates joined together by steel links or by cords. Square jointed plates protected their shoulders. Their legs were fitted with stiff 'greaves' of a sort, sometimes extending right above the knee, secured to the calf and heel by cords. The samurai wore bearkin shoes with studded soles and sometimes short boots of leather or lacquered wood. On their head was a steel helmet with a vizor, decorated with 'wings' at the sides (to deflect sword-thrusts) and fitted with a semicircular neck-shield made of three or five jointed metal plates. This helmet, often lavishly decorated, was embellished in front with chiselled metal horns and sometimes crested with a bronze effigy of an animal or a dragon. The equipment was completed by a quiver of arrows, a large bow, a dagger stuck into the belt and one or two swords (*tachi* and *katana*) with moderately long, forged steel blades. A short curved sword and various small accessories which the fighting man in the field might need (a change of bow-strings, a pouch) were also fastened to the belt.

The ordinary *bushi* who went on foot were much more lightly clad. Their armour was not as stiff nor were their helmets as magnificently decorated. They wore short breeches and padded leggings of strong hempen cloth, with a triangular leather section protecting the upper part of the foot. They generally went barefoot or wearing ordinary half-sandals made of straw (*ashinaka*). Their weapons usually consisted of a large halberd with a long, curved blade (*naginata*) and a sword. But some might also be armed with a bow and arrows.

The samurai always carried on them, either rolled up or folded, a doe or deer-skin which they used for sitting on, for marking their place during archery practices and, if one day they were to be executed, as a death-seat.

As for the *ashigaru*, they were generally armed some way or other, sometimes with spoils picked up on the battle-field, and later on with arquebuses. In short, their equipment was a rather strange medley:

'They were clad in mail with metal thigh and knee protections. Dragon-crested helmets were set on their heads, swords one-and-a-half metres long hung at their belts, and they had no difficulty in handling steel, octagonal shaped clubs more than two metres long, one part of which, sixty centimetres long, was rounded to provide a better grip.'[26]

The most famous and wealthiest war leaders had armour and weapons exceedingly rich in ornamentation:

'He carried a gold-hilted sword in a gilded scabbard fastened to a belt of silver chain made by the Imperial Bureau of Supplies, and protected by a tiger-skin cover. . . . At his back he carried a quiver of thirty-six arrows decorated with swan feathers, the bamboo shafts lightly lacquered between the nodes. His bow was rushbound at intervals throughout its length, with a silver hook fixed above the leather hand-grip to prevent the arrow from slipping.'[27]

The warriors never carried a shield, but the foot-soldiers made use of them in the field, especially for the defence of houses and fortresses. These shields were large, extremely heavy rectangles of wood (*tate*), sometimes decorated in a summary fashion and which the soldiers placed on the ground in front of them to protect themselves from enemy arrows. They moved them every time they advanced and set them on the ground where they were held upright by means of movable props.[28] Occasionally it was a servant who handled the *tate* to protect his master while the latter fitted an arrow to his bow-string.[29] These *tate* were sometimes covered with straw or hides.

There were several kinds of arrows, with either ordinary or forked heads, and sometimes with whistles fitted at the ends (*kabura-ya*). They were kept in an open quiver or in a lacquered wicker tube of water-willow or bamboo which protected them from the rain. A samurai's equipment had to include a banner, and a fan with a golden sun on a crimson ground painted on one side of it. War leaders waved it to signal to their troops.

Fire-arms, introduced in 1543 by some Portuguese passengers from a Chinese junk that had gone aground on the Isle of Tanegashima, to the south of Kyûshu, filled those who saw them for the first time with amazement, but it was not long before they were copied and used. This is how Nampo Bunshi records, in the *Teppô-ki*, the Japanese reaction to their first contact with these new weapons:

'There were two chiefs among the merchants, one called Mura-shukusha, and the other Kirishitamôta (Christian Mota?). In their hands they carried an object two or three feet long, straight on the outside with an inside tube, and made with some kind of heavy material, The inner tube ran the whole length of it, but was closed at one end. On one side there was a hole which was the opening for firing. I have never seen anything remotely like it in shape. To use it, fill it with powder and little balls of lead, fix a small white target on to a butt, stand firm and closing one eye, apply the fire to the hole. Then the bullet hits the target right in the middle. The explosion is like lightning and the report like thunder. The onlookers have to stop their ears. . . . Tokitaka was so interested in this weapon that he asked several smiths to inspect and study it for some months to enable them to make some. Outwardly the result of their experiments looked like the foreign weapon, but the smiths did not know how to seal the inner tube. Foreign merchants came again the following year to the Bay of Kumano, one of our islands. Fortunately, one of them was a smith whom Tokitaka regarded as a messenger from the gods. He ordered the commanding-officer, Kimbei Kiyosada, to learn from this smith how to seal the end of the gun. He learnt that there was a spring in the gun and this discovery led to the production of several dozen fire-arms (teppô) in little more than a year. Then all his vassals from far and near trained with the new weapons and soon, out of every hundred shots they fired, many of them could hit the target as many times. Later on, a man called Tachibana-ya Matasaburô, a merchant who stayed in our island for a year or two, learnt the art of making fire-arms. He became skilful at it and, on his return home, everyone called him, not by his real name, but Teppômata. Soon the provinces of the inner circuit mastered this art, and very quickly . . . the western and the eastern provinces learnt it too.'[30]

The horses the Samurai used generally came from the Kantô plains or the Tôhoku mountains where they were bred. Their owners were extremely proud of them and looked after them lovingly. They decked them with saddles of great value and with saddle-cloths trimmed with long tassels and silken fringes: 'The tail and mane of his light bay were very thick and strong, and on its back he had placed a saddle completely overlaid with lacquer powdered with gold-dust (*maki-e*) and newly-dyed tassels with great pompons hung down to the ground.'[31] The Samurai gave their horses pleasing names. If, during the Kamakura period, the combatants spared the samurai's mounts, during the second part of this medieval era, the *ashigaru* did not scruple to unseat the horsemen by plunging the long blades of their *naginata* into the horses' bellies or by slashing at their legs. When they were not making war, the samurai kept in training either by deer or boar-hunting (Yoritomo had been proud of the fact that his son, during a beat on the slopes of Mount Fuji had, unaided, despatched a deer with his arrows), or in proper training camps or during festivals. As the *Azuma Kagami* (1180–1266) records concerning Yoritomo, lords required their warriors to be 'proficient in the three virtues', meaning: to be of good family, to be a good bowman and a good horseman, and finally, to be of modest bearing. The 'Chronicle of Nitta Yoshisada' or *Yoshisada-ki* (1301-38) defines the difference that existed between nobles and samurai in this way:

'From days of old until the present time, military virtue and that of the artist's brush have been regarded as the two virtues comparable to Heaven and Earth. If a man lacks one of them, he cannot administer state affairs. Consequently, noblemen take up the study of literature as a matter of course and are trained in such arts as the composition of poetry and music. But for statesmen, the practice of arms is of supreme importance. They consist of archery, horsemanship and strategy.'

In the same way, among the twenty-one precepts of the Hôjô Sôun family (1432–1519), is this item: 'Cultural interests and the military arts, archery and horsemanship must be studied constantly. It is an ancient custom to study on the one hand literature and on the other the military arts. They must be studied at the same time.'[32]

Archery exercises mainly consisted in hitting three targets when shooting on foot (one large target, *omato*, a deer-target, *kusajishi*, and a large round target (*marumono*); and three targets when shooting on horseback: three targets placed in the path of a galloping horse (*yabusame*), shooting at hats placed at different distances (*kasagake*) and shooting at hounds (*inuoimono*). The archers practised at a distance of about fifty metres and the large fixed target (*marumono*) had a diameter of one-and-a-half metres. When they shot at dogs (with arrows with rounded heads so as not to wound them), thirty-six archers would split up into three groups which had to hit fifty dogs each in an area bounded by a barrier of bamboo enclosing a space of about a hundred and twenty metres in diameter.

They also trained daily in the use of sword and halberd as well as in wrestling (*sumô*). In peacetime the warriors devoted themselves to fowling (*oitorigari*) or to big-game hunting (*makigari*). And in wartime it was not unusual to see young boys (the legal coming of age was fixed at fifteen in Kamakura) accompanying their fathers on the battlefield to improve their knowledge of the military arts.

Many warriors also studied Zen philosophy which taught them the art of concentration, and not to fear death. Numerous contests, generally organized on the occasion of religious festivities (*matsuri*), gave them the chance to show their talents and skill and maintained a necessary spirit of rivalry among them.

WAR

War, which often brings to power military men anxious to preserve the prestige of their caste, generally begets a dictatorial government disinclined to consider the opinions of civilians. Nevertheless, in 1185 after Yoritomo had overthrown the might of the Taira clan – whose rise to power had seen the end of three centuries of political and peaceful domination by the Fujiwara aristocrats – he did his best to change from a man of war into an administrator. So it was with Ashikaga Takauji in 1334, Oda Nobunaga and Hideyoshi at the end of the sixteenth century and, from 1603 on, Tokugawa Ieyasu. The Japanese, a fearless and courageous fighter, despising death, was for all that not really a man of war. He was first of all a peasant in the noblest sense of the word, a 'countryman' who loved his small plot of native land, his province, and who rejoiced to see order and peace prevailing there. He was deeply distressed by a state of war, even shocked by its unseemliness and, although he did his duty in complete self-forgetfulness, he did not like fighting just for fighting's sake: he fought from a sense of duty – first towards his overlord, then towards his dependents. We have seen that he was anxious to reflect honour on his family by performing, at the risk of his life, heroic feats of arms, that he also looked for reward, but primarily with the object of making provision for his family and dependents. In adversity, he was philosophically resigned to suffer the lot of the vanquished or, sickened with fighting, he left this vale of tears to don the monk's habit and to pray, not for himself, but for the souls of those he had killed in battle. He fought to prove his gratitude to the one who ensured his livelihood, both his and his family's, and to whom he had sworn loyalty; and his heart was set on keeping faith: 'Now I give up my life for the safety of my lord. My life is as light as a crane's aigrette. I would rather die facing my enemy than live and turn my back on him,' says the *Mutsuwa-ki*,[33] a history of the first Nine Years' War (1051–62).

This pride and this sense of the honour, of the dignity of man, was nevertheless not put into practice for the benefit of the country, of a fatherland, for at this time, the idea of Japan as a nation had not yet gained ground in men's minds, and the concept of a fatherland hardly went beyond that of provinces belonging to the clan. But an event of cardinal importance was to weld together the warriors of the various clans and to mobilize, for a certain period of time, the moral and material forces of the entire country, with perhaps the exception of a few distant and unimportant provinces: the threat of the Mongol invasion. Although Samurai and *bushi* had answered the Regent's call as one man, in the hope of winning some reward or benefit in battle, the feeling of protecting more than their own immediate interests was developing without their being as yet fully aware of it: foreigners were attempting to invade their islands and this seemed unthinkable to them. The country, bled white by a watchful vigilance of more than twenty years, was ultimately to pay very dear for this mobilization of its kinetic energies, held in leash by the fear of invasion. From that moment only, the Japanese people realized that there were foreigners who might have warlike designs on them, and that it was advisable to make a clear distinction between the inhabitants of the Japanese islands and 'the others'.

But fortunately for Japan, it was not only Mongol troops which, not once but twice, in 1274 and 1281, attacked the islands, but more particularly Koreans and Chinese, at bottom not very anxious to fight for someone who meant nothing to them, in this instance the Mongol overlord of Pekin. Because the excellent boats of southern Chinese type required too much time to lay on the stocks, the Yüan dynasty had, as far back as January 1274, ordered Korea to build a fleet. Thirty-five thousand carpenters were set to work and constructed in all haste (and it must be admitted, taking no care over the work) 300 large junks, 300 fast ships, and 300 small craft.

Fifteen thousand Mongol and Chinese soldiers and almost as many Koreans were to embark in July of the same year, but the king of Korea died and sailing was postponed until October 3rd. Some Koreans forewarned the Japanese of the imminence of the attack, so the samurai resolutely awaited the invaders who, after laying waste the islands of Tsushima and Iki, disembarked as foreseen on the shores of Kakata Bay, on the north coast of Kyûshû.

However, the Japanese were utterly astonished to find that the Mongols did not fight in accordance with the laws of chivalry practiced by the samurai: the first horseman who advanced towards the disembarked Mongol troops, loudly shouting their names and challenging their adversaries to come and pit their strength honourably against them in single combat, were met by showers of arrows and promptly surrounded by a multitude of soldiers who massacred them. Moreover, the Mongol troops, as was their custom, had brought with them great drums whose deafening roll terrified the Japanese horses which were not used to this din. Finally, and although the Mongols, with the exception of their leaders, were not mounted and were lightly clad, they were better armed than the Japanese. This greatly astonished the samurai who had been used to single combat until then: the Mongol bows, small, powerful and easily handled, could shoot their short poison-tipped arrows up to a distance of 220 metres, while the best Japanese bows, very large and dissymmetrically curved, could hardly shoot their long and heavy arrows more than 100 metres.[34] But shortly after they had landed, the sea, becoming rough, drove the Korean boats on to the rocks around the coast, and being badly constructed, they broke up. This was disastrous for the Mongols who re-embarked with all possible speed in the remaining boats and returned to Korea, having lost, if the Korean chronicles are to be believed, about 13,500 men.

Rendered prudent and foreseeing by this adventure, certain that the Mongols would not be satisfied with this one attempt, the bakufu gave orders for Hakata Bay to be fortified by erecting all along the coast a stone rampart 2·10 metres high and 2·80 metres wide, buttressed on the inside by a mud embankment. The lords of Kyûshû had to play their part in the building of this line of fortification at the rate of thirty centimetres of wall for every *chô* of land they owned. Stakes were set in the beds at the mouths of rivers; attacking boats were built and reserves of arms, especially arrows and shields,

8   A samurai surveying the Mongol troops sitting on the stone rampart surrounding Hakata bay (Kyûshû)   *Drawing by Kikuchi Yôsai (1788–1878)*

were built up. The building of the wall took a great deal of time and, in actual fact, continued until 1332.[35]

The second Mongol attack, in 1281, was more serious, and this time Japan was in grave peril. But the irresolution and unwillingness of the Korean troops, the fact that the Chinese and Mongols had little experience of the sea, the carelessness with which, once again, the ships had been built, and above all a typhoon which demolished their fleet saved the Japanese who, despite all their courage, would have found it very difficult to withstand the overwhelming Mongol attacks, to say nothing of their balistas, their machines for hurling stone cannon balls and their gunpowder bombs. The explosion of these bombs terrorized the Japanese for this was their first contact with the effects of gunpowder. The 900 vessels and 40,000 soldiers that had sailed from Korea had joined forces at

Hirado and in Hakata Bay with a fleet of 3,500 ships from China carrying 100,000 Chinese and Mongol soldiers. A considerable number of them had disembarked. Desperate struggles took place at many points on the coast. The Japanese showed incredible daring and pugnacity, and succeeded in stemming the tide of invaders for almost seven weeks. Then came a typhoon which the Japanese called *kamikaze* 'divine wind'; it was of such force that it put the Mongols to flight and annihilated their fleet after causing the loss of a considerable number of men. All who were not able to re-embark were taken prisoner and a goodly number of them beheaded.

Hearing that Kubla Khan had still not abandoned his projects, the bakufu deemed it wise to maintain its troops on a war footing. All the same, one fact is a continual source of wonder: the Japanese, equipped with sadly inadequate weapons (except in single combat when their swords performed wonders), after their experience of the new weapons used by the Mongols – powerful bows, cross-bows, swivel-guns, bombs – did not think of equipping themselves with better arms! Which makes it abundantly clear that if the Japanese could individually give evidence of a courage second to none, they still did not think of war as other than an opportunity for winning personal glory. Poetic knights despising death, they were not really warriors at heart.

This victory, with no territorial conquests, was to prove disappointing for the samurai and the *bushi* whom the bakufu were in no position to reward. Many lords returned home ruined. From that time they began to lose confidence in the bakufu. Within fifty years conditions deteriorated to such a degree that the Emperor Go-Daigo, having an exalted idea of his 'divine mission', believed himself justified in raising a force of warriors against the Kantô. This was followed by a period of political unrest which did not end until the beginning of the seventeenth century and which resulted in military dictatorships of which the common people were the first victims. The egalitarian and altruistic spirit of the Kamakura bakufu had finally been sucked into the whirlpool of the family and clan rivalries which had followed its downfall. Later on, when Hideyoshi attempted to found his Far-Eastern Empire, invaded Korea and made preparations to bring China into subjection, he had no idea of the extent or the strength of this country, the disdainful Chinese having engaged only a very few men in the battle of Korea. So, in his ignorance, he counted his chickens before they were hatched and set about organizing the country before he had conquered it. In a letter he wrote on this matter to his nephew Hidetsugu on the eighteenth day of the fifteenth month of 1592, he said:

'The capital of Korea fell on the second day of this month. Therefore the time has come for you to cross the sea and to put the length and breadth of the country of the Great Ming under our dominion. It is my wish that Your Lordship crosses the sea so that you may become Civil Dictator of Great China.'

Later in this same letter, he still further anticipates his obsession with administration:

'The post of Civil Dictator of China will be assigned, as stated above, to Hidetsugu, who will be given a hundred provinces around the capital. The post of Civil Dictator of Japan will go either to the ordinary Councillor Yamato (Hideyoshi's half-brother, Hidenaga), or to the minister of Bizen (another of Hideyoshi's kinsmen) provided that they will declare their readiness to accept.'[36]

In the same way, when Tokugawa Ieyasu took over the control of the country after Hideyoshi's death and abandoned his predecessor's plans for conquest, his sole ambition was to govern Japan and to bring her order and peace. One wonders if the secret aim of the insensate war that Hideyoshi waged in Korea was not to rid himself of a surplus of warriors who, by their demands, might have interfered with his administrative projects in Japan itself. Then, influenced by his first successful campaigns in Korea, he succumbed to his megalomania and in the end really believed in the possibility of conquering China. This is a point of history that is still far from being elucidated.

If the battles and martial life of the samurai seem cruel to us, it is as well to remember that the warriors looked upon death either as an honour, or as a way of freeing themselves from a world of impermanence and suffering in order to enter another eminently permanent and peaceful world. For, contrary to warlike societies to whom a Valhalla promises a new life filled with fighting, feasting, hunting and sensual indulgence, the Japanese aspired only to a Beyond of peace and serenity. It can be claimed, therefore, at the risk of seeming inconsistent, that the samurai, despite their zeal in battle, at heart yearned for nothing but peace and order.

So that the bakufu might know exactly what manpower was available whenever the need arose, each family had to send to the lord of the district where it had settled down a list of the men and materials it could supply. The one we owe to G. B. Sansom[37] is typical of the kind of contribution an ordinary samurai family (owning sixteen *chô* of land) could make in the year 1276:

'Izeri Yajirô Fujiwara Hideshige, a vassal of the province of Higo, at the present time in holy orders (religious name Saikô) respectfully states as follows:

' "Men, bows, arrows, horses: Saikô, aged 85, cannot walk. Nagahide, his son, aged 65, has a bow, arrows and weapons (various). Tsunehide, his son, aged 38, has bow and arrows, various kinds of weapons, armour and one horse. Matsujirô, kinsman, aged 19, has a bow and arrows, various kinds of weapons, and two servants. Takahide, grandson, aged 40, has bow and arrows, various weapons, armour, one horse and one servant.

'The above are at his Lordship's command and will serve him faithfully. Humbly offered (and guaranteed correct) as above-mentioned. Fourth month of 1276.

The *Shami* (novice):
SAIKÔ (Seal)." '

Before going into battle, the samurai checked his equipment and clothed himself with care, blackened his teeth afresh, arranged his hair, powdered and perfumed himself (so that the enemy, if he took his head, would have no cause to mock at his dress) and sometimes concealed in his clothing, or his head-gear, the sacred image of a protective divinity (Buddhist) or a charm from a Shintô shrine. Thus assured, he took leave of his family and dependents:

'He had no fear of death, thinking that at least there would be someone to mourn him. His only worry was that, obsessed by this worldly desire, he might be doomed to follow the never-ending road (*Muryôgô-no-Michi*) of discontented spirits who pursue the living with their evil spells (monen). That he might be spared this fate, he continuously repeated the invocation: "O Buddha Amida! O Buddha Amida!" '[38]

181

9   Thirteenth-century samarai in everyday clothes, with his horse
Drawing by Kikuchi Yôsai (1788–1878)

Troop movements sometimes obeyed 'directional taboos' (*kata-imi*). Then detours were necessary in order to circumvent these prohibitions (*kata-tagae*). These were codified by the *ommyô-ryô* of the imperial court (*yin-yang* Bureau) and by regulations that various soothsayers and calendar makers had added. Although this is not particularly emphasized in the warrior chronicles of medieval Japan, it is quite evident that at least some of these regulations of a superstitious character were observed, if not by country folk, at least by some warriors. Moreover, they still hold today, although to a lesser degree.

So that they could be identified, warriors wore, fixed to their helmet or sleeve, strips of fabric on which signs or distinguishing symbols were drawn: 'Then Tadaaki's warriors took pieces of white silk, cut them into one foot lengths, wrote the symbol which stands for "wind" on them and attached them to the sleeves of their armour. . . .' The war-lords, both lesser and great, were followed by a standard bearer who held aloft the bamboo staff from which a banner hung. This was sometimes rolled up when they went into action.[40]

Leaders and samurai of important families wore special emblems either embroidered on their clothes or painted on their armour, emblems called *mon*, usually inscribed in a circle and enabling the family or clan to which the warrior belonged to be recognized at once. These *mon* have often been compared to the coats of arms of European knighthood, but they differed from them more particularly in that they were distinguishing marks rather than armorial bearings. Since there were no family names in ancient Japan (except in a few very special cases already mentioned), the clans had to be distinguishable by some sort of mark. On the battlefield, each samurai displayed his own *mon*, either on a banner or a standard, or on his clothing. The *mon* of high-ranking Samurai, of *daimyô* and war-lords was sometimes worn by their soldiers signifying their allegiance. Later on, staff and servants also took to displaying the distinguishing *mon* of the head of the family or the group which employed them. This is how the use of the *mon* spread rapidly to all classes of society. But people of the lower classes had no right to it.

When armies came face to face, the attacking side first despatched whistling arrows (*kabura-ya*) to warn the enemy (perhaps originally to frighten them), then, individually, the most intrepid of the samurai galloped forward and, as soon as he was within hailing distance, challenged a samurai of the enemy camp, one of the highest possible rank, to single combat:

'Then a single horseman emerged from the ranks of the imperial army wearing a lavender-coloured cloak over orange-tinted armour shaded off to white as it reached the underdress. He galloped in front of the enemy ranks, calling out his name in a mighty voice:

' "Since I am a person of little consequence, it may be that not one among you knows my name. I am a vassal of the lord Ashikaga, Shidara Gorô Saemon-no-Jô! If there is a vassal of the lords of Rokuhara among you who is willing to fight me, let him gallop forward without delay to test my skill!"

'Thus he spoke and, unsheathing a sword three and a half feet long, he raised it in front of his helmet as if to protect himself from arrows. And the two armies ceased fighting to wonder at this samurai whose war-like spirit was such that he dared to confront a thousand soldiers. Upon which, an old warrior aged about fifty came forward from the ranks of Rokuhara's army, clad in armour laced with black cords and wearing a helmet with a neck-shield of five metal plates. He was riding a nut-brown horse, its saddle-cloth decorated with blue tassels. And in a mighty voice, he cried out his name:

' "Although I am only an ignorant man, I have served for many years as Commissary of the Military Government. And although I am of inferior rank and may appear to be an insignificant foe in your eyes (for perhaps you despise me, thinking that I am only a lay-monk), I am descended from the family of General Toshihito, a family which, for many generations, has followed the Way of the Warrior. I belong to the seventeenth generation, I, Saitô Genki, the lay-monk of Iyo! Why should I hold life dear in this battle which is to determine the fate of our two armies? If any are to be spared, let them tell their sons and grandsons how honourably I fought!"

'As he was speaking, the two adversaries galloped forward and, with a clash of swords, came to grips so violently that they fell from their horses. Being the stronger, Shidara leapt upon Saitô and got ready to strike off his head when Saitô swiftly swung his sword upwards and wounded Shidara three times. Here indeed were mighty combatants who, even in death, did not relax their hold, but ran each other through with their swords and stretched out together on the same pillow . . .

'Once again a warrior rose from the Genji lines, a warrior clad in armour corded with Chinese silk, his helmet wrought with arrowheads. He drew out a sword five feet long, rested it on his shoulder and galloped his horse for fifty metres in front of the enemy lines. And with a great cry, he told his name:

"The glory of my family is not unknown. Since Lord Hachiman's times it has served generations of Genji, and yet today I have not been able to find an enemy worthy of my sword, for my name is unknown in this region. I am Daikô Jirô Shigenari, a personal vassal of Lord Ashikaga! Are Suyama, governor of the province of Bichû, and Kôno governor of the island of Tsushima here, who are said to have accomplished heroic deeds in battles gone by? Stand forth to meet me, and let us join in battle with our keen blades so that all may see and marvel!"

'Thus he spoke, tugging at his horse's bridle until its mouth foamed white. Suyama was not there for he had left in haste for the eighth gate (of Kyôto) to help the defenders of the Eastern temple.

'But Kôno Michiharu, governor of the island of Tsushima, was in the foremost ranks; he was a lusty, valiant man who could not hold back even momentarily, before Daikô's challenge: "Michiharu is here!"

'So he spoke, as he drew near to pit his strength against Daikô. But then Shichirọ Michitô, Kôno's adopted son, galloped ahead of him to bar his way (for he was thinking, perhaps: I must not let my father be killed!). Only fifteen years old at that time, he went right up to Daikô and gripped him wrathfully. Daikô lifted Kôno Shichirô up in the air by the straps of his armour, saying: "I do not choose to fight with a servant!"

'However, as he thrust the young man aside, he noticed the *mon* on his identity badge, a square within a square, with the number "3" written inside.

' "Surely this must be Kôno's son or nephew," he said to himself. And taking his sword in one hand, he cut off Shichirô's legs at the knee and sent him rolling three bow-lengths along the ground. Thereupon, digging in his spurs, the governor of Tsushima galloped swiftly forward to kill Daikô. What was left in life for him now that his beloved adopted son had just been slain before his eyes? In support of Kôno, his three hundred vassals rose up crying: "We must not let our Lord be laid low!" Likewise a thousand Genji vassals rose up, crying: "We must not let Daikô be slain!" Both the Minamoto and the Taira rushed upon each other in disorder, attacking and fighting in a great cloud of dust.'[41]

During the confusion which generally followed these single combats, when the mounted samurai sought above all to lay low the other samurai and casually cut down the rabble on foot, these last, armed with long halberds, struck at samurai as at foot-soldiers, showing wiliness and not scrupling to strike from behind or even to attack in numbers a single samurai, cutting off his horse's legs and men's too with great cutlasses called *naigama*. The important thing was to bring back as many heads as possible, sole proof of bravery that was certain of a reward . . . if the one who had taken them lived long enough to bring them back to camp!

Sometimes battles presented a different picture and we have just seen that, faced with Mongol troops, there could be no question of the rules of chivalry. With the advent of muskets and arquebuses and the proliferation of the *ashigaru* or infantry men, the technique of warfare developed continuously: unimportant engagements gave place to the confrontation of large, more or less disciplined armies. In 1600, during the battle of Sekigahara, which established the might of Tokugawa Ieyasu, the number of men facing one another in the field was estimated at nearly 230,000, cavalry and foot-soldiers in equal numbers, of which more than half were assembled on the battlefield, the others remaining in reserve. Already, at the beginning of the war of the Onin era in 1467, each of the two groups confronting one another around Kyôto had mustered an army of about 80,000 men[42] which, in those days and in view of the inexperience of war-leaders in the directing of great bodies of troops, was considerable. On sea, fighting methods remained virtually the same as on land. The *Gikeiki* describes one of these engagements in great detail, when various enemy vessels surrounded the boat in which were Yoshitsune and Benkei:

'Led by Teshima Kanja and Kôzuke Hangan, the assailants had approached within bow-shot in their small craft protected by rows of shields . . .'

After the ritual exchange of taunts, battle began:

'To his powerful bow he fixed a whistling arrow thirteen spans and three finger-breadths in length. He drew back the bow-string as far as he could and released it. The arrow sped towards Teshima with an ominous whine. Its forked head struck him beneath the vizor of his helmet, pierced right through to his neck and was checked by the upper plate of his neck-shield. The bowl of the helmet with the head inside, fell into the sea with a plop! Kneeling on the deck, Kataoka shot his arrows in swift succession. Fourteen or fifteen of his arrow-heads holed the sides of the enemy ships and three of them rapidly filled with water right to the brim. Urged on by Benkei, Hitachibô rowed furiously with his foot on the gunwale. When they were near enough to the enemy, Benkei seized one of the five enemy ships with a grappling-iron, leapt aboard and set about clearing a way for himself from stem to stern . . .'[43]

It is evident that the technique was of the simplest; it was primarily a question of being able to come to grips with the foe. On land, apart from battles in open country and encounters in single combat, the attack and defence of fortresses was regarded as of supreme importance, During long-drawn-out sieges recourse was often made to trickery and to less orthodox methods of fighting. The *Taiheiki*, that extremely valuable chronicle of the end of the Kamakura era, has left us many descriptions of sieges of this kind:

'In the end, the besiegers, filled with rage, grappled the wall on the four sides (of the fort) to scale it. But the men inside the fort cut all the ropes supporting the wall at the same time, for it was a double wall built in such a way as to let the outer one fall. . . . More than a thousand attackers were crushed under this weight. . . . While the besieged men hurled tree trunks and stones down on them. . . . Then all equipped themselves with shields covered with hides, held them up in front of them and advanced once again on the fort, saying:

' "To leap across the most to reach the wall will present no difficulty for the banks are not high nor the trench deep. But is this wall also going to fall on top of us?"

'They were filled with fear as they said this, hesitating to tackle the wall. They all went down into the water of the moat, threw grappling-irons on to the wall and pulled. But when it was about to fall (for it was made of mud and lath) those inside the fort took ladles with handles from ten to twenty feet long, plunged them into boiling water and poured this on to the besiegers' heads. . . . Every time the assailants drew near with a different method of assault, the besieged men defended themselves by new stratagems. . . .'[44]

Incendiary arrows and grappling-irons were the weapons most commonly used during sieges. If the fortress or castle held out for too long, the assailants tried to starve the defenders and filled in the trenches. When Tokugawa Ieyasu in 1614 laid siege to the castle of Osaka, his enemy's last place of retreat, he needed more than 200,000 men to fill in the trenches and beleaguer the position held by some 100,000 defenders.

In most cases, armies and *daimyô* alike made use of spies (*kanja*) who gave them information about the enemy's morale, its provisioning, and about the alliances and quarrels of its leaders rather than about troop movements. Sometimes war leaders employed specialists belonging to 'clans' of criminals who, by dint of training, had acquired an incredible skill as much in house-breaking as in covering up their tracks. These *ninja*, organized into associations, hired their services, temporarily, to one or another. At other times, a *daimyô* might order a warrior (samurai or not) to carry out some special mission. But there was not as yet any organized espionage or counter-espionage department.

In wartime, soldiers in the field made every effort not to lay waste the crops which they needed; but they sometimes behaved heedlessly towards the farmers and frequently burned down their houses, often without reason. Therefore, when an army was reported, the poorest farmers took to the mountains as quickly as possible or, if they belonged to a great landowner, sought refuge within the fortified walls of his *yashiki*. When the battle was over and the troops had left, the farmers rushed out on to the deserted battle-field to collect whatever they could find in the way of weapons, armour, horses or other abandoned possessions, which, in their eyes, represented a fortune. 'For half a mile along the road (of retreat), there was no room to put a foot down by reason of the horses and weapons left behind. There is no doubt that in this way immense wealth suddenly fell into the hands of the poor people of the Tôjô region,' says the *Taiheiki* at the end of the account of a bloody battle.[45] In some of the extremely poverty-stricken parts of the country, farmers had been known to despatch wounded soldiers ruthlessly in order to rob them. But these occurrences were relatively rare and the suffering that farmers endured owing to these battles outweighed any benefit they might derive from them. So much so that after the war of the Onin era, the farmers in the vicinity of Kyôto, worn out with the war, banded together and set up a temporary government at Uji and demanded the immediate withdrawal of the troops which were looting shamelessly. Afraid of being attacked by serfs and of meeting an inglorious death, the soldiers evacuated the district.

Although it was generally deemed shameful for a samurai to surrender, this was frequently the case, especially when a man was taken prisoner by surprise. As a general rule, a samurai who surrendered removed his helmet and rolled up his banner. In very many instances, a war leader made prisoner had the right (as in the Japanese game of chess) to enlist, together with all his vassals and warriors, under the victor's banner:

'And the lay-monk of Yuasa, now beset on all sides by his enemies, yielded his neck (meaning removed his helmet) as a sign of surrender. After Kusunoki had taken over this monk's warriors with his 700 horsemen, he brought into subjection the two provinces of Izumi and Kawachi and his army became exceedingly strong.'[46]

Sometimes prisoners were tortured, either to obtain information, or to make them confess some specific action or other:

'Thereupon, the monks were handed over to the samurai Tribunal to be tortured by the knife and by fire. For a while Monkan refused to give any answer to the questions. But, weakened in body and mind by the intense pain of water-torture, he murmured the words of confession. . . . Then they got ready to torture Chûen; but this monk, timorous by nature, did not wait for torture and wrote all that was asked of him.'[47]

Or else the prisoner was made to walk barefoot over live coals:

'A fire of wood charcoal was set ablaze in the northern sector of Rokuhara (the fortress belonging to the Kamakura samurai at Kyôto) like a raging inferno, with pieces of green bamboo laid on the top and dreadful flames shooting through the openings. Two low-ranking soldiers stood on either side so that they could stretch Tameakira's arms to the fullest extent and make him walk on the glowing embers . . .).[48]

However, prisoners of war do not appear to have been systematically tortured. When a victorious war leader refused to have recourse to torture, or if their leader had been killed in battle, prisoners were beheaded by a stroke of the sword, in accordance with the customary ceremonial. But from the Muronmachi period on, low-ranking prisoners accused of rebellion were very frequently put to the torture 'by crucifixion head downwards, sawing off limbs with bamboo saws, impaling, roasting, boiling or slicing. . . .'[49] Those of a higher rank were beheaded or forced to commit suicide. Sometimes, when it was a question of high-ranking prisoners, they were obliged to become monks. Soldiers, rather than surrender as warriors, preferred to do so as monks, but, although this appears to have been common practice, it was considered rather despicable:

'It would have been better for all these men to make a name for themselves by dying in battle, says the author of the *Taiheiki*,[50] for they had nothing to hope for that might make life dear to them, Yet their *Karma* was so bad that thirteen of the great Taira leaders became monks of the Ritsu sect in the monastery of Hannya-ji, donning the three religious habits, taking their begging bowls and giving themselves up. Sadahira-no-Ason received them, bound their arms tightly behind them, tied them across relay-horses and conducted them to the capital in broad daylight in view of the myriad soldiers of the imperial armies. . . . The same holds true of the other armies; when a father was killed, the son shaved his head to become a monk and vanished from the camp; and when a lord was wounded, his vassals looked after him and bore him home.'[51]

The names of the slain were always recorded on the battlefield in an effort to compensate the descendants and to find out the exact number of casualties. Special officials, assigned to this task, also counted the number of heads taken from the enemy: 'The number of dead and wounded in a single day was from five to six thousand; and when the war commissioner Nagasaki Shirô Saemon-no-Jô conducted his enquiry, twelve scribes were required to write down their names night and day for three days without putting down thier brushes.'[52]

Those of the defeated who had not been killed in action often had recourse to suicide. We are in possession of many accounts of these suicides, whether the warrior cut open his abdomen with his dagger (*hara-kiri* or *seppuku*), or threw himself on to his sword, or preferred to perish in his burning house with his most faithful servants and vassals (*junshi* or collective suicide). When he was about to be taken prisoner, Yoshitsune 'stabbed himself under the left breast, plunging the blade in so deeply that it all but came out again in his back; then he made three further incisions, disembowelled himself and wiped the dagger on the sleeve of his coat'.[53]

Thereupon his wife sought death at the hands of one of their vassals, Kanefusa (for in these heroic times women were often as resolute as men), who also killed his master's children before setting fire to the house and throwing himself into the blazing mass.

Collective suicides of this kind were not unusual. Clan chiefs involved in their death several hundreds of their warriors, retainers and vassals, as well as their family, who followed them into the Beyond of their own free-will. Some warriors' suicides were deliberately spectacular for the edification of their descendants:

'Yoshiteru climbed up on to the watch-tower of the second gate from where he made sure that the Prince was now far away (for he had taken his place and his clothes to deceive the enemy and to give his lord time to flee). When the time had come, he cut the hand-rail of the tower window (*yagura*) so that he could be better seen, calling out his lord's name:

' "I am Son-un prince of the blood of the first rank, Minister of Military Affairs and second son of Go-Daigô Tennô, ninety-fifth emperor since Jimmu Tennô, august descendant of Amaterasu Omikami. Defeated by the rebels, I am taking my own life to avenge my wrongs in the Beyond. Learn from my example how a true warrior dies by his own hand when fate plays false with him!"

'Stripping off his armour, he threw it to the foot of the tower. Next he took off the jacket of his underdress with its tight fitting sleeves . . . and clad only in his brocaded breeches, he thrust a dagger into his white skin. He cut in a straight line from left to right, cast his entrails on to the hand-rail of the tower, placed the point of his sword in his mouth and flung himself headlong towards the ground.[54]

This kind of death was admired by the samurai and deemed heroic and worthy of praise by generations to come. Therefore, many were those who put an end to their life in this way.

Archers slipped the last arrow of their quiver into their girdle before throwing themselves on to their swords, for tradition ascribed to this last arrow the power to destroy obstacles on the road of the Beyond.[55]

But the hazards of war resulted in many warriors being executed, whether they were accused of treason or by way of reprisals, or more simply because a collection of heads was needed. For war in Japan during the Middle Ages. was reduced to a kind of head hunt, as it were, interspersed with acts of heroism. Where executions were concerned, these had to conform to a certain ritual: the condemned man was entitled to write, as was customary, his farewell poem:

'Then, sitting upright on an animal skin, Tomoyuki picked up the inkstone once again and, serenely, composed farewell verses to the glory of the Buddhist Law:

> For forty-two years I have dwelt
> In this mortal sphere of non-action.
> Heaven and earth pass away
> When I say farewell to life.

He wrote: "the nineteenth day of the sixteenth month", laid down his brush and sat with body erect and hands joined. And as soon as Tago Rokurô Saemon-no-Jô passed behind him, his noble head fell forward.'[56]

It was customary for the place of execution (which could vary according to circumstances) to be surrounded by a *maku* or curtain. From his clothing the prisoner drew a sheet of paper with which he wiped his neck then, often on the same paper, he wrote his last poem. His vassals or servants attended to the cremation or burial of his body and took away his ashes or his head in order to restore these gruesome souvenirs, together with his last letter or farewell poem, to his family.

Troublesome prisoners might simply be assassinated in their jail, as in the end Go-Daigo's son, Prince Morinaga was at Kamakura. Head-hunting sometimes gave rise to falsifications: heads of unfortunate people were collected to add to the number of those of warriors genuinely slain in battle. The wounded were generally despatched ruthlessly, if they were unlucky enough for their vassals to have been killed or to have fled. And the *Taiheiki* provides yet another account of these fraudulent actions:

'Suda and Takahashi galloped through the streets of the capital to collect the heads of the wounded and the dead from the ditches, and to hang them in a row along the river, as far as the sixth gate. They were 873 in number. Some of them, however, were only heads brought along by Rokuhara warriors who had not taken part in the fighting but were seeking a way of

11 Nuns (Shintô *miko*) playing *kemari*, an old kind of football, in a temple courtyard. They wear an ancient costume with red pants; the ball is oval

winning honours: heads of commoners from the capital and other places, to whom divers names (of warriors) were given. Among them were five heads labelled "the lay-monk, Akamatsu Enshin" which were all hung in the same way, for they all belonged to unknown men.'[57]

When the heads of the defeated of high rank had to be kept long enough for the victorious general to be able to identify them personally, they were preserved in a lacquer container filled with *sake*.

Religious services, requested individually by families or collectively by the victorious clan, were held in memory of the dead of every battle. The geste of Yoshitsune gives this account of how he had a Buddhist service celebrated in honour of Tsuginobu and Tadanobu who had been killed in battle:

'Inscribe the names of all the men who died fighting at Shikoku and Kyûshû, heroes and cowards alike, so that we can offer prayers for them also! he said. Then Yoshitsune ordered a certain number of high-ranking monks to make the necessary preparations. . . . With much ceremony, Yoshitsune offered a copy of the *Lotus Sûtra*[58] written in his own hand.'

On the family altar of every Samurai family, a tablet (*ihai*) inscribed in the name of the dead man, recalled his memory, and a gravestone was erected in the garden or cemetery, even if the body of the deceased had not been found. A lock of hair or some object that had belonged to him was buried in place of his ashes:

'As the ringing of Gion's temple bell echoes man's vicissitudes, the fleeting glory of the flowering trees testifies that all that flourishes must decay. The proud do not last for ever, their life is like a summer night's dream. Warriors too must fall in the end, for they are like a lamp at the mercy of the wind . . .'[59]

CHAPTER VIII

RELIGION

The appearance on the Japanese scene of a new system of government, in complete contrast to that practised until then by the aristocrats of Kyôto, offered, from the spiritual and moral point of view, a kind of liberation which enabled new ideas to gain ground, and religions and philosophies to develop and win over the people. Many new ways of thought were superimposed on to traditional Japanese Buddhism, a form of Buddhism that was a blend of Shintô practices and beliefs of Chinese origin – the development of the pietist theories of Amidism, the uncompromising theories of Nichiren and the meditative theories of Zen. The samurai class adopted a Confucian moral philosophy and the revival of Shintô cults was purely Japanese. Powerful personalities provided a stimulus for the religious spirit of the Japanese people. Tempered by religion and spiritualized by Zen philosophy, the samurai spirit breathed strength into the new sects.

It cannot be said that there is a Japanese Buddhism, but rather that there are several kinds of Buddhism in Japan. If the nobles of Kyôto practised a form of Buddhism in which rites played a very important part, the samurai retained primarily philosophical concepts such as the one that emphasized the impermanence of all things. The masses saw in Buddhism only divinities to be worshipped, for the same reason as the *kami*, the spirits of the fields and mountains. As for the priests, their conceptions of Buddhism differed according to the sect to which they belonged.

The Japanese, traditionally tolerant from the religious point of view and as accommodating with regard to divinities as to foreign beliefs, never formulated any positive dogma, nor enforced recognition of any exclusive cult. They did their utmost to extract from each belief or philosophy, on the one hand ideas which seemed to them essential and valid to all, and on the other those which, fitting in with their own way of life, were likely to satisfy them morally and spiritually. This was only possible if, to the Japanese way of thinking, the sacred was regarded as something entirely different from the profane – which was indeed the case, although at certain times and in certain circumstances it might be difficult to separate the two. But here the Japanese reacted in their own way, by avoiding mixing elements which at first sight, appeared to them incompatible, and by juxtaposing them. In this way the majority of Japanese could at the same time be Shintôists, Buddhists and Confucians. At the end of the sixteenth century, they were all these, and sometimes Christians into the bargain.

The samurai, whose warrior code compelled him to kill, to eat meat, in a word (and according to religious ethics) to injure his neighbour, might seem to be in complete contradiction to the Buddhists teachings which forbade the taking of life. Nevertheless, he worshipped in the first place the ancestral gods of his clan or his family and the *kami* who protected both himself and his fellow men; in this respect he was Shintôist. The samurai also observed the moral principles of obedience, loyalty and filial piety which were derived from the Confucian system of ethics. He worshipped the Buddhist divinities, he believed in universal impermanence, in retribution of good and evil in a future life, and in a paradisian life after death and, in this, he could claim to be Buddhist. Yoritomo, while worshipping Hachiman, his *ujigami* (clan god), was at the same time a fervent Buddhist. There is even a tradition that he never set out to do battle without fixing a small image of Kannon in his hair-knot beforehand and that he was never without his rosary for saying Buddhist prayers.[1] And no matter how faithful a devotee of the *kami* of his clan, how mighty a slayer of enemies and cutter-off of heads a samurai was, he might all of a sudden retire to a monastery and become a monk.

For what mattered most of all to the Japanese was to have, after a very full life, what they called a 'good death' (*ojô*) guaranteeing their rebirth in the Paradise of Amida.[2] On the other hand, monks who considered themselves losers as far as their material interests were concerned, did not hesitate to go to war and to behave like coarse ruffians, at the same time reciting *sûtra*. An imperial prince, Morinaga, chief abbot of the Tendai monastery on Mount Hiei, when pursued by his enemies, recited incantations to a god in order to render himself invisible:

'In the hall of the Buddha, he saw three large Chinese chests on legs, containing scrolls of the *Daihannya* (sûtra) and left open at the place where a monk had started reading them. The lids of two of the chests were still closed. However, more than half the Sacred Scripture scrolls had been taken out of the one that was left open. The prince slipped inside this open box, pulled the Sacred Scrolls down over him and silently recited incantations so that he might be hidden from the sight of men. He held the cold steel of a dagger against his abdomen thinking: "If they find me, I shall take my life." '[3]

This miscellany of beliefs, these seeming contradictions, likely to amaze a Westerner used to more dogmatic coherence, are natural to a people for whom the idea of heresy does not exist. The religious outlook of the Japanese was essentially fluid, making it possible for them to identify the *kami* of the soil with the imported divinities of Buddhism. Their way of thinking did not necessarily at this time affect their way of life.

Buddhism in the Heian period was essentially aristocratic:

'Buddhist affairs were handled by the Ministry of Civil Administration; the emperor had the right to appoint priests (or rather monks) to posts in the ecclesiastical hierarchy and to bestow sacerdotal titles. The "civic" nature of the Buddhist Church arises from the fact that the ranks in the priestly and court hierarchies were precisely correlated, and that the superiors of great temples like that of Mount Hiei were usually imperial princes. . . . Nearly all the high ecclesiastical posts in monasteries were held by nobles of the third rank and above, and about half the remaining posts fell to lords of the first five ranks.'[4]

The masses only appreciated the simplest, generally syncretic, aspects of religion. The teachings of the esoteric Shingon and Tendai sects were only understood by a few of the initiated and the provincial monks themselves had only a very limited knowledge of them. The comparative democratization of power in the thirteenth century led to a like democratization of religion. Old sects reappeared (Ritsu and Kegon among others) and new ones sprang up, more suited to the understanding of the common people. These sects tried at the same time to simplify Buddhism by ridding it of the extremely elaborate rites which until that time had characterized its ceremonies. The 'aristocratic' forms of Buddhism continued, however, to be observed at Kyôto and by the provincial nobles. The new doctrines did not replace the old ones, but were merely juxtaposed and superimposed on them. And if the monasteries, through the medium of their soldier-monks, frequently engaged in bloody battles, their clashes were based less on doctrinal disputes than on conflicts of interest. Nevertheless, the new sects exerted a great influence on social life as well as on the development of thought in Japan during these confused times.

AMIDISM

The pietist belief in a Buddha saviour whose all-embracing Mercy was to welcome the faithful, at the last moment, into his paradise, a belief which became general during the Kamakura period, had appeared in Japan as long ago as the tenth century, when an imperial prince turned wandering monk, Kûya, travelled about the towns and villages chanting the name of Buddha Amida. This 'saint of the market-places' as he was sometimes called,[5] attempted at that time to spread Buddhism among the common people and to reconcile them to religion, thanks to a doctrine of salvation that was easily understood, not requiring any difficult studies but only a pure faith. Other monks after him, such as Genshin (942–1017), tried to rid the philosophies of the Tendai and Shingon sects of their excess of mystical ritualism and to replace them by a faith promising instant salvation in Amida, the Buddha of the West. In his *Ojôyôshû*, written in 984, Genshin sets forth the essence of this doctrine:

'When a pious person dies, the Buddha (Amida) appears before him. The Lord of Mercy (Kannon), one of his great *Bodhisattva*, brings a lotus flower on which to receive the pious soul, and the Lord of Power (Seishi) stretches forth his hands to greet him, while the other *Bodhisattva* and hosts of celestial beings sing hymns of praise and welcome. Born into the Pure Land, the pious man is like a blind man suddenly recovering his sight; he finds himself surrounded by rays of light and glittering jewels beyond price. . . . Amida Buddha is seated on a lotus flower; he is like a golden mountain in the midst of all the glories, with celestial beings thronging around him. The Lords of Mercy and of Power lead the new-born soul before the seat of the Buddha.'[6]

Meanwhile, the aristocrats had made this cult the excuse for splendid ceremonies, wherein dances and magnificent processions served more to testify to their aesthetic sensibility than to honour the divinity. The Amadism of the end of the Heian era no longer appealed to the masses. The belief, founded on an ancient prophecy, that the time was drawing near when the law of Buddha was to fall upon degenerate days, seemed, in the middle of the twelfth century, to be taking concrete form in the events and catastrophes that swept down upon the country. The corruption of religious institutions and their quasi-secularization, that of the court officials, the disturbances that followed, then the rise to power of the warrior class, inclined people to believe that the 'latter days of the Law' were at hand. As opposed to a difficult doctrine of self-improvement which would make it possible to attain to a land of salvation, a doctrine reserved for an elite, the common people had need of an easier method which would enable it, for its part, to reach the Pure Land of the Paradise of Amida by a single act of faith.

It was Hônen (Genkû, 1133–1212), a monk from Mount Hiei, who laid the foundations of this popular pietism for, he said, 'there are perhaps millions of people who would like to practise Buddhist discipline and themselves be led along the way of perfection, and yet, in these "latter days of the Law", there will be none who will be able to achieve the ideal of perfection'. And he advocated putting all one's trust in the person of the Buddha Amida, simply by repeating his name in the invocation *Namu Amida Butsu*, for 'there will be no distinction, neither between men and women, nor between the good and the bad, the mighty and the weak; all will enter into his Pure Land (*Jodo*) merely by invoking his name, Amida, with complete faith. . . .'[7]

Although in 1207 Hônen had been exiled at the request of the other monks of Mount Hiei, the simplicity of his teaching was of a kind to spread very rapidly, not only among the farming class but also among the warriors. To Masaki, Yoritomo's widow, he wrote:

'Think sympathetically and lovingly of all those who have a sincere desire to be born again into the Pure Land (*Jôdo*). Repeat the name of the Buddha Amida for their protection, as if they were your parents or your children, even if they live far away, even beyond the cosmos. Help those who have need of material aid in this world."[8]

Two days before his death, Hônen left this note, regarded ever since as his spiritual testament and as the exposition of the original teaching of Jôdo:

'The way of final salvation that I have taught is neither a kind of meditation such as was practised by many learned men in China and Japan nor is it a repetition of the name of the Buddha by those who have studied and understood its profound meaning. It is nothing else but the mere repetition of the *Namu Amida Butsu*, without any doubt as to His mercy, whereby a man can be born again in the Land of Perfect Bliss. The mere repetition, together with an ardent faith, takes in all the practical details such as the triple preparation of the mind and the four practical rules. If I myself, as an individual, held a more profound doctrine than this, I would not profit from the mercy of the two Honourable Ones Amida and Shaka and I would remain outside the vow of the Buddha Amida. Those who believe this, although they have a clear conception of all that Shaka (the Buddha Çâkyamuni) taught throughout his lifetime, must behave like simple people who do not know a single letter (of the alphabet), or like ignorant nuns whose faith is absolutely simple. In this way, without appearing pedantic, they must devote themselves ardently to the repetition of the name of Amida and this alone (must suffice).'[9]

For all that, his doctrine of the identity of the individual soul with that of the Buddha (the teaching of the Tendai sect) was sometimes disputed by his followers, among whom some maintained that the salvation of the believer was due entirely to the Mercy of Amida, while others attributed this to faith.

It was then that Shinran (1173–1263), also a monk from Mount Hiei and Hônen's disciple, founded his own sect, Jôdo Shinshû or New Pure Land Sect', of which the doctrine of 'natural' salvation was a huge success, declaring that it was possible for those who had never read the Holy Scriptures, like the veriest outcasts, to be saved at the last solely by the 'mercy' of Amida. 'Even the good will be born again in paradise: how much more the wicked!'[10]

> When a faith as hard as a diamond
> Is firmly established in you,
> The spiritual enlightenment of Amida will hold
> and keep you,
> And you will be free from Life and Death for
> evermore.[11]

And, for Shinran, the mere repetition of the *Nembutsu*, of the fervent invocation to the Buddha Amida at the point of death was sufficient to ensure to all the way of rebirth into the Pure Land Paradise.

'When the thought occurs to you to say "Homage to the Buddha Amida" (*Nembutsu* = *Namu Amida Butsu*) in the belief that aided by the wonderful vow of Amida[12], you will be re-born into paradise, then you are sharing in His Mercy, which embraces all beings and rejects none. Faith alone is required. . . . From that time onwards, if one has faith in the original vow (of Amida) there is no necessity for any other good deed, for no good deed can surpass the act of adoration (*Nembutsu*); there is no need to fear committing an evil action, for no evil act can stand in the way of the original vow of Amida.'[13]

It is easy to understand that such a theory was bound to find many followers, especially among the samurai and the warriors, calculated as it was to allay their scruples. Shinran spread his teaching chiefly by means of hymns (*wasan*) written in the vernacular:

> Infinite is the fearful ocean of births and
>   deaths,
> On which we are tossed from time immemorial.
> We cannot cross it,
> Unless we all set sail on the ship of Amida.[14]

One of Hônen's other followers, Ippen Shônin (Chishin, 1239–89) chanted the *Nembutsu* dancing the while with the common people in the villages, where special platforms had been built for this purpose not far from the temples.[15] His teaching included the notion that since in the midst of life one is in death, one must learn to live with death and recite the *Nembutsu* tirelessly. This belief had, as we shall see, a profound influence on the arts (paintings representing the *Raigô*, the Welcoming of the Faithful into *Jôdo* by the Buddha Amida followed by all the *Bodhisattva*) as on the literature of the times, utterly imbued as it was with a kind of fatalism and resignation, with the sense of man's powerlessness to be saved by his own merits, and with the brevity and transitoriness of all worldly things.

NICHIREN THE REFORMER

Quite different was the career of Nichiren, born in 1222 into a poor family of fishermen from the south-east coast of Japan, and

whose uncompromising doctrine conceded some degree of importance to the Scriptures, to popular cults and to Shintô beliefs,
contrary to Amadism which attempted to be simply and solely
Buddhist. Nichiren was first and foremost a reformer, a prophet,
and as such his behaviour was a combination of violence and
tenderness. Uncompromising violence towards the powerful and
the detractors of his teaching, tenderness filled with love and
forebearance in his dealings with the humble, his brothers. After
being driven from Mount Hiei because he had been presumptuous
enough to denounce the Tendai teachings of his day, and after
acquiring notoriety as a trouble-maker by showering sarcasms and
insults on the other sects Nichiren was, before long, attacking the
bakufu government itself. Arrested and condemned to exile he
there formulated the five points of his 'mission':

'In the first place, as his doctrine declared, his religion was
founded on the sole authority of the "Lotus Sûtra of the Good
Law" (Hokekyô), regarded as the sum total of all the Buddha's
teachings. Secondly, concerning the degree of understanding
of those who were to be instructed, the common man of this
"degenerate age of the latter days" was not likely to be attracted
to the Buddha's teaching unless it was put to him in the simplest
terms and not by means of complicated methods. Thirdly, as
regards the epoch, this was the age of the Latter Law (*Mappô*)
in which the "Lotus" alone was to remain efficacious for universal
salvation. Fourthly, as regards the country where this law was
proclaimed, Japan was the country wherein true Buddhism was
destined to prevail. Fifthly, concerning the ups and downs of the
types of Buddhism, the preceding forms had come to the end of
their mission and the way had been prepared by the old masters
for the triumph of the perfect Truth.'[16]

On his return from exile in 1263, Nichiren, who had won many
believers to his cause, became more uncompromising than ever
and was persecuted on all sides. He foretold (!) the Mongol invasions
but the government, taking him for a conspirator, condemned him
to death in 1271. A miracle saved him *in extremis*:

'As a warning to others, the prisoner was mounted on a horse
and led through the streets of Kamakura by his guards before
proceeding to the place appointed for his execution; he arrived

at Katase at dead of night. Many of his sorrowing disciples and followers had gathered together, weeping on the roadside, to bid him a final farewell. The devoted Kingo, with his brothers, held the horse's bridle. . . . In accordance with tradition . . . Nichiren, reciting the Scriptures tirelessly, knelt down on the straw mat and bared his neck to receive the fatal stroke. Just as the executioner raised his sword, a sudden clap of thunder shook the ground, the sky lit up and from the black clouds fell a ball of fire which broke the lifted sword into three pieces, paralysing the executioner's arm, and he fell to the ground. This miraculous intervention being naturally interpreted as a sign of divine wrath, a messenger was sent in haste to Kamakura to proclaim this miracle, a messenger who on the way met another entrusted with a full pardon, the regent Tokimune having had a dream ordering him to spare the prisoner.'[17]

The sentence was changed to exile to the island of Sado. But the isolation in which Nichiren lived for three years only strengthened his determination, and he declared:

'I shall be the pillar of Japan! I shall be the eyes of Japan! I shall be the well-spring of Japan! Just as now my mercy is vast and all-embracing, so will the adoration of the Lotus of Perfect Truth prevail in the ten thousand years to come, that is time without end. This is the merit I have acquired, which is destined to open the blind eyes of all who dwell in Japan, and to close the way to the deepest of hells (avici). These merits transcend those of Dengyô Daishi (the founder of the Tendai) and are far superior to those of Nagarjuna and Kascyapa. . . .'[18]

Pardoned, on his return from exile he retired to the slopes of Mount Fuji in 1274, where he devoted the rest of his life to the establishment of a kind of 'Universal Buddhist Church' and to the propagation of faith in the 'Lotus Sûtra'. His followers were ardent propagators of the faith and a number of them even went to Siberia to preach Nichirenism! Many warriors and farmers supported his doctrines; they travelled about the countryside chanting and beating their drums, while preaching the *Namu Myô-Hôrengekyô* or 'Homage to the Lotus Sûtra' at street corners and wherever the public was likely to assemble, often disturbing ceremonies in temples belonging to other sects. Their intransigence forced even the Amidists to 'militarize' themselves and to adopt, on their part too, a bellicose attitude, cause of many disorders in the fifteenth and sixteenth centuries.

ZEN

Although the contemplative doctrines of *Dhyâna* (*Ch'an* in Chinese) Buddhism had been known very early in Japan, they did not gain adherents until a Tendai cleric, the monk Eisai (1141–1215), on his return from China, founded monasteries in Japan so as to train disciples to become masters of Zen methods (Rinzai sect). In his preface to the *Kôzen Gokoku Ron* (Propagation of Zen for the Protection of the Country), he states precisely:

'As in India, as in China, this teaching has attracted believers and disciples in great numbers. This teaching spreads Enlighten-ment as with the Buddha of old, by the transference of truth from one man to another. In the matter of religious discipline, it practises the true method of the wise men of old. Thus it teaches Enlightenment, in substance as in semblance, and perfects the relationship between master and disciple. In its rules of conduct and discipline, there is no confusion between good and evil.'[19]

Dôgen (1200–53) followed after Eisai and in 1244 founded another Zen sect called Sôdô (or Sôtô). The philosophy of Zen which involved lengthy sessions of 'contemplative vacuity' seated and silent, and rather a difficult mental discipline, was unlikely to become very popular. Yet, the complete absence of self-hood required to attain the intuitive preception of the Supreme Reality appealed to many high-ranking warriors, who derived from it a foundation on which to base an art of fighting as well as an art of living and dying, without bothering too much about the cares of this world. Zen monks taught that as far as Supreme Enlightenment was concerned, it could not be communicated through words; it could only be understood by direct communication from soul to soul between master and disciple, between man and this supreme Enlightenment:

> Oh! poor lonely scarecrow
> Amid the mountain rice-fields!
> You do not know perhaps why you keep watch
> And yet you are not there in vain![20]

In actual fact, the author of this book is quite unable to explain what Zen is. It can only be lived, practised intuitively and does not in any way depend upon words or concepts. Musô Kokushi, a Zen priest and Ashikaga Takauji's intimate counsellor, who established Zen temples styled *Ankokuji* (Peaceful Country) in every province of Japan, said:

'The clairvoyant teachers of the Zen sects have no canon to which they have to refer on all occasions and at every turn. They offer instruction in accordance with whatever the occasion demands, and preach as the spirit moves them, with no set framework to guide them. If they are asked what Zen is, they may answer with quotations from Confucius, Mencius, Lao-Tzu or Chuang-Tzu, or else with quotations from other sects and also by using popular proverbs. At times they draw the attention to the immediate situation with which we are confronted, or swing their staffs crying *"katsu"*, or perhaps they just raise their fists or their fingers. These are the methods used by Zen masters and known as "the vigorous handling of Zen Buddhism". They are incomprehensible to those who have not yet ventured into this sphere.'[21]

Zen would not perhaps have met with such success in Japan if it had not had such remarkable men as interpreters. A number of them became counsellors whose advice was followed not only by Hôjô regents but also, and especially, by the Ashikaga shôgun. Their teaching had a profound influence on literature and the arts; apart from a set of ideals, it brought to them a love of Nature and simplicity: The Zennist's love of nature, says Anesaki Masaharu was nothing else but a discovery of beauty identical with our own soul, and in the same way its moral influence was nothing but a shedding of spiritual illumination over the world.'[22]

Zen monks, scattered throughout the country, proved equal to the task they had set themselves, establishing schools, alleviating the distress of the poor, and it was thanks to their influence that literature and art were kept alive; without them they would never have been able to survive the civil wars which in the fourteenth and fifteenth centuries laid waste the country and steeped it in blood.

SHINTÔ

Shintô, the Way of the Kami, the earliest form of religion in Japan, had undergone many changes since the ninth century, a time when her divinities had been put on the same footing as those of Budhism, Buddha the Great Illuminator, or Dainichi Nyorai (*Mahâvai-rocana*) being declared identical with Amaterasu Omikami, Kami of the Sun and ancestor of the line of Tennô or emperors. The Japanese were at times unable to make clear distinctions between Buddhism and Shintô, unless it was in the division of labour; upon Buddhism devolved everything concerning life after death, while Shintô turned its attention more particularly to life here on earth. All events relating to this life, birth, marriage, battles, festivals, were regarded as falling within the province of Shintô or rather of the kami, whom it was advisable to inform and proptitiate on every occasion, either by purifications (*harai*) or by offerings, dances and ritual invocations (*norito*).

But the increasingly sumptuous ceremonies of the Buddhist cult had made Shintô appear to be a religion of somewhat minor importance and, during the periods of ruthless conflicts between the Buddhists sects, the cult of the kami, although still observed in country districts and among the warrior class, seemed to have lost its autonomy. This was primarily due to the fact that there was no clearly defined concept of kami, the Japanese being 'intuitively aware of the kami in their inmost beings and communicating with them directly without ever having formed any clear notion of the kami, conceptually as theologically'.[23] And if Shintô has a myth-ology or even several which describe the activities of a multitude of kami, there is no absolute deity among them. Each kami has its own nature, considered as the 'spirit' of an object or a place, of an element or a phenomenon, a spirit which is 'the' object or 'the' phenomenon, or considered as protector of a group, of a clan (*ujigami*), or even of a family or again of a specific place. As such the kami are reputed to protect individuals as well as the whole country. When the typhoon of 1281 had destroyed the Mongol fleet, Fujiwara-no-Tameuji, the imperial messenger sent to the temple of Ise to thank the goddess Amaterasu, composed a *waka* in her honour:

> In answer to our fervent prayers for the
> favour of the Heavens,
> Our goddess, stirred by divine wrath
> Has swept the seas of the mighty enemy fleet
> And his ships are destroyed and shattered.[24]

Shintô, having neither Sacred Scriptures nor dogma, cannot claim to replace Buddhism which provided the people with a moral and a religious philosophy. For in Shintô there is no precise distinction between Good and Evil. This distinction depends upon circumstances. Man's soul is innately good and he only commits evil when he is momentarily out of harmony with Nature, with the Kami, because he is 'unclean'. And evil is sometimes regarded as a sickness which affects a human being temporarily, a sickness mainly due to a state of uncleanness which cuts him off from the world of the kami and which it is essential to eliminate by purifications. Nevertheless, despite the increasing ascendancy of Buddhism, Shintô remained inextricably bound up with the customs as with the ways of thinking and of living of the Japanese people. So it was that promises made among samurai and written under oath, brought various Shintô divinities into play depending upon clans, Hachiman in the case of the Genji, Hakone Gongen, and Izusan Gongen, Mishima Daimyôjin in the case of the Hôjô (of Taira stock), and that Hideyoshi in 1591 could write to the viceroy of Goa, though the intermediary of a Jesuit missionary:

'Our country is the country of the kami, and kami is the spirit. Everything in Nature comes into being through the spirit. There can be no spirituality without the kami. There is no Way without the kami. Kami reigns in times of prosperity as in times of adversity. Kami is positive and negative and unfathomable. Thus kami is the source of all existence. Buddhism in India, Confucianism in China and Shintô in Japan all proclaim it. To understand Shintô is to understand Buddhism as well as Confucianism.'[26]

However, each Buddhist sect developed its own form of syncretism and tried to absorb the kami in its own way. So it was that in the thirteenth century the Tendai sect formed the *Sannô Ichijitsu Shintô*, while the Shingon established *Ryôbu Shintô*; the Nichirenites themselves in the fifteenth century introduced *Hokke Shintô*. But the Middle Ages also witnessed the birth of a purely Shintô reaction with *Yoshida Shintô* which, in the fifteenth century, through the agency of Yoshida Kanetomo, proclaimed: 'First the kami, then the Buddha', and with *Ise Shintô* or *Watarai Shintô* which rejected all relationship between kami and Buddhist gods.[27]

Shintô, in close relationship with most of the festivals observed by the Japanese people, with farming activities as with important events affecting everyday life, played its part in no small way in the formation of Japanese Buddhism from the time this was adopted by the common people; and it gave to it a particular character. In the same way it is very probable that Zen itself would not have been likely to take root in Japan if minds had not been trained for a long time by Shintô to an intuitive understanding of Nature and its mysteries, and if they had not been used to communicating with the divine without having recourse to dogmas or complicated rites. In this sense, it is even possible to state that conceptions of an aesthetic nature attributed solely to Zen, are in actual fact typically Japanese, and that they were only revealed by Zen. Indeed, Zen in Japan seems to us to be like a spiritualized form of Shintô more than a purely Buddhist sect.

CONFUCIANISM

With Buddhism (and perhaps even before it) a number of Chinese beliefs made their appearance in Japan, beliefs belonging to the philosophical systems of Confucius and Lao-Tzu. The study of the Chinese classics helped to spread Confucian and Taoïst concepts among the more lettered Japanese, concepts which had a profound enough influence on their lives to change them appreciably. The bakufu samurai themselves took examples of heroism from these classics (such as the *Analectes*) and from treatises on military history which laid down as a basic principle that 'World peace cannot be ensured except by force and might of arms.' Yoshitsune tried by every means in his power to obtain a secret treatise on military science entitled *Liu-t'ao*, in the possession of a learned nobleman, in order to learn the Chinese art of warfare.[28]

Commentators of the Song epoch, in particular Chu-Hsi (1130–1200), imparted a new vitality to Chinese Confucianism and, thanks to Chinese monks who came to Japan, the doctrines of Chu-Hsi's neo-Confucianism, which flourished throughout the Middle Ages, were to continue to do so still under the rule of the Tokugawa. Learning, 'Knowledge needing to implement Faith', was the first essential of right conduct. The Zen monks, almost in spite of themselves, were active propagators of Confucian ideas; these were adopted by the rich and idle classes as well as by the influential warriors of the Ashikagas' entourage. Many other Chinese beliefs (among them those connected with Taoïsm) had supporters in Japan, and the Zen monks saw in Lao-Tzu's outlook 'To act by doing nothing' a kind of parallel to their own 'absence of system'.

These various Chinese beliefs had also influenced Shintô and introduced into Japan, long ago, theories on dualism and divinatory practices in vogue at the Court. These were codified by the '*Yang* and *Yin* Bureau', the *Ommyôr-yô*, which also controlled astrological observances. At first confined to the aristocratic circles of Kyôto, these had finally influenced the commoners who conformed to customs whose meaning they did not understand because 'for the greater number, the feeling that was bound up with *Ommyô-dô* divinities (*yang* and *yin*) was mainly based on the fear of misfortune and the search after good fortune.'[29]

Although for greater clarity we have been obliged to deal with each sect or religion separately here, it must not be forgotten that in Japan, especially during the Middle Ages, syncretism was the rule everywhere, even in the case of the uncompromising Nichiren: no doctrine is altogether pure, no believer belongs exclusively to a single faith or a single doctrine. The most ardent Amadist will also be a believer in Shintô, the Zen monk will at the same time be a follower of Confucian concepts, and the common man will follow all the cults to a certain extent, although he claims to be an adherent of this one or that one. And even the most intolerant of Nichirenites will not fail to worship the kami. For the Japanese cannot conceive of one thing being good to the exclusion of all others. With deliberate irony, he will find that every dogma has its good qualities and its faults:

> Zen likes sweeping,
> Shingon cooks,
> Monto (Jôdo-Shinshû) delights in flowers
> As Hokke in offerings
> While Jôdo has neither rhyme nor reason,

declares an old proverb in *tanka* form, in caricature of the main sects.[30]

MONKS AND MONASTERIES

In spite of continual conflagrations, destruction, pillaging and many diverse catastrophes which spared neither houses, palaces, nor religious buildings, the erection of temples and monasteries went on ceaselessly throughout this period of violence and religious ardour. After the rebuilding of the Tôdai-ji, destroyed by fire in

13　Portrait of Hideyoshi, about 1580. Colour on silk, by an
unknown painter. Osaka Museum

14 Calligraphy by Ikkyû Shôjun (1394–1481). *Sumi-e* (indian ink)
on paper

1180, many monasteries were founded or rebuilt, and countless buildings set up in all the provinces under the patronage of various sects; in particular, the followers of Zen persuaded the Shôgun Ashikaga Takauji to build an *ankoku-ji* (temple for the peace of the country) and a pagoda in every province. The Tôfuku-ji monastery in Kyôto, founded in 1264 and burnt to the ground in 1334, was rebuilt during the Oei era (1394-1427), and all over the country new constructions bore witness to the spread of faith. These monasteries and temples, it must be added, were both vast complexes of buildings sheltering thousands of monks and small country shrines, the refuge of only one or two priests.

The greatest temples, in spite of the corruption of their monks and the quasi-secularization of many of them, were nevertheless venerated, and the efficacy of the prayers offered by the monks continued to be much appreciated. These prayers were often highly syncretic:

'Then Benkei knelt on the threshold, blew his conch with all his might and began to chant in an impressive manner, as he rolled between his fingers the beads of the rosary hanging from his neck:

' "By the Kami of the three shrines of Kumano, who are the greatest miracle workers in Japan,

' "By the eight great messengers of the *vajra* of Ômine,

' "By the hundred thousand guardians of the Law of Katsuragi,

' "By the seven great monasteries of Nara, and

' "By the eleven headed Kannon of Hase-dera,

' "By the Kami of Inari, Gion, Sumiyoshi, Kamo, Kasuga and of the seven great shrines of Mount Hiei:

' "Grant that Yoshitsune may come this way,

' "May the barrier-guards of Arachi win everlasting fame by capturing him,

' "And may the magnificence of their rewards reveal to them the powers of the monk Sanukibô of the monastery of Haguro!"

'The guards listened with respectful attention, fortunately unaware of the moving prayer that Benkei was offering silently: "Hear me, Great *Bodhisattva* Hachiman! Show thyself like the countless protectors of the Law and grant that Yoshitsune may reach Ôshû safe and sound!" '[31]

Temples and shrines being regarded as sacred, people believed that their destruction or profanation was a bad omen. In fact, if temples and monasteries were frequently invaded, destroyed and burnt down by the soldiery, Shintô shrines were often treated with much more respect. In times of unrest, artists and learned men sought refuge in temples and monasteries. Moreover, a number of them had become important centres, as much from an economic point of view – their possessions as a rule being vast – as from a political and even military one. The unsettled times had led many monasteries to recruit troops from their own *shôen* to protect them.

The monks themselves, under the pretext of defending the Buddhist Law, did not hesitate to don the corselet under the religious robe and to transform themselves into warriors. Before long every temple of any importance had soldier-monks in its service. The monasteries took advantage of this to wage merciless war among themselves. It was to put a stop to the almost permanent hostilities between the Enryaku-ji of Mount Hiei and the monasteries of the Nara sect that the lords of Kyôto had appealed to the warriors of the East. The monks of Mount Hiei proved to be exceedingly unruly; they did not hesitate to swoop down on Kyôto and threaten the Court there, so that the Emperor Shirakawa was in the habit of saying that the only three things he was unable to control were the dice in the game of *sugoroku*, the waters of the Kama river and the monks of Mount Hiei. An army of 3,000 monks and religious was said to live in this monastery. Opposing forces sought the alliance of these formidable fighters whose conduct, as portrayed in epic poems, romances and illuminated picture scrolls, was frequently far removed from the Buddhist ideal:

'The leader of the monks was a warrior called Kawatsura Hôgen (this last word is a title meaning "Eye of the Law"). Although a man of religion, he was clad like an ordinary warrior in a light-green loose jacket and *hakama*, crimson armour and a helmet with a three-piece neck-shield. He wore a new sword in his belt and arrows feathered with plumes from an eagle's tail placed in a quiver of twenty-four arrows fastened high on his hip.'[32]

Instead of a helmet, monks sometimes wore a piece of white fabric which fitted round the head and concealed the lower part of the face. At other times they wore over their armour a kind of long, loose smock of hempen cloth dyed black or dark brown with extract of cloves. Their heads were usually shaved, although some ascetics or *yamabushi* let their hair grow, which distinguished them from the ordinary warriors who shaved their heads to the shape of a half-moon above their forehead.[33] Their favourite weapon was the large halberd *naginata* with a long curved blade; but, like the rest of the warriors, they also used bows, arrows, swords and sometimes iron clubs. They hardly ever rode horseback unless, like Prince Morinaga, they were war lords. Their 'code' was modelled on that of the warriors and they committed suicide in the same way as these by cutting open the abdomen in the form of a cross.[34]

The monks of the Tendai and Shingon sects, or those of the Nara sects, were not the only ones with the warrior spirit. Among the adherents of Shinran, religious men called *shami* who had the right to marry, there were some who, like Rennyo (1415–99), leader of the Hongan-ji, attacked by the monks of Mount Hiei in 1465, roused all the followers of the Jôdo Shinshû in the provinces to rebellion. These men formed independent communities determined to defend themselves both against attacks from the monks of other sects and against the lords who claimed to hold rights over their territories. These *ikko ikki* or 'bands of disciples with a single mind', as their adversaries called them, stirred up a number of armed rebellions in the country districts throughout the sixteenth century. Entrenched in the Ishiyama Hongan-ji (Osaka), they did not finally surrender until 1580. But in the meantime, in 1571, Nobunaga, provoked by the behaviour of the monks of Mount Hiei, had razed their monasteries to the ground and slaughtered all those who lived on 'the mountain'. It was the end of the warrior-monks. Thenceforward religious bodies no longer interfered in political and military matters, at least by taking up arms:

> In all Mount Hiei's buildings, great and small,
> The Law had been dishonoured;
> How sad to see the triple scourge of fire, sword
>   and death
>
> Send them swirling skyward in smoke.
> Even the waters of the lake (Lake Biwa) which
>   laves the eighty-four provinces
>
> Grew warm;
> The once hot ash and embers of three thousand
>   temples
> Are now cold[35]

THE BEGINNINGS OF CHRISTIANITY

About 1545 Portuguese traders accompanied by Jesuit missionaries began to arrive in Kyûshû, alerted by men who, shipwrecked there in 1534, had introduced fire-arms into the country before returning to China. The *daimyô* welcomed these foreigners most affably for they brought them many novelties, and their only reason for coming to Japan seemed to be to trade and to preach the Gospel. In the minds of the Japanese of this era these two activities seemed to be bound up with the 'barbarians of the south'. They deemed it good policy, therefore, to accept the religion in order to derive profit from the trade. The traditional religious tolerance of the Japanese(Nichiren's intransigence apart, which is only the exception that proves the rule), inclined them to look favourably on the new doctrines offered by these men in black.

Francis Xavier landed in their wake in 1549 and was equally well received, not only in Kagoshima by the *daimyô* of Satsuma, but also in Hirado and Yamaguchi, in the *daimyô* of Ouchi's castle. In Kyôto, however, he could see no one in authority, the Shôgun being away and the Emperor in seclusion. He returned, therefore, to the south of Japan and, after more than a two-year stay, went back to Goa, taking with him some Japanese converts. Then, at the same time as the traders, Jesuit missionaries landed in ever-growing numbers and began their work of conversion. Although these first missionaries had some successes, before long they came up against the opposition of the religious of the Hokke (a Nichirenite sect) and the Zen monks. Trade with the foreigners was highly profitable for the *daimyô* of the provinces where the Portuguese landed; it procured them those fire-arms which the feudal lords, always warring, so badly needed.

At first Christianity was accepted as being part and parcel of foreign civilization, like the religion which had come from India and which the Japanese in those days called by the name of its country, Tenjiku-shû. 'The success of the missionary work was partly due to the new life these champions of the counter-reformation infused into the Gospel they brought with them, but also to the warm welcome given to foreign goods imported by the Portuguese traders who accompanied the missionaries,' says Anesaki Masaharu.[36] Certain aspects of the new religion, although accepted, nevertheless offended the deepest feelings of the Japanese: original sin, the celibacy of the priests, the oneness of an all-powerful God able to give orders to emperors, all these features, to quote only the most characteristic, very quickly resulted in the Japanese mistrusting a 'strange' religion which it behoved them not to encourage too much. After a warm welcome there appeared an ill-concealed reticence.

Yet, many Japanese were converted, Christian mysticism providing them with something new. Oda Nobunaga welcomed Catholic priests graciously – even befriended them. In less than ten years, more than eighty-four Jesuit Fathers reached Japan, the number of their faithful being at that time nearly 150,000. Two hundred churches had been built.[37] Perhaps Nobunaga thought favouring the Christians would check the intrigues of the Buddhist monasteries. Some of Nobunaga's sons embraced the new religion. But although Hideyoshi, after Nobunaga's assassination, had not declared himself openly against Christianity, he was chagrined to see his vassals giving their allegiance to a foreign power, the Papacy, of whose nature he could form no idea. He also feared the Spanish fleet anchored off Manila. In 1587, dissensions between the Portuguese Jesuits and Spanish Franciscans furnished him with an excuse to prohibit the work of the missionaries. And in 1591, in reply to a letter from the Viceroy of Goa, he stated:

'A few years ago, the so-called Fathers came to my country seeking to bewitch our men and women, both lay and religious. On this occasion they were punished, and they will be so again, if they return to our lands to preach their faith. Whatever their sects or denominations, they will be wiped out. It will be too late then to be sorry. If you have any wish to establish friendly relations with this country, the seas are free from the threat of pirates and traders have permission to come and go as they will. Bear this in mind. . . .'[38]

Nevertheless, Hideyoshi did not take any serious steps to enforce this edict and the missionaries, in hiding in the homes of their flock, pursued their work of spreading the Gospel in secret. While foreign trade was encouraged, conversions were discouraged. In 1596 the fervour of the Franciscan missionaries was to bring matters to a head, together with the business of the *San Felipe*, a Spanish galleon whose sailors, somewhat exasperated, threatened to appeal to the might of Spain. Hideyoshi, perhaps fearing an invasion and convinced that the missionaries were spies, therefore had thirty-six of them, mostly Franciscans, crucified. Portuguese Jesuits probably had a hand in the business.

But, when Hideyoshi died in 1598, persecution stopped abruptly and the Christian priests went on with their preaching, mainly at night, going from house to house. In 1605 the number of converts rose to nearly 750,000, an enormous figure in those days, representing practically 4 per cent of the population of Japan. Dominicans and Augustins had arrived to participate in this missionary zeal. The arrival of Dutch and English ships (enemies of the Papacy), whose aims were purely commercial, further aggravated the situation. The Christians were denounced as Papists by the new arrivals, who were obviously trying to eliminate Spanish and Portuguese trade for their own profit. It was left to Ieyasu to banish all the missionaries in 1614, the Christians having been accused of conspiring with foreign powers. Ieyasu, it must be added, treated one of the Nichirenite sects in the same way. But one is at liberty to think that the main reason for the failure of Christianity in Japan was the absolute incompatibility between Christian teaching and the Shintô way of thinking. The other reasons were purely incidental.

CHAPTER IX

THE SPIRIT OF MEDIEVAL JAPAN

JAPANESE CULTURE

It might be tempting to think that the advent of the uncultured warrior society of Kamakura, then the struggles which followed the setting up of the Muromachi bakufu, would result in the brilliant culture of the Heian era being engulfed in the general chaos. However, if political events and the hazards of war brought about profound and lasting social and economic changes, the spirit of Japan, all that constitutes what is now known as *bunka*, Japanese 'culture', survived these vicissitudes at the same time being influenced by disorders which affected the life of the whole country. The refined elegance, the affectation, and in a word, the decadence which characterized society during the latter part of the Fujiwara epoch could, without doubt, have led to the impoverishment of the arts and of the spirit, to a real decadence. Under the influence of Kyôto's aristocracy, the strength of purpose and the simplicity of manners of the new rulers of the country were soon to undergo a transformation.

In actual fact, far from vanishing amid the turmoil, the culture of the Heian era received on the contrary an impetus which enabled it to develop afresh instead of being lost for ever in a sterile conservatism. After a brief period of stagnation, the spirit re-established itself, and in Kyôto particularly, was given new life by contact with the 'eastern barbarians'. Then a new spirit began to develop, less superficial, more heroic, something of a contrast to the effeminacy of the preceding epoch. There was a return to fundamentals, an attempt to go back to the beginnings of purely Japanese concepts, and the marvellous Nara epoch (marvellous because endowed with the glamour of ancient things) then serves as a model. Thus, throughout the Kamakura period the Heian spirit was transformed, became, as it were, more virile. The warriors once more repaired to the capital. Coming into contact with the court nobility, their still untutored minds mellowed, became more perceptive and, with the help of luxury, underwent almost a conversion. On the one hand, therefore, a democratization of culture occurred and, on the other, an ennoblement of the samurai spirit. Then the authority of the new religious sects and the influence of their monks was all prevailing.

If certain art forms which had originated in Kyôto, continued to be cultivated with a new energy, aesthetic forms were none the less also created. The cult of pure sensibility, the *mono-no-aware*,[1] dear to the nobles of the capital, changed; it found its fulfilment in artistic forms as seemingly different as poetry, drama, the tea-ceremony or the way of flowers. While formerly religion was the well-spring of all the arts it was now, in the words of G. B. Sansom, only 'their foster mother'.[2] In times of disruption, artists and men of letters had found refuge in the monasteries but, now that Zen was rejecting the Scriptures, their works turned more towards Nature than towards esoterism and there was a great temptation to imitate Chinese masters. Like them, and principally at the instigation of Zen masters, the Japanese turned to descriptive rather than imaginative forms, as much in the sphere of art as in that of literature. In brief, artists had learnt to see and this faculty was going to enable their minds to free themselves from abstract rituals in order to formulate 'visual' codes.

'If the eye is clear, it functions quickly. If the vision is keen, the one who sees is freed from doubt. Doubt engenders thought; thought clouds the vision. To face a thing is to see clearly. If we see clearly we do not hesitate for one second. Thus, seeing is believing. We believe because we see clearly. The revelation of the reality of the thing leads to belief in this thing. . . .'[3]

Thus were born the contemplative arts, whose inner meaning sometimes eludes us, but whose beauty, if we do not always understand it, cannot fail to move us.

It is difficult to define the concept of art as the Japanese of this epoch understood it, unless by the word *yûgen* which could be approximately translated by the phrase 'profound beauty'. This *yûgen* is something which is not subject to change but is, on the contrary, what is at the heart of all things, eternal, universal. It is an aesthetic sentiment which transcends the shape of things in order to find their hidden meaning:[4]

> 'The essence of *yûgen* lies in the true quality of beauty and graciousness. . . The *yûgen* of a discourse resides in the charm of speech and in the complete mastery of the spoken word . . . so that the most ordinary of the phrases uttered will be pleasing. With regard to music, a melody can be said to be *yûgen* when it flows magnificently and when the sounds seem sweet to the ear. There is *yûgen* in dancing when its discipline has been completely mastered and when the audience is enthralled by the beauty of the dancer's movements and by his look of serenity.'[5]

This epoch of such contradictory tendencies, which witnessed the triumph of a refined aestheticism, was lacking in neither grandeur nor lapses of taste. If, at the beginning of the Kamakura era, life seemed rather too 'utilitarian' and dull, with the return of prosperity it was not long before extravagance was the rule. And the last of the Hôjô regents, whom we have already seen finding enjoyment in watching dog-fights, did not hesitate to summon companies of actors and musicians to Kyôto. The Ashikaga shôgun themselves staged great festivals. Oda Nobunaga, after his victories, gave free rein to his extravagant tastes. Hideyoshi organized gorgeous festivals like the prodigious *hanami* (flower viewing) of March 15, 1598, held at the Daigo-ji in Fushimi near Kyôto, attended by all the *daimyô* in Japan, and which is still famous. Certainly these great festivals originated from the desire to shine, but also from the need to see and to see into: to see things, the blossoming of spring, a pottery bowl, a trifle, but by reaching beyond the tangible form, by seeing clearly into the nature of the thing. The *bunka* of the Middle Ages, contrary to that of the Heian period, based entirely on a contrived emotion and thereby rather artificial, sought to understand Nature intuitively, to become one with her, to see the true beauty hidden beneath the surface of things. To achieve this, man must conform to rules, to a law. And it is in the strict observance of this law that he can attain to complete freedom, for this law (the way of flowers, of tea, of *Nô*) transcends the individual. And, according to the aesthetes of medieval Japan, perfect freedom can only be found by observing a law perfectly. This basic conception determined not only the evolution of art and literature but that of Japanese society in its entirety.

MUSIC, DANCE, THEATRE

There were few festivals or gatherings, however modest, without a musical accompaniment. The Japanese people, artistic by nature, because sensitive, found it quite natural to express the feelings stirring within them through the medium of a flute, a *biwa* or a *koto*. There were social gatherings whenever an opportunity presented itself for making music and for singing. Certain instruments were reserved for the exclusive use of women, others for men. The flute for instance was accounted a typically masculine instrument and women did not learn to play it. Yoshitsune's wife, disguised as a page, was in the utmost confusion when some monks asked her to play the flute, believing her to be a young man.[6] The Japanese had a great regard for musical instruments:

> 'Then he gave her a heap of precious things, in particular a fine drum of sandal-wood, with a sheepskin cover and multicoloured cords.
>
> ' "I value this instrument highly," said Yoshitsune. "During the reign of the ex-emperor Shirakawa a monk of the temple of Hôjû-ji brought back from China two rare treasures, a *biwa* called Meigyoku and this drum known as Hatsune. Meigyoku was kept in the imperial palace until it was burnt down, during the Hôgen war. . . . Hatsune was given to Taira-no-Masamori, governor of Sanuki, who took great care of it. After Masamori's death Tadamori inherited it. . . . I meant to keep it always but I want you to take it, now that the end has come." '[7]

Things of great value like swords, musical instruments and tea cups, were given names, just as in our medieval historical romances we see gallant knights endowing their swords or their hunting horns with a personality. A musical instrument was like a living person, creative, the sound being the very essence of life. It was as essential for a samurai of high standing to be able to play at least one instrument (the flute) as to know how to compose a poem. On every occasion, and especially during festivals, profane and religious, there was dancing to music. Troubadour monks (*biwa-hôshi*) travelled the roads of medieval Japan in every direction, singing gestes like the *Heike Monogatari*, or accompanying themselves on the *biwa*, a kind of lute with four or five strings. Other instruments used were the *koto*, a great wooden zither modelled on the Chinese *kin*,

10 Shizuka-no-Gozen, mistress of Yoshitsune and famous dancer
Drawing by Kikuchi Yôsai (1788–1878)

with thirteen strings of equal tension which movable bridges
allowed of tuning according to the required mode, many kinds of
flutes, straight, cross, fipple (one of them, the *shakuhachi*, was
introduced from China in 1335[8]), and tambourines and a variety
of drums.

The *Gikeiki* has left us an excellent description of an orchestra
improvising to accompany Shizuka's dance; she was Yoshitsune's
mistress, one of the finest dancers in Japan at that time:

The three musicians withdrew to get ready for this ceremony and reappeared one by one. Suketsune . . . was carrying a sandal-wood drum covered with sheepskin, hung with six cords . . . Then Kajiwara made his appearance. . . . He began to accompany the drum with a sound like a chirruping insect, using a gong hanging from a multicoloured cord and decorated with golden chrysanthemums. . . . Hatakeyama took "Pine-breezes", his long bamboo flute. . . . A splendid orchestra, judged Yorimoto from behind the screen.'[9]

The *Taiheiki* tells us that towards the end of the Kamakura era at Kyôto the dance known as *dengaku* was exceedingly popular with men and that this entertainment had an enthusiastic following in high and low classes alike.[10]

Japanese scales were composed of five notes. They came on the scene, according to Noël Peri[11] towards the thirteenth or fourteenth century, adapted from Chinese scales called *ritsu* and *ryo*. The intervals between the notes were very unequal and we find at least three types of scales whose intervals corresponded more or less to those of the European scales of F sharp minor, B minor and E minor.[12] The 'variable' notes were obtained by altering the tension of the strings by finger pressure or, in the case of the flute, by changing the position of the lips on the mouth-piece. As a rule Japanese music was made to emphasize a song so the interval differences between the notes, however displeasing they may be to Western ears, flow quite smoothly. Court music probably came from Korea. We do not know the origin of popular music.

The musicians, who were generally priests, nobles or samurai, were members of the highest classes; from the fourteenth century on, they formed kinds of confraternities which 'secularized' religious music. They shaved their heads as monks did. Strolling companies came into being as a form of entertainment given in the houses of nobles, great warriors and *daimyô*. These musicians accompanied one or several female dancers (*shirabyôshi*) who also chanted poems called *imayô* or *saibara*. There were other kinds of more popularly inspired dance music, like *sarugaku* and *dengaku*. Entertainments where poetry, dancing and music blended harmoniously, and which the aristocrats of the fourteenth century appreciated keenly, gave rise to a drama form set to rule which was called *Dengaku-no-Nô*, or more simply *Nô*.

Stage dances originated in the rustic peasant dances usually performed when the rice seedlings were planted out to ward off evil spirits. When these dances were adopted by the shrines, their actors put on magnificent costumes and texts were assigned to them which they had to recite in ritual fashion, chanting in time with the beating of the drums. *Sarugaku-no-Nô* companies (*Nô* means roughly Art, Ability) attached to the great shrines acquired a reputation which varied according to the quality of their actors. The troop attached to the Kasuga-Jinja at Nara was, at the end of the Kamakura epoch, very highly rated; its actors perfected the *Sarugaku-no-Nô* and the *Dengaku-no-Nô* by giving them rules. We have already seen that art in Japan cannot be left to the whim of the individual, but must conform to certain canons. Art consists above all in making the feelings of the interpreter and the spectator thrill in unison, within a fixed framework. In this way, in every kind of Japanese art, the state of mind of the person who looks or listens is every bit as important as whatever is represented.

'Among those who watch a *Nô* performance [wrote Ze-ami in 1420], connoisseurs see it with their mind, while those who have not learned see it with their eyes. What the mind perceives is the essence; what the eye sees is the representation. . . . There can be no true representation without this inner meaning. The connoisseur understands that the representation lies in the inner meaning and is not a thing apart. . . . He understands Nô.[13]

The theme of the entertainment and the actor's personality counted for little. In order to symbolize the personnages of the drama, the leading actors wore masks.

It remained for Kan-ami, a Shintô priest and his son Ze-ami (1363–1443 or 1445) to discover the laws and formulate the rules, still unchanged, of this form of drama. Already in 1349 'polished' performances of *Dengaku-no-Nô* were very much in vogue. That year the Shôgun Ashikaga Takauji had put on a magnificent performance to help finance the building of a bridge. Several thousands attended it, from the regent to the humblest citizen. The stage was draped with green and crimson fabrics. It was decorated with tiger and panther skins imported from China and hangings of gold brocade. The air was fragrant with incense. Two companies of actors were competing against one another, each actor being sumptuously dressed, powdered and painted, and with blackened teeth. *Sarugaku* actors leapt and twirled. The spectators were so carried away with excitement that the stamping of their feet, to manifest their delight, resulted in the stands collapsing. Panic ensued, robbers took advantage of it and swords were drawn from their scabbards. The celebration ended in bloodshed.[14]

The Shôgun Yoshimitsu, a great amateur of *Nô* and who delighted in watching the dance movements of young men on the stage (women taking no part in theatrical performances), encouraged the production of these shows; actors formed themselves into family guilds known as *za*. Five schools of *Nô* developed at that time: Kanze (founded by Ze-ami and his father), Komparu, Hôshô, Kongô and Kita. The Shôgun made these entertainments a pretext for magnificent festivals sometimes lasting a week. At times the shows were staged with unparalleled extravagance. When, in 1568, to thank him for his military support, the Shôgun Yoshiaki invited Nobunaga to a great performance of *Nô* which was to comprise thirteen acts, Nobunaga, sickened by this display of wealth while the country was still suffering the effects of war, left the theatre after the fifth act.[15]

The passion for *Nô* spreading to the provinces, great families took care that it should not tempt the young lords to spend too much money. The House Law of the Asakura (*Asakura Toshikage Jûshichikajô*) states in article 5: 'Actors of the Komparu, Kanze, Hôshô and Kita schools of *Nô* are not to be summoned frequently from Kyôto for performances. The money intended for this kind of venture is to be assigned to the training of young dancers of the region and for the permanent benefit of the latter.' Article 6 adds: 'Performances will not be permitted in the castle at night-time.'[16] These laws led to the increase of *Nô* companies in the provinces and to the spread of certain popular forms of drama and dance.

At the beginning of the sixteenth century, *Nô* was still the prerogative of a few aristocratic families The actors, warmly applauded, were the pride of the families under whose patronage they were. They were richly rewarded at each performance, mainly by gifts of clothing:

'When these dancers took part in a festival, the lay monk of Sagami and his close relatives and captains took off their robes and their breeches (the upper ones) and tossed them to the actors, none of them wishing to be outdone (in generosity). The garments were piled up mountain high and in this way no one can tell how many thousands and dozens of thousands (of coins) they had spent.'[17]

ACCOMPLISHMENTS

The polite attainments of this epoch, like the dramatic arts, had some of the characteristics of the *yügen* concept of beauty and of the meaning of *wabi* or 'restrained expression'. From the middle of the fourteenth century, one of the most popular pastimes consisted in a gathering of aesthetes for the *cha-no-yu* or tea-ceremony. These meetings, when one drank tea, also gave the samurai and the aristocrats of Kyôto, an opportunity for admiring works of art – especially porcelain – newly arrived from China and with which the lords of that era were infatuated. But, thanks to the Zen monk Jukô (1422–1502) and his followers Joô (1503–55) and Rikyû (1521–91), the tea-ceremony was soon given strict rules: it became an art, in the Japanese meaning of the word.

Special pavilions were built in the gardens of mansions in order to preserve the intimate and peaceful atmosphere essential to the celebration of this ceremony. These *chashitsu*, whose rustic style was inspired by *wabi*, in their turn soon had their own specially designed private gardens. The tea-house, which was extremely simple, consisted of just one small room, originally of four and half *tatami*, but in which each item had been chosen with extreme care. The whole arrangement had to reflect the tranquility favourable to meditation, to allow the mind to seek relaxation far from the restlessness of life, to recollect itself. 'Tea-rooms' were taken into account in the general lay-out of the plan of some great mansions and castles: the simplicity of these rooms was a contrast to the opulence of the rest of the dwelling. The modesty of this rustic style of architecture pleased many of the nobles who, under Zen influence, were enamoured of simplicity. They took it into their heads to build mansions modelled on these *chasitsu*: whence the *Sukiya* style which, by developing and adjusting itself to *Shoin* architecture, led to the style called 'Grand *Shoin*' which was immensely popular, especially in the seventeenth century.

The ceremony itself was taken very seriously, every movement which the host and his guests had to make following strict rules, a prescribed form of etiquette which none might infringe under pain

223

of being pronounced boorish and being excluded from the company. Every *chasitsu* was embellished by a *tokonoma* where a precious vase, a painting or a bouquet of flowers was displayed. To drink tea here was a way of recollecting oneself and appreciating things that were simple and elegant, rather than a way of quenching one's thirst. And the style ultimately codified by Rikyu, Hideyoshi's tea-master friend (who in 1591 committed suicide by his order, for having displeased him), is still followed today in minutest detail. All the same, just like the theatre, this tea-ceremony became a costly pastime. It finally led to great festivals such as the one Hideyoshi, then at the pinnacle of his renown, organized in the pine woods of Kitano-Ten-mangû at Kyôto in 1587; this was an immense and sumptuous tea-ceremony to which everyone from the highest to the lowest was invited, each guest having to bring a kettle, a tea cup and a mat to sit on. At this time, the refined art of the fifteenth century, perfected under the patronage of the Ashikaga Shôgun, was beginning to decline.

Concurrently with the spread of the art of tea-drinking, *kadô*, the way of flowers, blossomed. The art of *ikebana* (flower arrangement) was nothing new but it was regarded as a pleasant pastime or an act of adoration rather than a real art. The bouquets arranged according to certain principles were mainly used as offerings on Buddhist altars. The technique known as *rikka* was then codified for the decoration of *tokonoma* in palaces and tea-houses. In the fifteenth century, Ikenobô Jukei created in Kyôto a new style of flower arrangement based on Confucian concepts symbolizing Sky, Earth and Man (*tenchijin*), a style called *nageire* or again *seika*. But floral art did not come into its own until the seventeenth century, when a number of schools were founded and when *Kadô* began to form part of the education of women in nearly all classes of Japanese society.

Other accomplishments, intended to encourage gatherings of people with artistic tastes in common, consisted in distinguishing one incense perfume from another, in comparing shells or iris bulbs. The art of calligraphy, so highly prized during the Heian period, had by no means lost its hold: it was practised in writing letters and especially poems or maxims at that time regarded as works of art. A variety of pastimes, less artistic although still imbued with aesthetic feeling, were in vogue: such as poem card games, *sugoroku* (a kind of backgammon), *shôgi* (a game of chess in the Chinese style) or *igo* (now just called *go*) for which they used a great chess-

11　The game of *gicchô*　*Drawing by Kikuchi Yôsai (1788–1878)*

board on which the players move the pawns in an attempt to surround their opponents' pieces.[18]

Among open-air amusements were horse-racing, bouts of *sumô* (a ritual contest), a kind of polo (*dakyû*) and a game of pall-mall (*gicchô*) mainly played on New Year's Day. Nobles and commoners alike delighted in watching these games and in betting on cock fights (*tori-awase*) or on boat races. In winter, snowball fights were very popular with both old and young. But one of the nobles' favourite sports was *kemari*, a game similar to football in which the ball must not touch the ground before reaching the goal, the use of the hands not being allowed. The commoners had little in the way of amusement, but they took part in ritual festivals (*matsuri*) and sometimes they watched races or archery contests organized by the Samurai and nobles. The kite game resulted in spectacular contests of *tako*, the tails being fitted with sharp blades meant to cut the cord of the opponent's kites.

SCULPTURE AND PAINTING

If, in the political sphere, there was a clear-cut division between the period of the Fujiwaras and the Kamakura period, Yoritomo's advent to the shôgunate had no immediate effect upon art, which continued to develop in accordance with the aristocratic and religious traditions of the previous centuries. Nevertheless, the resumption of relations with Song China led to the appearance of many new styles in Japan. Although Buddhism at that time experienced a kind of rebirth, a restoration more than anything else, the new sects, without being aniconic, were of a practical and simple character so they did not look kindly on representations of the gods. These continued to be sculptured or painted by artists supported by the Tendai and Shingon sects. The tendency being towards portraiture, as during the Nara period, idols lost something of their mystery and became more human, sculptors taking it into hte aeridsh to inlay the eyes of their creations with glass or painted crystals in order to give them more life, a technique known as *gyokugan*.

Two tendencies made their appearance then, one of Chinese inspiration, primarily Buddhist, the other, more popular, showing a return to the realistic style of the Nara epoch (eighth century). This last trend was to raise the realistic works of Unkei and the sculptors of his school to the pinnacle of art. Divinities, prominent Chinese personalities, monks, *daimyô*, kami or animals were then sculptured from nature, came to life, The works of this period and school can be numbered among the most priceless masterpieces in the world. The first, more traditional trend, represented by the En-Pa (or *Shijô*) school, led to the over ornamentation of statuary and to a kind of coarsening of the forms used previously. This period witnessed the beginning of decadence in Japanese sculpture. The popularization of Zen, a doctrine which rejected the Scriptures and conceded little importance to representations of the gods, Amidism whose pantheon was reduced to images of Buddha and his two acolytes, and Nichirenism, were so many more factors against the success of sculpture. From the Muromachi period onwards, apart from the work of a few sculptors of *Nô* masks, Japan virtually ceased to produce sculptures of any value.

The same tendencies are shown in painting, with this difference that, replacing sculpture and benefiting from the demand for ornamentation shown by the new leisured classes as from the ceaseless Chinese contributions, it developed without a break and initiated various genres to meet the mood of the time. During the Kamakura epoch, painting, following the example of works brought back from China, achieved with the art of portraiture (*chinsô*, portraits of clergy, portraits of nobles or of samurai) a realism modified by formalism, a realism which did not become complete until the following period. As for religious painting, it followed the

226

style of the painters of the Song dynasty or 'vitalized' the works of the end of the Heian epoch, by humanizing divinities and by giving them animation. But towards the end of the period the abuse of gold-leaf and of pictorial methods led to a certain decadence of style which became conventional and spiritless.

On the other hand, the illuminated picture scrolls or *emakimono* dating from this period show as great a diversity of styles as subjects. These *emakimono*, popular as they were, were often designed and used by the clergy for instructing the faithful, and portrayed not only aristocratic scenes but also, for the first time, scenes of everyday life and of the warriors' lives. Military subjects, lives of famous monks as well as literary and religious subjects were then handled with charm and liveliness, frequently with humour, in *sumi-e* (indian ink washes) or in colour. The fashion for these illuminated scrolls faded during the Muromachi period to give place to that of the *kakemono* or hanging pictures, in imitation of paintings of the Chinese Song and Yüan dynasties.

During the Muromachi period, the shôgun's wealth, of which Zen monks approved, led to a kind of secularization of painting. Japanese painters visited China and brought back numerous styles: the art of *suiboku* (Indian water ink), inspired by that of Chinese painters, is devoted to the representation of landscapes or to the detailed observation of Nature. The paintings were very often accompanied by beautifully and ornamentally written poems, known as *shi-jiku*. This kind of painting, like religious portraiture, was held in high esteem in Zen monasteries. Most of the artists at that time were either monks or painters attached to temples. Sesshû (1420–1506) was one of the most prolific artists of his day; he left us not only illuminated scrolls but also standing screens and *kakemono*, marvels of concision and wit, whose subjects drawn in simple lines soon became typically Japanese.

Almost at the same time, other schools developed which, during the following periods, were to assume considerable importance. A warrior, called Kanô Masanobu (1434–1530), introduced a truly Japanese style, different from Sesshû's, and his son added colour, at that time typical of the *Yamato-e* school, which until then had limited the talents of its painters to the illustration of *emakimono*. But it was Kanô Eitoku above all who, at the end of the sixteenth century, created the true style of the Kanô school. Japanese painting did not acquire its patent of nobility until the sixteenth century, when it became truly resplendent with colour. While the art of the Muromachi attempted to symbolize Nature, that of the Momoyama period (or of the Dictators) tried to reproduce her in minutest detail and as gorgeously as possible. Castle walls and *fusuma* had to be embellished to satisfy the 'nouveau-riche' tastes of the lords of the time. Decoration became merely a profusion of flowers, birds, animals, and landscapes on golden backgrounds. The castle Nobunaga had built for him at Azuchi was lavishly decorated, on five floors, with paintings executed by Kanô Eitoku and his pupils. The epoch was one of splendour, which did not prevent many paintings also being executed in the Chinese manner (in *suiboku*). Nevertheless, more classical styles persisted in Kyôto and the provinces; painting more or less inspired by that of sixteenth-century Europe began to develop in Kyûshû through contact with foreign missionaries. These *nambanbyôbu* (the folding screens of the southern barbarians) had practically no influence on Japanese painting, the foreigners' stay when all is said and done having been of short duration. On the other hand, a style of painting came into being which accurately portrayed the various strata of society and which delighted the class of newly rich merchants.

The combined artistic production of medieval Japan, apart from that of the *emakimono*, was none the less essentially aristocratic. At the end of the sixteenth century, however, a slight tendency towards the democratization of art appeared. The schools became varied. But the Momoyama was the most magnificent period in Japanese painting, during which, in Kondo Ichitarô's apt words, 'the glorious, ambitious, brilliant, vigorous expressions of the power of the spirit, were rediscovered in art'.[19]

LITERATURE AND POETRY

Period of transition, period of formation, the time of the samurai (which actually starting with the advent of a militarist government at Kamakura, continued until 1868, but after 1603 took on a permanent complexion which turned the samurai into the ruling and administrative class) witnessed a transformation in literature at the same time as in society and the arts. Literature, usually considered the reflection of an epoch and a people, nevertheless only provides us with what the aristocrats, the samurai and the monks contributed to it. Although the education of the people

228

became more widespread, the lower orders still only followed their rulers. All the same, two main trends can be detected in the literary spirit of medieval Japan: one, somewhat decadent and aristocratic, retained the characteristics of the romantic literature of the previous epoch; the other, new and more vigorous, was an expression of the two major preoccupations of the period, religion and the cult of heroism.

The written language itself evolved: the study of Chinese, although not entirely abandoned, became the prerogative of a minority of men of letters. Whereas during the Heian period Chinese was used solely in aristocratic circles, from the twelfth century the written language became a compound. A number of Chinese words were added to purely Japanese phonemes, while grammar remained indigenous. While in the tenth century only women wrote in Japanese – and with what felicity at times! – from the thirteenth century onwards Sino–Japanese was used by all who wrote which, contrary to what might have been expected from a popularization of culture, simplified neither the language nor its written expression.

The return of the 'golden age' of the Nara epoch, in religion (renewal of Kegon and Ritsu sects) as in sculpture (realism), was revealed in literature by a certain interest in the past: ancient forms were copied and the 'gestes' drew their material from the history of the clans. It was no longer the nobles alone who devoted themselves to literary exercises but monks and warriors also. Romantic works, chiefly inspired by Lady Murasaki Shikibu's celebrated *Tale of Genji*, with its time-worn amorous intrigues, were from the thirteenth century on replaced by the *gunki-monogatari*, heroic tales of warfare in which the spirit of the samurai was glorified, and by *otogi-zôshi*, tales of imagination. These, often heroic, chanted by troubadours or on theatre stages, were sometimes known as *mai-no-sôshi* (dance narratives) or *kowakamai*. Purely historical narratives (*rekishi-monogatari*) were popular everywhere, as were Buddhist stories, moral anecdotes which served to illustrate religious teachings.

The sense of the transitoriness of all worldly things, the feeling that the world was entering an era of degeneracy of the law (*mappô*), resignation before a state of affairs that one is powerless to change, inspired the monks to write popular essays wherein they described life's struggles, the lives of the 'saints', Buddhist paradises and hells.

The terms they used were simple and forceful, devoid of the intellectual witticisms or literary allusions which abound in the classical romances:

> 'The country people, writes Shinran, do not know the meaning of the characters and are extremely slow witted. Consequently, I have written the same thing over and over again so as to help them to understand. Educated persons will think that this is strange and no doubt they will make fun of me. But I do not care about their opinion, for I have written with the intention of making my meaning clear to stupid people.'

There were, of course, other literary genres, such as the *nikki* or intimate diaries, and the *kikô* (travel note books) but, in works of this kind, few achieve as consummate an art as those of the classical period. As for philosophical writings, little in number, they form the rearguard of those of the Heian period. The *Tsurezuregusa* ('Idle Thoughts') remains the best of these essays.

At the time of the Ashikaga shôgun, under the influence of Zen masters, there was a tendency in literature, as in painting, towards imitation of the Chinese; but this was little more than a fashion and, after 1400, Zen monks turned their abilities mainly to historical or philosophical studies. Plays (*Nô*) began to be written, the majority drawing upon history for their theme, through more or less lyrical poems that were already known. As for poetry, which continued to be a form of literature which every educated man was expected to discuss intelligently, it scarcely departed from the forms, nor the style so patiently elaborated during preceding centuries, and remained dependent to a great extent upon private or imperial anthologies. The nobles used to write their poems in note books which were handed down from father to son: 'I wrote these notes in the little poetry books written and preserved from generation to generation, I chose the best of them and, setting them in order, I forwarded them to the Councillor . . .' says Lady Abutsu-ni in her *Izayoi Nikki*.[21] The most famous texts were learned by heart, whence the extreme difficulty in understanding the most trifling *tanka* (a poem of thirty-one syllables – 5, 7, 5, 7 and 7) if one is unacquainted with both the poems of the innumerable Japanese anthologies and the Chinese classics.

Romance, travel diaries, notes and essays are sprinkled with poems, drama handbooks are full of them; they formed to some extent part of everyday life, and developed into a game in the course of which a number of friends vied with one another in wit – and memory. Poetry became virtually a social duty. The man who was not moved by it was unworthy. The fiercest of samurai, however limited his education (and he owed it to himself to acquire some so that he could pride himself on it), had to be incapable of remaining insensible to the charm of a few well-turned lines, of an elegantly worded thought.

The *Taiheiki* relates the story of a nobleman who, about to be put to the torture, was saved *in extremis* by the farewell verse he wrote for the occasion:

> 'The Lord Tameakira asked for an ink-stone; and they gave him one with some paper, thinking to themselves that he wished to write a confession. However, it was not a confession he wrote, but a poem saying:
>
> > It is beyond my belief!
> > I am questioned not on the art of poetry
> > But on the things of this transient world!'

Tokiwa, governor of Suruga, was struck with admiration at this and bowed before Tameakira's nobility of mind. So did the two messengers from the east (Kamakura) whose eyes filled with tears when they read this. Thus Tameakira escaped torture and was judged innocent.

The art of poetry mattered little to the military for theirs was the 'Way of the Bow and the Horse', while the court delighted in Chinese and Japanese verses. Nevertheless, because it is in the nature of things that one action affects another, a single poem rescinded Tameakira's sentence and softened the hearts of the eastern barbarians. Therefore, it is not without justification that Kino Tsurayuki wrote in his preface to the *Kokinshû* (in 905): 'Poetry has effortless dominion over heaven and earth and fills both the invisible gods and demons with compassion. Poetry brings harmony between man and woman; it "soothes the savage breast" of the warrior.'[22]

But anything indulged in too freely is harmful. For lack of inspiration the poets, innovators in other days, turned their art into a profession. Son succeeded father as poet, disciple succeeded master and schools were formed, all second rate. Having become hereditary, poetry also became sterile in form as in meaning. Great lords and monks shared the privilege of 'making poetry'. But from the end of the fourteenth century the common people, weary of these arid exercises, began to bestow its favours on new genres, religious hymns (*wasan*) or popular ballads from which *Nô* texts drew inspiration. At the same time a kind of poetic game or *renga* was initiated in which several poets improvised in turn *tanka* parts of seventeen or fourteen syllables, to produce 'linked verse'. The *Haiku*, a short poem of seventeen syllables, immortalized by Bashô in the seventeenth century, was born of these poetic games. The *tanka* still remains the basic form of all Japanese poetry which is also poetically known as 'the Way of Shikishima':

> The heritage
> Handed down by our fathers,
> Help us to preserve it
> Oh Kami, you who know
> The art of poetry . . .[23]

CONCLUSION

The setting up of the new bakufu in Edo in 1603 and the taking of Ôsaka Castle by Tokugawa Ieyasu in 1615 marked the end of the Middle Ages in Japan. The era of political disturbances, of internal wars appeared to be at an end. Japan had found a master, a shôgun who, after proving himself a great warrior, once peace was established, became an administrator like his predecessors. Japan retired within herself in her new found peace, and developed a virtually closed economy which, to some extent, brought the country's progress to a halt. Out of this isolation arose an introspective civilization which left a deep mark on the life of the people and gave them the special character that we recognize as theirs. Confucianism, given official status, took precedence over Buddhism and Shintô without, however, destroying them. The samurai way of thinking became a moral philosophy, the Way of the Bow and the Horse, *Bushidô*, 'the Way of the Warriors' which compelled them to maintain peace despite themselves. Then, after two and a half centuries of dictatorship, the Europeans reappeared in Japanese waters to threaten her.

The Japanese spirit wavered from then on between the lure of the West and the need to preserve her territorial integrity. Slowly, inexorably, Western civilization covered up with its veneer this other civilization patiently built up in the course of centuries, long nurtured in suffering and in pride by generations of men and women. But this was only in semblance. The Japan of old still dwells deep in the soul of every inhabitant of her islands and manifests itself at every turn in some euphuistic subtlety or an exquisitely delicate courtesy. Nichiren had prophesied:[1] 'Foreign power will come, will win over Japan as the hawk makes after and captures the pheasant.' But Nichiren had reckoned without the *kamikaze*! And Japan, restored to life after her ordeal, derived new energy from despair itself.

The spirit of Japan, conceived in the Nara epoch, carried in the womb of her islands throughout the Heian period, delivered in the anguish of the Middle Ages, schooled by the rod of iron of the Tokugawas, fully grown now, benefited from all her past experiences. She cannot forget them.

We cannot conclude otherwise than by quoting these lines from Fujiwara Shunzei's *Flowers of My Native Land*:[2]

> Though wave after wave of desolation
> Has hurled itself upon the city,
> The cherry tree still blooms
> As in days gone by.

BIBLIOGRAPHY

The bibliography given here is far from being exhaustive. In point of fact, it only concerns the works we have most often consulted for the realization of this book. Before each reference we have indicated, in capitals, the abbreviations that we have made use of in the notes which follow this brief bibliography.

A. *Untranslated Japanese Works*

NIHON SHOKU WATANABE MINORU: *Nihon Shoku Seikatsu Shi*, 'A History of Food in Japan', Yoshikawa Kôbunkan, Tôkyô, 1964.

KOGO JITEN KINDAICHI KYÔSUKE and HARUHIKO: *Kogo Jitem*, 'A Dictionary of Ancient Japanese', Sanseidô, Tôkyô, 1966.

BUSHIDAN TOYODA TAKESHI: *Bushidan to Sonraku*, 'Bushi Clans and Villages', Yoshikawa Kôbunkan, Tôkyô, 1963.

NIHON HÔKEN MAKI KENJI: *Nihon Hôken-seido Seiritsu-Shi*, 'A History of the Growth of Feudalism', Tôkyô, 1941.

NIHON NO FUKUSÔ SUZUKI KEIZÔ, YAMABE TOMOYUKI, TAKADA YOSHIO: *Nihon no Fukusô* (1), 'Japanese Dress', Yoshikawa Kôbunkan, Tôkyô, 1965.

NIHON NO REKISHI *Nihon no Rekishi*, Collected work in twenty-six volumes, Chûôkoronsha, Tôkyô, 1965.

    VI: *Bushi no Tôjô*, 'Formation of the Bushi';
    VII: *Kamakura Bakufu*, 'The Military government of Kamakura';
    VIII: *Môko Shûrai*, 'The Mongol Attack';
    IX: *Nambokuchô no Dôran*, 'War of the Nambokucho Period';
    X: *Gekokujô no Jidai*, 'The Era of Social Disorder';
    XI: *Sengoku Daimyô*, 'Daimyô of the Civil War';
    XII: *Tenka Tôitsun*, 'Unification'.

NIHON JÔMIN SHIBUSAWA KEIZÔ: *Nihon Jômin Seikatsu Ebiki*, 'Illustrated Dictionary of the Life of the People of Japan', Kadokawa Shoten, Tôkyô, 1966–7.

SENMEN Koshakyô: End of the twelfth century.

BAN DAINAGON Ekotoba: Twelfth century.

CHÔJUGIGA: End of the twelfth to thirteenth century.

SHIGISAN-ENGI Emaki: Twelfth century.

GAKI-ZÔSHI: Twelfth century.

KITANO-TENJIN Engi Emaki: Thirteenth century.

IPPEN SHÔNIN Emaki: End of the thirteenth century.

KOGAWA-DERA Engi Emaki: Twelfth century?

SAIGYÔ Monogatari Emaki: Thirteenth century.

KIBI-NO-OOMI Nittô Ekotoba: Twelfth to thirteenth century.

BA-I SÔSHI Emaki: Thirteenth century.

TAIMA MANDARA Emaki: Thirteenth century.

ISE SHINMEISHÔ uta Awase Emaki: 1295?

OBUSUMA SABURÔ Ekotoba: End of the thirteenth century.

TENGU-ZÔSHI Emaki: End of the thirteenth century.

ISHIYAMA-DERA Engi Emaki: Scrolls 1–3: fourteenth century; scrolls 4–7: fifteenth century.

SHINRAN SHÔNIN DEN-E: Fourteenth century.

GOSAN-NEN Kassen Emaki: Fourteenth century.

ESHI-ZÔSHI: Fourteenth century.

HASEO-KYÔ SÔSHI: Thirteenth to fourteenth century.

NAOMIKI Môshibumi: Thirteenth to fourteenth century.

KASUGA GONGEN Kenki-e: 1309.

FUKUTOMI SÔSHI: Fourteenth century.

Among the other *emakimono*, we must also mention the *Hônen Shônin Emaki* (1307), the *Yamai-no-Sôshi* (thirteenth century) and the *Naki Fudô Emaki* (Museum of Kyôto, thirteenth century), which are not found in the Nihon Jômin, I-IV.

B. *Translations of Texts*

TAIHEIKI   *The Taiheiki, a chronicle of mediaeval Japan,* translated by H. McCullough, Columbia University Press, New York, 1959.

YOSHITSUNE   *Yoshitsune, a fifteenth century Japanese chronicle,* translated by H. McCullough, Tôkyô University Press, Tôkyô, 1966.

TRANSLATIONS   *Translations from Early Japanese Literature,* by E. O. Reischauer and J. K. Yamagiwa, Harvard University Press, Cambridge, Mass., U.S.A., 1951.

SOURCES   *Sources of Japanese Traditions,* by Ryusaku Tsunoda, W. Th. de Barry, D. Keene, Columbia University Press, New York, 1958.

SEI SHÔNAGON   *The Pillow-book of Sei Shônagon,* translated by Arthur Waley, London, 1960.

GENJI   *Lady Murasaki's The Tale of Genji,* translated by Arthur Waley, London, 1935.

TANNISHÔ 'The Tannishô, translated by Ôtani Chôjun and G. Renondeau, in *France-Asia*, No. 168, pp. 2289 ff.

C. Sundry Books

AKIMOTO AKIMOTO SUNKICHI: *The Japanese Way of Life*, Tôkyô, 1961.

ANESAKI ANESAKI MASAHARU: *History of Japanese Religion*, Tôkyô, 1963.

RELIGIOUS LIFE ANESAKI MASAHARU: *Religious Life of the Japanese People*, K.B.S., Tôkyô, 1963.

NICHIREN ANESAKI MASAHARU: *Nichiren the Buddhist Prophet*, Harvard University, Cambridge, Mass., 1916.

ASAKAWA ASAKAWA KANICHI: 'Some Aspects of Japanese Feudal Institutions' in *Transactions of Asiatic Society of Japan*, 1st series, 46, Tôkyô, 1918.

MONASTIC SHÔ ASAKAWA KANICHI: 'The Life of a Monastic Shô in Mediaeval Japan', *Annual Report, American Historical Ass.*, I, 1919.

ASTON ASTON (W. G.): *Shintô, the way of the gods*, London, 1905.

HÔNEN THE SAINT COATES AND ISHIZUKA: *Hônen, the Buddhist Saint*, Chion-in, Kyôto, 1925.

EMBREE EMBREE (J. F.): *A Japanese Village, Suye Mura*, London, 1946.

KATA-IMI FRANK (BERNARD): 'Kata-imi and Kata-tagae', *Bulletin Franco-Jap Publishers*, New series, Vol. V, Nos 2–4, Tôkyô, 1958.

FORTIFIED CASTLES GUILLAIN (F.): 'Japanese Fortified Castles', *Bulletin Franco-Jap Publishers*, XIII, 1, Tôkyô, 1942.

HALL HALL (J. C.): 'Japanese feudal laws, the Hôjô code of Judicature' in *Trans. Asiatic Soc. of Japan*, 1st series, 34, Tôkyô, 1906.

HAUCHECORNE HAUCHECORNE (A.): 'Japanese Music' in *The History of Music*, Vol. I, N.R.F., Paris, 1960.

KAMAKURA ISO MUTSU: *Kamakura, Facts and Legend*, Tôkyô, 1929.

EAST-WEST JOÜON DES LONGRAIS (F.): *East and West, Japanese Western Institutions Compared*, Paris, 1958.

CHIVALRY JOUON DES LONGRAIS (F.): 'Eastern and Western Chivalry in Japan' (outline of comparative sociology) in *Collection of Social Studies published in memory of Frédéric Le Play*, Picard, Paris, 1956.

OBUSUMA JOÜON DES LONGRAIS (F.): *Description of an Emakimono 'Obusuma Saburô'* (National Museum of Tôkyô) reproduced by the Kichô Tosho Fukusei Kai, Society for the reproduction of precious books, with notes by Yamada Yoshio, Tôkyô, 1942.

KAMAKURA AGE   JOÜON DES LONGRAIS (F.): *The Kamakura Era: Sources 1150–1333*, archives, ancient Japanese Charters, Franco-Jap Publishers, Tôkyo 1950.

WOMAN   JOÜON DES LONGRAIS (F.): 'The Status of Women in Japan in the twelfth and thirteenth centuries, according to the Iwashimizu Monogatari', in *Rec. of the Jean Bodin Soc.*, Vol. XI *Women*, p. 322, Brussels, 1959.

ÉDUCATION   KAIGO TOKIOMI: *Japanese Education, Past and Present*, K.B.S., Tôkyô, 1965.

KATÔ GENCHI   KATÔ GENCHI: 'Shintô, National Religion of Japan', *Ann. Guimet Museum*, Vol. L, Paris, 1931.

MOCK   MOCK JOYA: *Things Japanese*, Tôkyô, 1964.

TAIKÔ-KENCHI   MORÉCHAND (GUY): 'Taikô Kenchi', in *B.E.F.E.O.*, Vol. LIII, Part I, Paris, 1966.

MORRIS   MORRIS (IVAN): *The World of the Shining Prince*, New York, 1964.

MATSUDAIRA   MATSUDAIRA (N.): *Seasonal Feasts in Japan*, Paris, 1936.

SHINTÔ   ONO SOKYÔ and P. WOODARD: *Shintô, the Kami Way*, Tôkyô, 1968.

ARCHITECTURE   PAINE and SOPER: *The Art and Architecture of Japan* London, 1960.

WARRIOR-MONKS   RENONDEAU (G.): *History of the Warrior-Monks of Japan*, Bibl. Inst. Chinese Higher Studies, Vol. XI, Paris, 1957. *The Shugendô*, Assiatic Society Books, XVIII, Paris, 1965.

SANSOM HIST   SANSOM (G.): *A History of Japan*, Vols. I and II, London, 1961.

SANSOM   SANSOM (G.): *Japan, A Short Cultural History*, New York, 1943.

SHÔGUNAT   SHINODA MINORU: *The Founding of the Kamakura Shôgunate, 1180–1185 with selected translations from the Azuma Kagami, Records of Civilization, Sources and Studies*, Vol. 75, Columbia University Press, 1960.

TUGE   TUGE HIDEYOMI: *Historical development of Science and Technology in Japan*, K.B.S., 1961.

UNESCO   UNESCO: *Japan, its land, people and culture*, Tôkyô, 1964.

WANG-I-T'UNG   WANG I-T'UNG: 'Official relations between China and Japan, 1368–1549', *Harvard Yenching Institute Studies*, No. 9, Harvard University Press, Cambridge, 1953.

NOTES

Complete notes for such a work would require a volume to themselves. Therefore we have been obliged to limit these to what is strictly necessary. The abbreviations used are those indicated in our bibliography. Roman numerals refer to the volumes or to the chapters of the works concerned or, as regards the *emakimono* to the number of the illuminated scrolls. Arabic numerals refer to the pages of the works mentioned. Finally, numbers in italics refer to the numbers of the illustrations.

CHAPTER ONE

For the whole of this chapter, abridged here for lack of space, see Sansom Hist., I and II and Sansom, 1–431.

1. The best known of these romances are: *Genji Monogatari* by Lady Murasaki Shikibu; *Makura-no-Sôshi* by Lady Sei Shônagon;

Kagerô Nikki by a Fujiwara Lady; *Sarashina Nikki* by a Sugarwara Lady; *Izumi Shikibu Nikki; Ochikubo Monogatari*, etc.

2. Morris, 45.
3. Taiheiki, VII, 194–5.
4. Sei Shônagon, 10, 18.

CHAPTER TWO

1. Embree, 133.
2. This custom is found in south-east Asia, as also in Siberia.
3. Gaki-zôshi (Tokyo scroll, Nat. Museum). Nihon Jômin, *94*, Nihon Jômin, *141*, *142*, Kitano Tenjin, VIII.
4. In Japan, the willow is believed to have healing vir-

tues. In actual fact, salicylic acid is derived from it.

5. Morris, 91, 92.
6. Mock, 362.
7. East-West, 382.
8. Mock, 728.
9. Mock, 693, 694.
10. Yoshitsune, VII, 274.
11. Taiheiki, I, 9.
12. Genji, 136.

13. Embree, 136.
14. Mock, 122.
15. Nihon Jômin, *19*, Senmen.
16. Nihon Jômin, *561*, Naomiki.
17. Nihon Jômin, *17*, Senmen.
18. Nihon Jômin, *545–6*, Haseo-kyo.
19. Nihon Jômin, *17*, Senmen: *369*, Saigyô.
20. Nihon Jômin, *369*, Saigyô.
21. Nihon Jômin, *637*, Chôju Giga.
22. Nihon Jômin, *681*, Fukutomi Sôshi.
23. Mock, 145.
24. Taiheiki, I, 12.
25. Yoshitsune, I, 72.
26. Yoshitsune, VII, 242.
27. Nihon Jômin, *430*, Obusuma Saburo; *75*, Shigisan.
28. Sansom, 373.
29. Education, 21.
30. Education, 30.
31. East-West, 382.
32. Yoshitsune, II, 86.
33. Mock, 125.
34. Naki-Fudô, Engi Emaki, thirteenth century, Kyôto Museum.
35. Taiheiki, VI, 169.
36. East-West, 328, 329.
37. East-West, 322.
38. Nihon Shoku, 155 ff.
39. Only from the end of the Muromachi era. In the twelfth and thirteenth centuries, the ceremony was held in the brides parents' home.
40. East-West, 317.

41. Kamakura, 117.
42. East-West, 340.
43. Mock, 718, 719.
44. Translated into French by Bernard Frank under the title *Narayama*, Paris, NRF, 1959.
45. Katô Genchi, 92, 93.
46. Mock, 369.
47. Nihon Jômin, *146*, Kitano Tenjin, VIII.
48. Nihon Jômin, *149*, Kitano Tenjin, VIII.
49. East-West, 76.
50. East-West, 442.
51. East-West, 372.
52. East-West, 326.
53. Woman.
54. Translations, Tsutsumi Chûnagon, 172.
55. Poem by Minamoto Saneakira (910–70) in the *Gosenshû*; Translations, Tsutsumi Chûnagon, 171, note 59.
56. Translations, Tsutsumi, 172.
57. Morris, 34.
58. Genji.
59. Translations, Izayoi Nikki, 43. Miura Hiroyuki, Zoku Hôseishi no Kenkyû, XII, 1061–1136. *Kamakura-Jidai no Kazoku Seido*.
60. Translations, Izayoi Nikki, 52.
61. East-West, 470.
62. East-West, 385.
63. East-West, 372 ff.
64. Nihon no Rekishi, VII, 401–3.
65. East-West, 306.

66. Jôei Shikimoku, article 9.
67. Jôei Shikimoku, article 15.
68. Jôei Shikimoku, article 34; East-West, 306.
69. Nihon no Rekishi, VII, 405, 496.

70. Nihon no Rekishi, VIII, 375 ff.
71. Nihon Jômin, *273*, Ippen, VIII.
72. Nihon Jômin, *274*, Ippen, II
73. Nihon Jômin, *267*, Ippen, VIII.

CHAPTER THREE

1. Sei Shônagon *Makura no Sôshi*, Kaneko Motoomi, ed. 1075, 1076, *Makura no Sôshi Hyôshaku*.
2. Hyakurenshô, quoted by Watanabe Minoru, Nihon Shoku, 115.
3. Nihon Shoku, 125 ff.
4. Hanazono-in Gyoki and Gukanki of January, 1379.
5. Morris, 149.
6. The fact is made quite clear in the *Tsurezuregusa* (1330-1); Nihon Shoku, 125.
7. *Imagawa Daizôshi*, Nihon Shoku, 140.
8. This is perhaps the origin of the triple gesture made with the right hand by *sumô* contestants when they receive their prize after a bout.
9. Nihon Shoku, 141.
10. Sôgo Daizôshi, Nihon Shoku 141.
11. Morris, 147.
12. Translations, Tsutsumi Chûnagon, 265.
13. Nihon Shoku, 118.

14. Renchû-Shô, Nihon Shoku, 133.
15. Shûkai-Shô, Nihon Shoku, 133.
16. In his work *Kissa Yôjô Ki*, Nihon Shoku, 126.
17. Sources, Eisai, *Kissa Yôjô Ki*, 244.
18. Hanazono-in Gyoki of June 1332, Nihon Shoku, 126, 128.
19. Sansom, 307.
20. Nihon Jômin, *529*, Gosan Nen; *453*, Ishiyama-dera V.
21. Mock, 314.
22. Nihon Shoku, 119.
23. Nihon Shoku, 143.
24. Sansom, 433, note.
25. East-West, 184, 185, For this Chapter see the numerous *emakimono* of the period, *Ippen Shônin Emaki, Yamai-no-Sôshi, Kokawa-dera Engi, Ishiyama dera Engi, Gazi Zôshi*, etc.
26. Casal, 9 and note 8.
27. Translations, Tsutsumi Chûnagon, 186 ff.

28. At least according to relatively late Dutch sources (seventeenth century)
29. Translations, Tsutsumi Chûnagon, 256, 257.
30. Taiheiki, II, 60.
31. Casal, 24.
32. Nihon Jômin 478, Ishiyamadera, III.

33. Nihon Jômin, 247, Ippen, III.
34. Nihon Jômin, 93, Gaki Zôshi.
35. Translations, Tsutsumi Chûnagon, 217.
36. Nihon no Rekishi, VII, 459 ff.
37. Nihon Jômin, 186, Ippen, XI.

CHAPTER FOUR

1. Gunter Nitschke: Kyôto . . . esoteric town planning in East-Orient, Vol. I, 1, p. 30, Tôkyô, 1967.
2. Architecture, 196, 197.
3. Saibara, quoted by Fujiki Kunihiko: Heian Jidai no Kizoku no Seikatsu, 117; Morris, 23.
4. Taiheiki, XII, 347, 348, 349.
5. Here the narrator attributes to Antiquity a fact which dates only from the end of the eighth century. But these anachronisms were quite common in the writings of Japanese men of letters at that time, steeped in Chinese culture and anxious to link up their history with that of the heroes of China. Ts'in Che-houang-ti, founder of the Ts'in dynasties, lived about 221–207 (210) before our era. His capital, Hien Yang, situated near Chang-An, was the starting point of the Silk Route.
6. These measurements are obviously exaggerated and are not based on evidence of any kind.
7. Taiheiki, XII, 347 to 350.
8. Taiheiki, XII, 363.
9. Governor Mosher: Kyôto, a contemplative guide, Tôkyô 1964, pp. 130 to 132.
10. Poem of 1467, quoted by Sansom Hist, II, 226. Free translation by the author.
11. Pageant of Japanese Art, Architecture and Gardens, Tôkyô, 1957, p. 51.
12. Nihon no Rekishi, VII, 473.
13. Translations, Izayoi Nikki, III, 88.
14. Translations, Izayoi Nikki, II, 87. Free translation.
15. East-West, 222.
16. Nihon no Rekishi, VII, 476 ff.
17. Taiheiki, X, 289, 290. Japanese bows not being capable

of a range of more than 100 to 120 metres, this distance is exaggerated.
18. Taiheiki, X, 292.
19. Nihon no Rekishi, VII, 474.
20. Kamakura, 205.
21. Kamakura, 107.
22. Sansom Hist., II, 302.
23. Sansom Hist., 295.
24. Nihon no Rekishi, VIII, 235 ff.
25. Yoshitsune, III, 126.
26. This garden, like those of the Tenryû-ji and the Tôji-in, have been attributed to the Zen monk Musô Kokushi.

27. For all these descriptions, see the *emakimono* and for greater detail the *Ippen Hijiri-e*.
28. Nihon Jômin, *537*, Eshi Zôshi.
29. Nihon Jômin, *585, 586*, Kasuga Gongen XIV.
30. Nihon Jômin, *621*, Kasuga Gongen XVI.
31. Nihon Jômin, *666*, Fukutomi Sôshi.
32. Translations, Tsutsumi Chûnagon, 262 to 265.
33. Nihon Jômin, *574*, Kasuga Gongen XIV.

CHAPER FIVE

1. Nihon no Rekishi, VIII, 256.
2. East-West, 243.
3. Nihon no Rekishi, VII, 398.
4. East-West, 245–8.
5. East-West, 252.
6. Nihon no Rekishi, VII, 175.
7. East-West, 244.
8. Sansom, 302.
9. Nihon no Rekishi, VII, 133, 148.
10. East-West, 249, 250.
11. Nihon no Rekishi, VII, 183.
12. East-West, 56–60.
13. Or *Buyaku*. Cf. *Nihon-Shi Shô-Jiten*, 611.
14. Nihon no Rekishi, VII, 401; East-West, 135.
15. Nihon no Rekishi, VIII, 375.

16. Nihon-Shi Shô-Jiten, 672.
17. East-West, 133, 134.
18. East-West, 61.
19. East-West, 254–8.
20. Sansom, 361.
21. East-West, 258.
22. East-West, 258.
23. Sansom Hist., II, 251–3.
24. Taikô Kenchi, 13 ff; Sansom, 430.
25. Sources, *Kokushi Shiryô Shû*, III, 280, 281.
26. Bushidan, 74. Plan of a Village of the Yamato 1306–8).
27. Embree, 9–25.
28. Bushidan, 75. Plan of a Settsu Village (1342–5).
29. Sansom Hist., II, 334; Bushidan, 56; Taikô Kenchi, 61.

30. Translations, Izayoi Nikki, 71.
31. Nihon Jômin, *221*, Ippen.
32. Yoshitsune, VII, 262, 263.
33. Nihon Jômin, *11*, Senmen.
34. Nihon no Rekishi, VIII, 268 ff. The price of rice varied according to districts and eras from 8 to 14 *mon* per *shô* (1 1. 8 or 2 kg); but this price was subject to considerable variations in times of famine.
35. Nihon no Rekishi, VIII, 262–4.
36. Called Hsüan-ming (*Semmyô* in Sino-Japanese).
37. Nihon Shoku, 116.
38. Nihon Shoku, 116, 117.
39. Maize was not imported to Japan until about 1573.
40. Nihon Jômin, *477*, Ishiyama Dera.
41. Nihon Shoku, 136.
42. Mock, 404.
43. Embree, 203.
44. Nihon no Rekishi, VIII, 208.
45. Nihon no Rekishi, VII, 73.
46. Nihon no Rekishi, VII, 207. Free translation of a *tanka* (thirty-one syllables).
47. Nihon Shoku, 136.
48. Translations, Izayoi Nikki, 95.
49. Translations, Izayoi Nikki, 55, note 110.
50. Nihon Jômin, *230*, Ippen, VII.

CHAPTER SIX

1. P. Huard and Ming Wong: *Chinese Medicine*, Paris, 1964, pp. 49, 51, 52. The *I-Shin-pô*, written according to medical treatises of the Suei, comprised thirty volumes. It was presented to the Emperor En-yû in 984.
2. Tuge, 34.
3. Mock, 65, 67, 71.
4. Nihon Jômin, *633*, *634*, Kasuga Gongen.
5. Taiheiki, V, 140.
6. Kamakura, 205.
7. Nihon Jômin, *233*, Ippen, VII.
8. Nihon Jômin, 52, 53, Chojû Giga, IV.
9. Nihon Jômin, *401*, *402*, *403*, Taima mandala; *469*, Ishiyama, I.
10. There are many books dealing with Japanese lacquer. Among them we quote only: Herberts (Dr Curt): *Oriental Lacquer, Art and Technique*, London, 1962. YOSHINO (T.): *Japanese Lacquer ware*, JTB, Tôkyô.
11. See on this subject one of the numerous works which have been devoted to it by

specialists and in particular
GORMAN (H. H.): *Japanese and Oriental Pottery*, Yokohama, SD.

LEACH (B.): *A Potter's Book*, London.

MITSUOKA (T.): *Ceramic Art of Japan*, JTB, Tôkyô, 1949.

FUKUI (K.): *Japanese Ceramic Art*, Tôkyô, 1926.

12. Also to be consulted on this subject:
YUMOTO (J. M.): *The Samurai Sword*, U.S.A., 1958.

JI (H. J.): *Japanese Sword*,

National Museum, Tôkyô, 1948.

HAKUSAI (I.): *Nippontô*, Tôkyô, 1948.

13. See: SALWEYS (C. M.): *Fans of Japan*, London, 1894.
14. Tuge, 11–13.
15. Nihon Shoku, 138.
16. Sansom, 359.
17. Nihon no Rekishi, VIII, 23 ff.
18. Sansom, 355, note.
19. Yoshitsune, VII, 250 ff.
20. Taiheiki, I, 6.
21. Taiheiki, I, 7.

CHAPTER SEVEN

1. Nihon no Rekishi, VI, 77, 78.
2. East-West, 204.
3. *Azuma Kagami*, quoted in East-West, 226 (Zoku Kokushi Taikei, Tôkyô, 1903, Vol. 4, p. 122).
4. Taiheiki, VI, 165. Distances like the number of soldiers, are very much exaggerated and do not square in any way with the facts.
5. Taiheiki, V, 131, 133.
6. Nihon Hôken, 82 ff.
7. East-West, 208.
8. Taiheiki, IV, 108.
9. Casal, 21.
10. East-West, 145.
11. Yoshitsune, V, 176.
12. East-West, 150.
13. East-West, 234.
14. Taiheiki, VI, 169.

15. Taiheiki, VI, 168.
16. Sansom, 291.
17. Nihon Jômin, *176*, Ippen, VII.
18. Nihon Jômin, *168*, Ippen, VII.
19. Taiheiki, III, 85.
20. Taiheiki, VI, *171*, *172*.
21. Taiko Kenchi, 12.
22. Fortified Castles, 39, 40.
23. Taikô Kenchi, 12.
24. Nihon Jômin, *539*, Gosan Nen.
25. Taiheiki, VII, 186.
26. Taiheiki, VIII, 224.
27. Taiheiki, XII, 343.
28. Nihon Jômin, *425*, Obusuma Saburô.
29. Nihon Jômin, *597*, Kasuga Gongen.
30. Sources, 319, 320, 321.
31. Taiheiki, XII, 343.

32. Education, 19, 20.
33. Education, 24. The *Mutsu-waki* is a war chronicle by an unknown author (1051–62).
34. Nihon no Rekishi, VIII, 86 ff.
35. Nihon no Rekishi, VIII, 101.
36. Sources, 327, 328.
37. Sansom, 315, 316.
38. East-West, 314.
39. Taiheiki, VIII, 230.
40. Nihon Jômin, *532*, Gosan Nen.
41. Taiheiki, IX, 253 to 255.
42. Sansom Hist., II, 220.
43. Yoshitsune, IV, 163–5.
44. Taiheiki, III, 88, 89.
45. Taikeiki, III, 87.
46. Taikeiki, VI, 153.
47. Taikeiki, II, 35.
48. Taikeiki, II, 32.

49. Sansom, 428.
50. Taiheiki, II, 334, 335.
51. Taiheiki, VII, 187.
52. Taiheiki, VII, 181.
53. Yoshitsune, VIII, 290.
54. Taiheiki, VII, 179.
55. Taiheiki, I, 22.
56. Taiheiki, IV, 95.
57. Taiheiki, VIII, 214.
58. Yoshitsune, VIII, 277.
59. Appearance of the *Heiki Monogatari* and of many other gestes of the time. Text quoted in different ways according to:
Sansom, 291; SADLER (A. L.): 'The Heike Monogatari, in *Trans. As. Soc. of Japan*, Series I, XLVI, 1918; Turrettini, in *Atsume Gusa*, Geneva, 1871, etc.

CHAPTER EIGHT

1. Kamakura, 17.
2. East-West, 233.
3. Taiheiki, V, 135, 136.
4. Morris, 104.
5. Anesaki, 151, note 1.
6. Anesaki, 152.
7. Anesaki, 174, According to '12 articles of Hônen'.
8. Hônen the saint, 461.
9. Hônen the saint, 728, 729.
10. Tannishô, III.
11. Tannishô, XV.
12. The original vow of Amida (Hongan) in forty-eight points, states that, when he will have reached the state of Buddhahood (this vow being made when he was as yet only Bodhisattva), all who call upon him and long to be reborn in the Pure Land (Jôdo), his paradise, will be heard. This vow is recorded in Chapter I of the *Muryôju Kyô* or 'Eternal Life Sûtra'.
13. Tannishô, I.
14. Anesaki, 185.
15. Nihon Jômin, *292*, Ippen, IV; *293*, Ippen, VI; *294*,

295, Ippen, VII.

16. Anesaki, 195.

17. Kamakura, 229, 230.

18. Nichiren, 119, 120.

19. Sources, Eisai, preface to the *Kôzen Gokoku Ron, Taishô Dai-Zôkyô*, Vol. 80, Zoku Shoshûbu, 2, p. 242.

20. Anesaki, 208.

21. Sources, 261 *Kôsô Meicho Zenshû, Muchû-mondô*, XVI, *Musô Kokushi hen*, p. 145.

22. Anesaki, 214.

23. Shinto the Kami Way, 8.

24. Katô Genchi, 96.

25. East-West, 233.

26. Shintô the Kami Way, 87.

27. Akiyama, Sources, 326. See note 38.

28. Yoshitsune, II, 97 ff.

29. Kata-imi, 38.

30. Akimoto, 179. *Zen Sôji, Shingon Ryôri, Monto Hana, Morimono Hokke, Jôdo Jidaraku.*

31. Yoshitsune, VII, 254.

32. Yoshitsune, V, 180.

33. Taiheiki, V, 141.

34. Taiheiki, VIII, 221.

35. Sources, 317. Poem by Sakunen of Western Kyoto, from the *Hoan Nobunaga-Ki*, IV, in *Dai-Nihon Shiryô*, 10, Vol. VI, 874.

36. Religious Life, 80.

37. Anesaki, 243, 244.

38. Sources, 326. Akiyama, *Nisshi Kôshô-shi Kenkyû*, 66, 1939

CHAPTER NINE

1. This expression, *Mono-no-Aware*, is untranslatable. It is the feeling which gives rise to an emotion (shared by others) and which involves a certain melancholy due to the transience of all worldly things. An autumn landscape, with its falling leaves, the rain, the mist are typical of *Mono-no-Aware*, literally 'the pity of things'. But according to Hisamatsu Senichi, it is also the feeling inspired by a sunny spring morning, delight mingled with a shade of melancholy. See note 4.

2. Sansom, 378.

3. Soetsu Yanagi, 'The Way of Tea', in *Art around Town*, Vol. VII, No. 4, p. 2, Tôkyô, 1959.

4. Hisamatsu Senichi: 'The characteristics of beauty in the Japanese Middle Ages', in *Acta Asiatica*, Tôhô Gakkai, Tôkyô, 1965, Vol. VIII, 40–53.

5. Sources, 289, in Nosé, '*Zeami Jûrokubushû Hyôshaku*' I, 358–66.

6. Yoshitsune, VII, 256.

7. Yoshitsune, V, 168.

8. Hauchecorne, 313.

9. Yoshitsune, VI, 233.

10. Taiheiki, V, 131.
11. PÉRI (NOËL): *Essay on Japanese Scales*, Paris, 1934.
12. Hauchecorne, 308, 309.
13. Sources, 302, 303. Zeami, *The Book of the Way of the Tallest Flower*.
14. Sansom, 385, 386.
15. Sansom Hist., II, 279.
16. Sansom Hist., II, 252.
17. Taiheiki, V, 131.
18. This game, still extremely popular, is now known as *go*.

19. Kondô Ichitarô, 'Painting fourteenth to nineteenth centuries' in *Pageant of Japanese Art*, Tôkyô, 1957, pp. 32, 33.
20. Sansom, 327.
21. Translations, Izayoi Nikki, 55.
22. Taiheiki, II, 32, 33.
23. Translations, Izayoi Nikki, 84. Shikishima, the poetic name for Japan, is used here for the poetic art of the Yamato.

CONCLUSION

1. Katô Genchi, 198.
2. *Senzai Wakashû*, anthology of imperial poems compiled by Fujiwara Shunzei (1114–1204) and presented to the emperor in 1188.

LIST OF SHÔGUN, REGENTS AND DICTATORS FROM 1185 TO 1603

Shôgun of the Minamoto Clan

Yoritomo	1192
Yoriye	1202
Sanetomo	1203

Hôjô Regents (Taira Clan)
(Shikken)

Tokimasa	1203

Shôgun of the Fujiwara Clan

Yoritsune	1226
Yoritsugu	1244

Yasutoki	1225
Tsunetoki	1242
Tokiyori	1246

Shôgun Imperial Princes

Munetaka	1252
Koreyasu	1266
Hisa-Hira	1289
Morikuni	1308
Morinaga	1334

Nagatoki	1256
Masamura	1264
Tokimune	1268
Sadatoki	1284
Morotoki	1300
Takatoki	1315

Shôgun of the Ashikaga Clan

Takauji	1336	Yoshihisa	1474
Yoshiakira	1358	Yoshitane (1)	1490
Yoshimitsu	1367	Yoshizumi	1493
Yoshimochi	1395	Yoshitane (2)	1508
Yoshikazu	1423	Yoshiharu	1521
Yoshinori	1428	Yoshiteru	1545
Yoshikatsu	1441	Yoshihide	1565
Yoshimasa	1449	Yoshiaki	1568

Dictators-Administrators

Oda Nobunaga	1573
Hideyoshi	1582
Hideyori	1598

Shôgun of the Tokugawa Clan

Ieyasu	1603
Hidetada	1615

HISTORICAL PERIODS OF JAPAN

A. Prehistory and Protohistory

Jômon	about 7500 BC – about 300 BC
Yayoi	about 300 BC – about AD 300
Kofun (megalithic tombs)	4th–7th centuries of our era

B. History

Asuka Period	552–645	
Nara Period	645–794	
Heian Period	794–1185	
Fujiwara Regents	890–1185	
Kamakura Period	1185–1333	*(the Hôjô Regents)*
Muromachi Period	1333–1573	*(the Ashikaga Shôgun)*
Momoyama Period	1573–1603	*(the Dictators)*
Edo Period	1603–1868	*(the Tokugawa Shôgun)*
Contemporary Period:		
Meji Era	1868–1912	
Taishô Era	1913–1924	
Shôwa Era	1924 up to the present day	

JAPANESE CURRENCY, WEIGHTS AND MEASURES
(TWELFTH TO SIXTEENTH CENTURIES)

A. *Linear Measures*

Rin	= 0·303 mm
Bu (10 *Rin*)	= 3·03 mm
Sun (10 *Bu*)	= 3·03 cm
Shaku (10 *Sun*)	= 30·303 cm
Ken (6 *Shaku*)	= 1·818 m in Nagoya
	= 1·908 m in Kyôto
	= 1·757 m in Edo

Cloth

Tan	= from 25 to 30 *Shaku*
Kujira-Shaku	= about a quarter longer than a *Shaku*
Hiki	= 2 *Tan*

Land

Chô (60 *Ken*)	= from 109·08 m to 105·42 m according to district
Ri (36 *Chô*)	= from 3·9 km to 4·3 km according to district

B. *Square Measures*

Tsubo (or Bu)	= 1 sq. *Ken*	= about 3·35 m²
Se	= 30 *Tsubo*	= about 1 are (100 sq. m)
Tan	= 10 *Se*	= about 10 ares (1,000 sq. m)
Chô	= 10 *Tan*	= about 1 hectare (10,000 sq. m)
Sq. Ri	= 36 sq. *Chô*	= about 16 km²

C. *Measures of Capacity*

Shaku	= 1·80 cl
Gô (10 *Shaku*)	= 1·80 dl
Shô (10 *Gô*)	= 1·80 l
To (10 *Shô*)	= 18 litres
Koku (10 *To*)	= 180 litres
Hyô (4 Koku)	= 720 litres (special for rice)

D. *Weight*

Momme	= 3·75 grammes
Kin	= from 100 to 180 *Momme* according to district
Kan (1,000 *Momme*)	= 3·75 kilos

E. *Currency*

Wadô-Kaiho (from 708 to 958): Copper currency (sometimes gold
or silver) struck in Japan
Mon (Chinese *Sen*): from 958 to 1587–91: imported from China
Kan: String of 1,000 *Mon*

Japanese Money: 1587 = Tenshô Tsûhô: silver or gold
 1592 = Bunroku Tsûhô: silver
 1606 = Keichô Tsûhô: silver.

INDEX